CHOICE WORDS

Borgo Press Books by ROBERT REGINALD

Across the Wide Missouri: The Diary of a Journey from Virginia to Missouri in 1819 and Back Again in 1822, with a Description of the City of Cincinnati, by James Brown Campbell (ed. as Michael Burgess with Mary Wickizer Burgess)
Ancestral Voices: An Anthology of Early Science Fiction (ed. with D. Menville)
Ancient Hauntings (ed. with Douglas Menville)
The Arms Control, Disarmament, and Military Security Dictionary (with Jeffrey M. Elliot)
The Attempted Assassination of John F. Kennedy: A Political Fantasy
BP 300: An Annotated Bibliography of the Publications of the Borgo Press, 1976-1998 (with Mary Wickizer Burgess)
California Ranchos: Patented Private Land Grants Listed by County, by Burgess McK. Shumway (ed. as Michael Burgess with Mary Wickizer Burgess)
Choice Words: The Borgo Press Book of Writers Writing on Writing (editor)
Classics of Fantastic Literature; or, Les Épines Noires: Selected Review Essays (ed. with Douglas Menville)
Contemporary Science Fiction Authors
Cumulative Paperback Index, 1939-1959
Dreamers of Dreams: An Anthology of Fantasy (ed. with Douglas Menville)
Forgotten Fantasy: Issues #1-5 (ed. with Douglas Menville)
FutureVisions: The New Golden Age of the Science Fiction Film (with Douglas Menville & Mary A. Burgess)
A Guide to Science Fiction and Fantasy in the Library of Congress Classification Scheme
The House of the Burgesses (as Michael Burgess with Mary A. Burgess)
If J.F.K. Had Lived: A Political Scenario (with Jeffrey M. Elliot)
King Solomon's Children: Some Parodies of H. Rider Haggard (ed. with Douglas Menville)
Mystery and Detective Fiction in the Library of Congress Classification Scheme
The Nasty Gnomes: A Novel of the Phantom Detective Agency
Phantasmagoria (ed. with Douglas Menville)
The Phantom's Phantom: A Novel of the Phantom Detective Agency
R.I.P.: Five Stories of the Supernatural (with Douglas Menville)
San Quentin: The Evolution of a California State Prison (ed. with Bonnie L. Petry)
Science Fiction and Fantasy Book Review (ed. with Neil Barron)
The Spectre Bridegroom and Other Horrors (ed. with Douglas Menville)
The State and Province Vital Records Guide (with Mary Burgess & Daryl Mallett)
Tempest in a Teapot: The Falkland Islands War (with Jeffrey M. Elliot)
They: Three Parodies of H. Rider Haggard's She (ed. with Douglas Menville)
Things to Come: An Illustrated History of the Science Fiction Film (with Douglas Menville)
¡Viva California! Seven Accounts of Life in Early California (ed. with Mary Wickizer Burgess)
Western Fiction in the Library of Congress Classification Scheme (with Beverly A. Ryan)
The Work of Robert Reginald (as Michael Burgess with Mary A. Burgess)
The Work of Katherine Kurtz (as Boden Clarke with Mary A. Burgess)
Worlds of Never: Three Fantastic Novels (ed. with Douglas Menville)
Xenograffiti: Essays on Fantastic Literature and Other Divers Topics

CHOICE WORDS

THE BORGO PRESS BOOK OF WRITERS WRITING ON WRITING

Edited by

Robert Reginald

THE BORGO PRESS

An Imprint of Wildside Press LLC

MMX

Borgo Literary Guides
ISSN 0891-9623

Number Four

Editorial Contributions Copyright © 2010 by Robert Reginald
[p. 9-10 shall constitute an extension of this copyright page]

All rights reserved.
No part of this book may be reproduced in any form
without the expressed written consent
of the authors and publisher.

www.wildsidebooks.com

FIRST EDITION

CONTENTS

Acknowledgments 9
Introduction: "Choice Cuts," by Robert Reginald 11
1. "Dispatch from the Front: Never Waste Anything," by Ardath Mayhar 15
2. "Paperback Writer," by Victor J. Banis 18
3. "Tipping the Odds in Your Favor," by Charles Allen Gramlich 33
4. "Writing Is Fighting the Familiar; or, 47 Years in the Wake of Adelbert Ames, Jr.," by W. C. Bamberger 42
5. "Slanting Can Be Fun and Dangerous; or, Art vs. All That Other Stuff," by Charles Nuetzel 56
6. "A Few Words, a Very Few Words, on Writing," by Robert Reginald 66
7. "Writing with Purpose," by Charles Allen Gramlich 71
8. "Preparing and Writing," by Charles Allen Gramlich, Y. Du Bois Irvin, and Elliott D. Hammer 74
9. "Images," by Damien Broderick 81
10. "Emotion and Intellect in Poetry," by Michael R. Collings 89
11. "Making Things Happen," by Ardath Mayhar 93
12. "Plotting a Science Fiction Story," by Brian Stableford 97
13. "Saying Much with Little: Some Practical Suggestions for Tightening Bulky Lines in Poetry," Michael R. Collings . 104
14. "The Two-Headed Author: The Challenges, Risks, and Rewards of Collaboration," by John Howard Weeks 109
15. "Love, Anyone? or, How to Write Sex Scenes," by William Maltese 116
16. "Writing for the Stage," by Francis Jarman 147
17. "On Translation," by Frank J. Morlock 169
18. "In Other Words...: Editing Borgo Press," by Robert Reginald 180
19. "How Not to Starve as a Writer," by Ardath Mayhar 187

Index, by Mary Wickizer Burgess 191

About the Authors 201

DEDICATION

For my other half,

The TRUE *editor in the family,*

MARY,

Without whom....

And for

JOHN GREGORY,

Who opened a new door....

ACKNOWLEDGMENTS

A NUMBER OF these pieces have been previously published, in whole or in part, and are reprinted by permission of their authors:

"Paperback Writer," Copyright © 2007, 2010 by Victor J. Banis, first appeared in the author's book, *Spine Intact, Some Creases: Remembrances of a Paperback Writer, Second Edition* (Borgo Press, 2007), one of the best autobiographies of a writer I've ever read—funny, poignant, and full of insights.

"Images," Copyright © 2005, 2010 by Damien Broderick, is adapted and expanded from a chapter in the author's book, *Ferocious Minds: Polymathy and the New Enlightenment* (Borgo Press, 2005); Broderick always offers unique insights—it's well worth reading.

"Emotion and Intellect in Poetry" and "Saying Much with Little: Some Practical Suggestions for Tightening Bulky Lines in Poetry," Copyright © 2009, 2010 by Michael R. Collings, first appeared in the author's book, *The Art and Craft of Poetry: Twenty Exercises Toward Mastery, Second Edition* (Borgo Press, 2009), an excellent guide to writing and editing quality verse.

"Writing with Purpose," Copyright © 2009, 2010 by Charles Allen Gramlich; "Tipping the Odds in Your Favor," Copyright © 1994, 2009 by Charles Allen Gramlich; these both appeared in the author's book, *Write with Fire: Thoughts on the Craft of Writing* (Borgo Press, 2009), another first-rate guide to the art of writing publishable commercial fiction.

"Preparing and Writing" Copyright © 2009, 2010 by Charles Allen Gramlich, Y. Du Bois Irvin, and Elliott D. Hammer, first appeared in the authors' book, *Writing in Psychology: A Guidebook* (Borgo Press, 2009); a very sound and thorough guide on publishing in scholarly sources, with an application far beyond psychology.

"Dispatch from the Front: Never Waste Anything," "How Not to Starve as a Writer," and "Making Things Happen," Copyright © 1992, 2009, 2010 by Ardath Mayhar, first appeared in the Second Edition of the author's book, *Through a Stone Wall: Lessons from Thirty Years of Writing, Second Edition* (Borgo Press, 2009), a guide to the art that is simply one of the best books on the subject that I've ever read—it should be on every penman's shelf.

"Slanting Can Be Fun and Dangerous; or, Art vs. All That Other Stuff," Copyright © 2007, 2010 by Charles Nuetzel, first appeared in the author's book, *Pocketbook Writer: Confessions of a Commercial Hack* (Borgo Press, 2007); Nuetzel's look at the 1960s' paperback scene in Los Angeles is well worth a visit.

"A Few Words, a Very Few Words on Writing," Copyright © 2006, 2010 by Robert Reginald, is adapted and expanded from a chapter in the author's book, *Trilobite Dreams; or, The Autodidact's Tale: A Romance of Autobiography* (Ariadne Press, 2006), a short, reflective work telling about Reginald's personal journey as a writer, and how he was touched by a near-fatal illness.

"Plotting a Science Fiction Story," Copyright © 1989, 2010 by Brian Stableford, first appeared in 1989 in *Interzone* and also in the author's book, *The Way to Write Science Fiction* (Elm Tree Books, 1989), a standard guide to the subject.

Published here for the first time are:

"Writing Is Fighting the Familiar; or, 47 Years in the Wake of Adelbert Ames, Jr.," Copyright © 2010 by W. C. Bamberger.

"Writing for the Stage," Copyright © 2010 by Francis Jarman.

"Love, Anyone? or, How to Write Sex Scenes," Copyright © 2010 by William Maltese.

"On Translation," Copyright © 2010 by Frank J. Morlock.

"In Other Words…: Editing Borgo Press" and "Introduction: Choice Cuts," Copyright © 2010 by Robert Reginald.

"The Two-Headed Author: The Challenges, Risks, and Rewards of Collaboration," Copyright © 2010 by John Howard Weeks.

INTRODUCTION

Choice Cuts

I have the best job in the world.

Each day, I sit down in front of the computer, access my email, and discover what treasures have drifted my way that day. There might be an original fantasy or western novel by Ardath Mayhar, a collection of dark tales by Kathryn Ptacek, a translation by Frank J. Morlock of a hitherto unknown eighteenth- or nineteenth-century French play, a book of literary criticism or novel by Damien Broderick or Brian Stableford or Charles Allen Gramlich, an epic poem or fantasy novel by Michael R. Collings, an adventure by Charles Nuetzel, a modern thriller or cookbook or romance by William Maltese, a contemporary play or nonfiction work by Francis Jarman, a humorous piece or horror novel by Victor J. Banis, or…well, almost anything really, on any subject or in any genre imaginable. I cast my editorial net very widely.

But I'm leaping forward when I should, perhaps, be glancing backward. How did this all begin?

On 22 March 2006, John Gregory Betancourt, the Publisher of Wildside Press and a well-known fiction writer, phoned me out of the blue with a proposition. He was looking to expand his print-on-demand offerings, and wondered if I'd be willing to edit a line of reprints derived from the leavings of the old Borgo Press and Starmont House lists. He knew that I still had contact with some of those writers, since my wife, Mary Wickizer Burgess, and I had once owned Borgo, and had had many conversations with the late Ted Dikty, Starmont's Publisher; and he thought that it would be a relatively easy process for us to find them again.

(We'd operated the original Borgo Press from 1975-99, shutting it down when we reached a point where we needed to start planning for retirement. We'd then sold the BP imprint to Wildside for a dollar in the Spring of 2003, just a few months before I experienced a near-fatal heart attack, dumping me into a long period of recuperation.)

I didn't want to be involved in any business way with Wildside Press, and I told John that up front; at our age, we just can't essay any kind of financial risk. On the other hand, the thought of getting back into the game in some small fashion excited me, and I told him that too. I'd certainly be willing to give it a try.

Within a few months, I discovered that many of the BP and SH authors were more than willing to sign agreements bringing their books back into print—"and oh, by the way, Rob, I have some other titles that have never been published. Can you...?"

So I posed this question to John, and received an affirmative reply. Instead of just cannibalizing bound copies of previously published works, I was now beginning to accept and format the e-copy of brand *new* works, including original volumes never before published anywhere.

John and I both derive from the SF world, so it's not surprising that most of our contacts derived from that sphere, at least at first.

But within a year of starting the Borgo Press Imprint of Wildside Press, I was being approached by writers who had *other* wares to peddle, including original and reprint books of fiction and nonfiction outside the realms of fantasy, science fiction, or weird supernatural and horror fiction.

The thing about POD publishing is this: *if*, as an editor, you can imagine a niche market for a particular work, it's immediately viable as a product. The initial investment in production is so slight, compared to offset or any other kind of regular printing, that it's almost negligible as a factor.

So again I went to John and asked the question: could I contract for publications outside the genre categories that Wildside had customarily mined in the past? And the answer once again was "Yes."

So now, some three and a half years later, I've turned in over 750 monographs to Wildside, and they've all been published under the BP label, more than doubling the number of titles that we issued under the original Borgo Press.

* * * * * * *

TWO YEARS AGO my dear life companion and collaborator, Mary, suggested that I put together an anthology of essays on writing by Borgo Press writers. We had done several volumes in '07 that included material on that subject. She even offered a possible title—the same one, coincidentally, that appears on page three of this book! Fancy that! (More recently, she also suggested the title of the essay on editing that I've penned for this volume.)

But for various reasons, I never did anything with the idea—until suddenly, in the midst of 2009, we published almost simultaneously four more original works on writing—and once again I recalled Mary's original proposal.

Thus was *Choice Words* (re)born!

Both she and I envisioned this book as focusing only on writers that had been published by The Borgo Press (old or new). There are certainly many good words penned by other writers for other lines on the art and science of writing and editing and translating—and I urge you to find and read them.

But the intent of *this* volume—and the sequels on related topics that I hope to edit in the near future—is to showcase the thoughts and talents of our *very* talented Borgo Press list, a group of men and women who share in common an abiding love of language in all its forms, and a passion to write and write and write.

That passion—those ideas—the sheer ability—come through quite clearly in each of the essays included herein. So do the different personalities of the individual writers, and the wide range of interests that each has pursued during their often lengthy careers.

None of these folks is a household name today, but between them, they've sold and published more than *1,000* books in professional markets during the last forty-five years.

Think of it: a thousand volumes of fiction and nonfiction that were published and paid for. Six of these writers have more than 100 book credits each. It's an astonishing record.

So it wasn't difficult to assemble the various pieces of *Choice Words*. They almost chose themselves. Some were commissioned from the writers, while others were reprinted from existing Borgo Press books. Indeed, I had so much good material that I couldn't use it all. So there'll be at least one more volume of *CW* in the not-too-distant future.

The advice of these experts is based upon decades of experience in different types and styles of writing and editing. I tried to choose pieces that complemented each other, and that covered unique facets of the craft. So there's an essay on translating, another on poetry, and another on play writing, another on collaboration, another on writing for technical markets, and another on editing, among others.

I also included some general observations on writing by the likes of Victor J. Banis and Ardath Mayhar, because their wisdom is so evident to even the rawest of beginners that I need say nothing more. These are the kinds of authors that understand their craft so completely, and express themselves so succinctly and lucidly, that anyone seriously interested in the art will find something of value here.

Finally, I tried to balance the several long, theoretical pieces with those of a lighter tone offering practical tips for the neophyte.

I hope you have as much fun reading these essays as I had assembling them. And I hope that some of you will take the time to locate the original works from which a number of these pieces have been excerpted.

The next book in this series will focus on autobiographical reminiscences by Borgo Press writers. I already have a number of pieces slated for that volume, and I'll start working on it seriously within the next month or two.

Until then…good reading, dear friends!

—Robert Reginald
San Bernardino, California
14 November 2009

I.

DISPATCH FROM THE FRONT

NEVER WASTE ANYTHING

by Ardath Mayhar

FOR TWENTY YEARS I have advised my writing students never to waste anything that happens to them, be it pleasant or painful. I thought I had taken that advice as far as it could go on my own, but, as life has a habit of doing, I learned that I hadn't even begun.

In September 1999 I lost my husband of forty-one years. He had been terribly ill for many years, but I learned then that sometimes death is a friend, not something to grieve over. In October I swerved to miss a small animal in the road, lost control, and wrecked my car. That was when fresh material began to pour in, uninvited, unwanted, but hopefully not to remain unused.

I know how it feels to be that guy bound solidly to a backboard, staring at the roof of the ambulance while EMTs work on you. (Note: They bind your head down so tightly that it feels as if a quarter-sized bit at the back of the skull is slowly turning into mush.) I understand what it feels like to wait, still bound to the board, while the ER team assesses the injuries and waits for an opening in X-ray to make sure just what all you broke. I did a pretty good job on myself, too: fractured ankle that needed surgery to put the jigsaw puzzle back together, using six screws and a plate, plus a compression fracture in the spine at T-5, which is just where the lungs work hardest in breathing.

The term "Guarded Breathing" meant nothing to me before. Now I understand. This means that the pain is so intense that your lungs refuse to expand more than the minimum amount needed to supply oxygen. You breathe in short gasps, which makes eating all but impossible.

When that term was used on a rerun of the old *Emergency* show a while back, I understood exactly what the victim was feeling.

Now if I can only get it onto paper in a story, this experience will prove valuable. Waste nothing, remember?

Have you heard about pain management specialists? Bless them all! One came to my rescue after the ankle surgery and did a Thoracic Epidural, injecting a cocktail of drugs directly into the compressed disk. IT STOPPED HURTING, comparatively speaking. I intend to use this rather new medical discipline in a story or book, before I am too old to attack the computer. In addition, I can sympathize with anyone wearing a plastic back brace and describe its man-eating habits. This thing encased my entire torso, though the bosom could have contained at least one more woman of my dimensions. If I could sing, I could have stood in for a Wagnerian soprano. I carried my purse, a book, *etc.* in it when going to the doctor, as using what I have been given is an old habit.

I suspect the slug from a .350 Magnum wouldn't penetrate the thing, and I could have fallen off the roof without reinjuring my back, I feel certain. Never again will I turn a turtle onto its back, for now I understand the helplessness such a big, thick shell entails.

Going to the bathroom and getting out again while wearing it was simply impossible. My sister and her husband took me home from the hospital to recuperate and put me in their room, by day when they were at work, so I could get to their small bathroom, using the walker. The first time I went wearing Matilda, the brace, I sat down without a problem. Though my brother-in-law had installed a bar to grab, my arm motion was so curtailed and my leg so unstable that when I tried to pull myself up again, it didn't help.

The space was too narrow to get my elbows down so I could undo the six Velcro straps that held Matilda on. Luckily my sister came home for lunch and freed me from the trap. This was no situation for a long-time claustrophobe!

Speaking of Velcro—I now know how it might feel to wrestle an octopus. Using the wheelchair, I went to the bathroom (the larger one), but shed Matilda after entering.

When I was ready to leave, I decided to save my sister some effort by taking the brace back to the bedroom with me; I picked it up.

Those straps grabbed everything—pants legs, hair, skin, cast—until I threw it away in desperation and fled as fast as I could wheel my chair.

When I got into a walking cast, it, too, had a set of Velcro straps. Getting caught between Matilda and the walking cast was something like being in the middle of a fight between King Kong and Godzilla.

Emancipation from Matilda gave me a bit of insight into what it would feel like to be let out of a straitjacket. Getting out of the cast was almost as satisfying. I thought I was on the road to recovery at full speed.

Then I discovered I had a staph infection, as often happens after surgery. I learned, to my utter disgust and despair, what fragility feels like. Having been strong (East Texas dairy farmers have to be that) and active all my life, being incapacitated, not to mention WEAK, was a revelation, and gave me a lot of material that may prove useful, given time. A lot of time. Some things have to "cool off" quite a bit before you can bear to go back into them in depth.

Now, five months after the accident, I am truly recovering and can walk without a cane. The back, having been abused to its limit while I was dairying, got better on its own without surgery, and my spirits are good. Being an incurable optimist helps there.

I turned seventy in February, and my doctors, all the way, have been boggled at the way I heal. One of the neurologists came into my hospital room in the middle of the second night and asked me to squeeze his hands as hard as I could.

Never assume that an old woman lying flat on her back is weak. Remember that I milked cows for ten years and a goat after that.

I squeezed, and he flinched, said, "That is enough of that!" and retreated.

In March I attended AggieCon, a science fiction convention at Texas A&M, driving myself there and back. I walked up and down stairs as if the ankle was completely well (it isn't quite, but getting there).

After being unable to write for almost three years, drained by my husband's illness as well as keeping our bookshop afloat without help, I can now sit down at the computer and START SOMETHING NEW without wanting to scream and run. The con recharged my batteries.

The most valuable thing I have learned is that a positive attitude will carry you through almost anything. You can make stories out of the strangest and most painful things, if you remember them. I made mental notes all the way along, and I intend to use them all before I sink forward, dead, with my nose in the keyboard.

II.

PAPERBACK WRITER

by *Victor J. Banis*

It is late at night when you pull into your garage, only to be confronted by two men in ski masks and bearing a chainsaw. Do you:

1) Invite them up for a nightcap—the saw is the clue; forestry is such exhausting work;
2) Have a serious discussion with them on their fashion consciousness—ski masks are so last season;
3) Interview them for your memoirs?

All right, it was a trick question. A writer never stops writing no matter what he appears in the eyes of others to be doing. Which is to say all of the above are correct answers—just make notes while you are about it.

* * * * * * *

SOMEONE, I'VE forgotten who, once boasted that he could teach anyone how to write at least one novel. Wallace Stegner was famously less convinced. His opinion was:

"1. It can be done. 2. It can't be done to everybody."

(I once said almost the same thing, but it had nothing at all to do with writing, and really must be saved for another book.)

I would add the caveat—we're back to writing by the way—that this would-be writer must come to me with at least a reasonable command of the English language. And a copy of Strunk & White's *The Elements of Style* wouldn't hurt either.

James Jones once said, "No one can help you. A writer is alone with it, by the nature of it." To which I would say, yes and no. All of the writers I tutored in the sixties were familiar with the language, and all of them without exception went on to see a novel sold and published. Some of them, it's true, were one-book wonders, but most went on to write multiple books, and some enjoyed long and productive careers.

I guess this is probably as close as we can get to the question of whether anyone can be taught to write a novel. Whatever else you may think of my experience as a writing instructor, a one hundred percent success rate is hard to beat. I would be surprised indeed to learn that anyone else has matched it.

Yes, I know that some of you are thinking, "But this was only paperback pulp fiction; his writing advice won't help me with my bestseller-to-be"—but you would be wrong on two counts.

For starters, the paperback publishers of the sixties and seventies were open to new themes, particularly (but again, not exclusively) sex-related themes, but they weren't otherwise much interested in experimental writing styles, and they certainly weren't looking for bad writing. Even in the paperback pulp field, editors looked for the same conventions of plot structure, characterization, pacing, *etc.*, as their kin at the more prestigious houses. Among the writers creating erotic fiction at that time for Greenleaf (though under house pseudonyms) were Donald Westlake, John Jakes, Marion Zimmer Bradley, Evan Hunter, and Harlan Ellison—a roster that surely suggests Greenleaf took writing skills seriously.

Further, like the roster listed above, the writers that I taught were not confined to that one area. Many of them went on to write mainstream novels for the New York houses, both hardcover and paperback. And they followed the same teaching I had given them when they started in the pulp field.

I myself went on from the pulp field to write mainstream novels that sold well and were much praised by critics. I don't pretend that I was a Hemingway, but I do in all modesty think I was a good writer and, more to the point here, a good teacher of the craft of writing as—again—my success with my students proved.

I don't think that there is anything particularly mysterious about my success in teaching the craft of writing. My own focus had always been on the nuts and bolts of technique. For the most part I was a self-taught writer, but I did read many books on writing. And sometimes still do; there's always room to grow.

I know that writing instructors at the tonier workshops decry the mere idea of learning from a book, but that seems to me nothing more than a sort of academic chauvinism. I don't say that a book can give anyone the talent that they don't have to start with, but neither can a writing class. One supposes that those instructors from time to time offer suggestions or advice on technique; they will be mostly the same sort of suggestions you can find in the right book.

Certainly there are books that can help you improve what you are doing. Writing is not entirely about bolts of lightning striking you from above; most of it, to be blunt, is mastering the craft and working your butt off. You can get some help with that craft from an instructor, or you can get it from a good book on writing. I might add, by the way, that many of those same instructors who insist you can't learn about writing from the printed page are not at all reluctant to pen how-to articles for magazines and newspapers.

I can say for sure that I found some books that helped me. One of the best of these, and one which I urged all my writers to read at that time, was *Writing to Sell* by Scott Meredith, published in 1960 by Harper, reissued in 1977, reprinted by Writer's Digest Books in 1995.

In his day Meredith was a big-league literary agent, who, as I have mentioned earlier, was one of the founders and owners, albeit a silent one, of Greenleaf Classics. He had a reputation for never missing a penny in charging back expenses to his clients. Jay Garon used to tell a story that once, when one of Meredith's big name authors died, he sent a lavish floral arrangement to the funeral. When the widow got her next statement from the agency, she found that she had been charged for the flowers.

I never knew the man, so I can't tell you if the story is true (and I hasten to add the Scott Meredith Agency is still a much respected agency in the business, though he himself is gone).

Be that as it may, Meredith's book had not so much to do with the fine points of producing literature. Rather, it was a clear, concise, and to the point primer on the elements that go into producing a commercially successful novel, in particular plot skeleton.

Writing to Sell devoted several chapters to plot skeleton. Let me give you my own version in just a few words: your lead character has a problem, one that he must solve and that seemingly he cannot. That is The Problem. Mind you, it is not called The Annoyance. The problem facing your protagonist must be urgent, and the obstacles to its resolution formidable.

He makes a number of efforts to resolve The Problem, but his efforts only make matters worse. These are The Complications. The efforts must be the protagonist's own, they must be real efforts, and the situation must worsen progressively as a result of them, one atop the other.

At The Climax he makes some extraordinary effort *of his own*—and this is where many first-time novelists fall on their faces. The *deus ex machina* is not allowed, The Problem cannot resolve itself, and Superman cannot show up to open the door unless you have already made clear that because of something your hero has done earlier in the novel, Superman owes him the favor. Nor can your hero escape the pit in the ground "with a mighty leap," if you have heretofore described the pit as so deep to be inescapable. Whatever means you employ to resolve The Problem, you must have laid the groundwork for it earlier on. If it is a matter of your protagonist running faster than a locomotive, you will have needed to show his track speed somewhere previously in the book.

This is, then, The Resolution, in which the hero is finally able to resolve that Problem, by his own efforts and using no skills or tools that you have not already shown the reader, though you can be subtle indeed in providing the reader that peek.

I cannot stress too much that you mustn't with your Resolution reveal that The Problem—the mystery, the tragedy, the loss of the family homestead, whatever—was of no consequence after all. There is an old Edward G. Robinson movie, *The Woman in the Window* (1945), which builds up suspense with a terrific story only to reveal at the end that it was all a dream. More recently, I read a novel in which the well-respected author (since I am a fan, I will not name names) spent three hundred or so pages building up an intriguing mystery regarding a young character in the story—literally a case of was he or wasn't he?—only to leave the question entirely unresolved in the end.

This is cheating your readers. If your Problem isn't a major one in the beginning, your readers won't care. If you lead them to believe it is, and so enlist their sympathy and concern, they don't want to be mocked at the end by a writer chortling "Ha, ha, got ya." They will finish the book with a bad taste in their mouth and evil thoughts of its writer.

Without the coherence of plot structure, you risk writing not a story but an anecdote. Without resolution, you risk undoing everything you have done up to the end and losing your reader's faith in you.

This is not to suggest that the prince and the damsel must inevitably live happy ever after in their castle, though there is nothing wrong with a happy ending. If your protagonist is an anti-hero who has been a cad and a rotter from page one, the right ending might have him getting his full comeuppance—though in a sense that could be said to be a happy ending.

Sometimes even a worthy protagonist may lose out in one sense and yet triumph in another, nobler way. Think of Barbara Stanwyck in King Vidor's movie, *Stella Dallas* (1937), marching away from her daughter's wedding, smiling bravely through her tears. She sacrifices her relationship with her daughter in order to give her daughter, as she sees it, a chance at a better life—never mind that the daughter isn't worth it. Stella loses in a way, but triumphs in having done what she believes is the right and good thing to do.

What is important, and it is doubly so if your ending is not a conventional happy one, is that the character comes out at the end in some way a better or at least a wiser person.

There you have it. Of course I could go on for hundreds of pages enlarging upon each of these points, but this is not the place for that. You might scour some used bookstores or shop around on the internet and see if you can find Scott Meredith's book. Or you could spend some time pondering the above, which really does pretty well cover the matter.

There are other books as well from which an aspiring writer can benefit. John Gardner's *On Becoming a Novelist* (Harper Colophon, 1985) and his *The Art of Fiction* (Borzoi/Knopf, 1984) ought to be required reading for any would-be author. W. Somerset Maugham's *The Summing Up* (1938) has much of value to say on the craft of writing, among other things.

Alas, I have read a great many books on writing that were a waste of time, and a few that I thought were likely to do more harm than good. Today it seems as if an entire generation has succumbed to what I call The Natalie Goldberg Syndrome. You see them in coffee houses and cafés, jotting lines in their notebooks or tapping away at their laptops.

I think this is a pleasant enough way to spend your day if you are interested less in becoming a writer than in posing as one in the hope of eliciting the admiration or envy of others. (Be forewarned: not everyone admires or envies writers.) Jonathan Kellerman has a character in one of his novels (I presume speaking for Mister Kellerman) remark that when an aspiring student says he wants to be a writer, he knows there is no hope for him; but when he says he wants to write, there is at least a slight hope.

If you are really serious about writing, for Heaven's sake go home and write. Jones had that right, at least—when you get down to the bottom line, you are "alone with it."

Writing is a solitary business, like leprosy or a broken leg, and can be every bit as painful. Sharing it with others is likely to weaken the impulse. That may be in part why alcoholism has often been called "the writer's disease." Certainly there has never been a shortage of writers with liver ailments.

I personally think there may be a number of factors that contribute to this problem. For one thing, it can be difficult to get the mind to relax enough for the ideas to come, and alcohol relaxes inhibitions. Undoubtedly a sip or two is going to get the ideas flowing. I certainly know that often when I drink I get ideas, though not all of them are related to books except in a peripheral way. My lesbian friend, Laura, used to say on bad weather days, "there are only two things to do on a day like this, and I don't feel like reading a book." But it's probably best that I keep some of these thoughts to myself. I don't have too good a reputation to begin with.

The difficulty is that, as time goes by, a sip or two isn't enough to get the writer's juices going. The muse can be stubborn and as coy as a sailor on Saturday night. It doesn't take long at all before your creative juices require not a sip but a glass or two, and in time the only idea you can focus on is having another drink while you wait for the inspiration that never comes. My advice? Save the juice to celebrate finishing a good day's work.

Personally I think, too, that part of the problem is tied up in all that right-brain, left-brain business. Generally speaking, the right side of the brain is the seat of creativity and imagination, the left side of the brain the processing of words and logical reasoning.

The left side is also the site of the more intense experiences, whether of words or emotions—which, as it happens, practically defines the writer's lot in life. It is why writers experience highs at a higher level than most, and lows way down lower. They are living life at a souped-up level.

When you read the lives of great writers you find, among a long list of uncanny similarities, that many of them suffered from what was once commonly called "nervous exhaustion." It can be wearisome, to say the least, to live with your motor constantly redlining.

But wait, there's more! At the very same time that the left brain is commuting at warp speed between heaven and hell, the right brain is running at full throttle as well. For most people, most of the time, one of these brains gets to mostly kick back and watch the other work. Even artists in other fields get a break. If you are a painter you are mostly using your left brain (words, logical reasoning) when you argue with the landlord, and are deeply involved with the right brain, the creative side, when you are daubing oil on canvas.

The writer is blessed (or cursed, it's all about perspective, isn't it?) with having to do his creating with words. So while the left brain is getting all worked up over the words and emotions the writer is putting on paper, the right side is working up a sweat trying to shape it all into a wonderful creative vision. Which just means that when one is writing—certainly when one is writing fiction—both sides of the brain have to hustle their behinds at the same time, and I've no doubt they are both soon pooped for their trouble. It may well be that this is when that touch of the grape begins to look appealing.

* * * * * * *

I NEVER DID take any writing classes, though I have talked to numerous individuals who have and to some who teach them. Much of what I've heard I find worrisome. The practice, for instance, which apparently is fairly common to these classes, of sharing your idea or a part of your story with the class, after which everybody gets to kick it—and, presumably you—around a bit. Writing, as I said before, is mostly a solitary business. As Stephen King so neatly put it, "It is, after all, the dab of grit that seeps into an oyster's shell that makes the pearl, not pearl-making seminars with other oysters."

I don't pretend to know everything about how the mind works, but I do know that one feels the urge to write because one has something one wants to express and can't think how to express it any other way. Someone once said that those who are successful at life live it, and those who aren't, write about it. That may be a little harsh, but I think the writer and indeed the artist in every field is responding to an itch that he hasn't been able to successfully scratch otherwise.

The process is a bit like a steam cooker. The pressure grows within you, and writing allows you to let off some of the steam. You can release the pressure as well by talking it out. The problem is that as the pressure wanes, so does the need to write that drives the writer to the word processor and keeps him there.

I don't say that you can't ever pick someone else's brain or occasionally talk out some knotty plot twist that has stymied you; but for myself, I have never discussed a novel or any aspect of it at length with anyone else without losing some of that urge, that inexorable drive, to get it down on paper.

I mentioned John Gardner's books above, and I must mention also that he taught creative writing at a number of universities and workshops to considerable acclaim. Which is to say that, despite any demurrers from me, it can be done; but except for Gardner and myself, I have never heard of another instructor whose classes I would care to sit through.

I will concede the writing class one thing, however, and it is a major thing. I think it is good for the writer to be around other writers. It's hard for non-writers to understand what you are going through. If you are like me, you get crabbier and more anti-social as a book progresses. If you don't, there is probably something wrong. I don't know of any writers of any consequence who don't look for ways to shut themselves off from the world while they are writing. I have read that Simenon would check himself into a hotel for two weeks, and even set up a work table in the bathroom so that the maids could come in and clean without interrupting him.

Not every writer goes quite that far, but the deeper and deeper you get into the world of your novel, the harder and harder it becomes to relate to the day-to-day issues in your non-book world. The characters in your novel become more real to you than your next-door neighbors and your friends.

This is a necessity. In order for you to make these characters and their world real to the reader, they must be real to you; shuttling back and forth between two worlds becomes increasingly difficult and wearisome.

Another writer knows all this in a way that non-writers do not, because he has been there too. Non-writers expect you to go to the party and be witty as if you were interested in the people around you—and indeed you might well be, but just not at this time. They will expect you to carry on an intelligent conversation about something having nothing to do with the world in which you are currently immersed. They will want you to care about, to love, and be friends with them, and will be unable to understand that your entire attention and your every emotion is focused on some individual trying to escape from inside your head onto a piece of white paper. These are situations that can lead to divorce, to murder—possibly even to a chapter in your next book.

Writers are good for one another as well because they have wonderful conversations together. It's usually hard to find anything in which they haven't some interest (after all, what another might regard as insignificant trivia may be fodder for the writer's next book). On the other hand I've known writers to spend entire evenings together exchanging no more than a few spare words, each absorbed in the scenes, the situations, the people of his current project. Even so absorbed, however, there is comfort to be taken in the company of another understanding individual. You don't have to explain to him why you are mumbling and looking off into space.

Which is perhaps the hardest part of all, so far as mixing with non-writers is concerned. Non-writers tend to think you are not working if your fingers aren't moving over the keyboard. Many of them don't think you are working even then. As a writer you get used to hearing, "You don't work during the day; couldn't you pick up the dry cleaning?" Worse, no matter how you explain that you want to be left alone for the next two or three hours, as soon as your fingers grow still you are fair game for conversation. Every writer understands exactly what Jack Nicholson was doing in *The Shining*, typing the same phrase over and over. It kept the wife out of the room and negated the need for conversation.

Writers invariably suffer from what the French call *l'esprit de l'escalier*. Literally translated, that is "the spirit of the stairs," but what it really means is that you have gotten home and are on your way up to bed before you think of what you should have replied to that snotty remark two hours earlier at the party. Too late in the physical world—but not too late to put it down on paper. A writer may, out of the blue, respond to some comment that his writer friend made two weeks before, and the friend will understand exactly. You can't count on that with everybody.

Perhaps most important of all, only another writer truly understands that you are always writing, day and night, even in your sleep. You may be having a heated quarrel with your lover and really be into it, but there is still that little part of your brain taking notes ("Aha, that's good, I can use that in Chapter Six….").

In the middle of making love you are conscious of which way the toes point and the raspy sound of excited breath in the ear. The taste of a wonderful *cioppino* is not just a gustatory pleasure, but fodder for the voluminous files in your writer's memory. Without these files you can't bring your story to life in a way that makes connection with the reader.

The writer is the classic split personality whose sanity is saved—at least most of the time—by the efficiency of the switching system that allows him to shuttle back and forth. Sometimes that system breaks down. Then we're back to the bottle, or worse. Every writer of any experience feels a certain empathy for Dr. Jekyll and Mr. Hyde.

* * * * * * *

THERE IS ONE point on which every writing book, every writing instructor, agrees. You must write every day. Writing, as I said earlier, is not about bolts of lightning striking from the ether. Inspiration may occasionally come to you in just that fashion, and you will find yourself dashing to the typewriter or the word processor, your fingers flying to keep up with the ideas as they pour through you.

Great writers—actually just plain old professional good writers—do not wait for those lightning bolts. Or rather, they train themselves to go to the source of those bolts on demand, in a manner of speaking.

In metaphysics it is understood that you cannot train yourself to enlightenment, or go out looking for it and expect to find it. (The same could probably be said for finding Mr. Right, but that's another story.) Enlightenment comes to you; but you can prepare yourself for it, with meditation for instance, so that you are open to its approach.

Writing inspiration is much the same, and the way that you prepare yourself for it, the chief way, is to write every day. When you write you are relying upon that muse, your subconscious mind, the creative self, the higher self, the right side of the brain, however you want to call it and think of it.

It is like waiting at home for visitors that you would like to see. You can just go about your business, and hope that the time they pick to stop by is the time that you are at home. Or you can let them know when you will be there.

By writing every day you are saying to that other self, "Okay, this is when I am ready for you, when you can best get through to me—just in case you would like to come to call."

Now it goes without saying that some days you will feel inspired and some days you will not. Just go ahead and do what you can do. If nothing at all comes, don't force it. If you don't know, say, how to get your heroine and the villain alone together in a car on a dark country road, do not doggedly make up the scene. Ask yourself—aloud is best, if you are alone—"How do I...?" and let it go at that; which is to say, let your subconscious mind go to work on it.

If the problem comes back to nag at you, just ask yourself again, "Okay, fine, but how do I...?" Sooner or later your subconscious mind will get the hint, and you will generally find that the answer appears to you.

That is not to say that if you stare at the blank page for a few minutes and no words pop into your mind, you should jump right up and go water the garden. Stay at the typewriter, at least for a while.

Have a drink of water—that may sound like trivial advice, but those whose work depends on inspiration have found it helpful. The brain works better when well watered, and when in doubt about when more will be coming, it tends to hoard what it's got. When you take a sip of water (*water*, mind you, not coffee or carbonated sodas or alcohol in any form), the mouth immediately signals the brain that help is on the way, and the brain releases the fluids it has been hoarding—*et voilà*, ideas start to come.

Edit something you wrote the day before. Type out a line or two about a possible character, maybe for this book, maybe for the next one. Invent someone and give him a physical description. Doodle some titles or write a limerick.

If you can do nothing else, just reread what you have already written. Let the elusive muse know that you are still there waiting for her appearance. Waiting patiently, without aggravation, but waiting nonetheless, at her convenience.

Of course, if you can, you want to get words down on paper. And here is something you may find difficult to believe but is true all the same, as every writer knows who has followed this prescription. When you have finished the book and go back to read it through, you will have a hard time recognizing which pages you wrote on those inspired days and which came out of you ploddingly, when you thought nothing you were writing was going to be worth saving.

This is the whole point of writing every day, of making a habit of writing, so that skipping it feels just as uncomfortable and "not right" as not brushing your teeth—the muse does get in the habit of visiting, even on days when you are not aware she is whispering to you. This is professional writing, and this is why I have already said you want to be home alone doing it—that voice in your ear can be tiny indeed and hard to hear. It is easy to miss it in the chatter of a coffeehouse, however delightful that chatter may be.

Walter Mosley says that writing a novel is working with smoke. Or ghosts. In any case the ideas, the characters, the words, are ephemeral. When they first come to you, they are indeed no more than wisps, and you must do the best you can to get something of their nature down on paper.

You must come back to them by the next day. Your subconscious mind will have worked on them and hopefully fleshed them out just the slightest bit. With each day they become more substantial.

Wait a week, however, and those initial scribblings will likely be meaningless to you when you read them back. They are only words. The ghost that wanted to enliven them for you has given up and departed. They are jealous, these spirits, and easily offended.

Physical athletes often rely on the body and the subconscious mind to duplicate winning moves for them. So you see a tennis player, before she serves the ball, go through exactly the same ritual each time. Three bounces of the ball, maybe a tug at her pigtails, two stomps of the left foot. This is what she did when she served that killer ace, and hopefully the exact same routine will produce the exact same results. It may be "body-memory," as some coaches believe, or it may be mere superstition, but whatever it is, it sometimes works.

In the same vein, some instructors think it is essential to write at the same time each day. I don't know if it is essential or not, but since you are trying to establish mental habits, it's probably a good idea.

How long to write? Again, experts say to set aside the same amount of time each day, or to write until you have produced the same number of words or pages. I am less convinced of the importance of this—some days, if you can, you may want to write for hours. Personally I myself never could invest more than two or three hours of actual typing—but remember, you are not writing just when you are at the keyboard. I think an hour is a good minimum, or even a half hour, but there have been times when I could spare only ten or fifteen minutes and managed to get in some good work. What is most important here is that you are making yourself open at a regular time for the ideas and the words to come to you.

Do this with unfailing regularity for a while and you will almost certainly find that they do come. Great novels have been written in a few minutes each day. I can't say for certain, but I doubt that any have been written in hours scattered randomly throughout the months.

Of course, it goes without saying that every writer is different. If I drink coffee late in the day, it keeps me awake at night, but a former doctor used to tell me that, when he woke up during the night, the best thing to get him back to sleep was a cup of hot coffee.

Writers sometimes develop elaborate fetishes. John Cheever liked to write in his underwear and Hemingway wrote standing up. Flannery O'Connor liked to face the back of a clothes dresser. Kent Haruf likes to pull a stocking cap down over his eyes and write—literally—blind.

The best system for you is the one that works. These suggestions are aimed primarily at the beginning writer (though unlike old dogs, writers never stop learning new tricks). In time you will discover your own way. While I think it is important, for instance, especially when you are beginning as a writer, to spend the time every day at your typewriter or word processor, you may be one of those writers who finds it better to just get away from the blank page altogether from time to time.

If, after a day or two of staring in frustration at the keyboard, nothing seems to be happening, try going for a walk—alone, or you are likely to be distracted by a companion's conversation when the voice you really want to listen for is the one from within. The brain needs lots of blood to do its best work, and in addition to drinking plenty of water, a bit of exercise can only benefit your thought processes by upping your circulation.

Again, don't wrestle with your plot problem. Continuing to hammer at your brain for an idea is like chasing your shadow. It is tension and fear that is blocking the flow of ideas, and you are only adding to them by nagging yourself to death. Enjoy the sights, the sounds, the smells—let the ideas for your novel come to you when they are ready.

For others relaxation is the key. Writer's block is really nothing more than that same fear and tension freezing up the creative juices. I usually meditate a bit before I start writing; I find that stilling the mind makes it easier for the muse to be heard.

Over the years I have done a great deal of my writing in my head while lying in bed at night. A bit of dialogue comes to me or a narrative patch, and I go over and over it—editing, polishing, and most importantly making sure it is imbedded in my memory so that when I sit down at the word processor in the morning I only have to get the night's work on paper. What I usually find surprising is that a scene I spent an hour or so on during the night and that seemed like half a book at least, turns out to be no more than a paragraph or perhaps two when I finally get it typed. It is usually a good paragraph, however, written in a truly relaxed state, and done over and over until the flow and the rhythm are well nigh perfect.

Sometimes I do the same sort of polishing in my head when I am up and about—while taking a walk, for instance. When you put words on paper or enter them into your computer, they take on a finality, a reality, that makes it a bit more difficult to change them or, if you must, discard them. In your head they are still ideas you are playing with, and often for me the "playing" improves the final result.

There are occasions when it seems that nothing will jar the ideas loose. As a final measure there is one trick that almost never fails to get you past that blockage. If you have an earlier, published book, pick it up and begin copying from it, preferably from the beginning. You are reminding your writing self how you did it. Usually after a few pages you will find yourself back in gear.

If this is your first novel, then use a book by someone else, preferably something in a similar vein to what you are trying to create—*i.e.*, if you are writing a mystery, copy from a mystery by an author whose work you admire. At the very least you may be polishing up your own style a bit, and it should get your creative juices flowing.

On a rare occasion, however, nothing will serve to get a manuscript past a certain point. For me this usually means I'm just not ready to write this book at this time. Generally I wait to begin actually writing a book until I have had some time to chew over it in my head. I like to get a handle on the characters, decide whose viewpoint to utilize, most often settle on an opening line or even a paragraph, and have a pretty clear idea of my ending so I know what destination my writing road is headed toward.

Some writers prefer not to know how things are going to end—James Lee Burke says he never knows more than a chapter or two ahead where he is going, though I will say frankly that his plots sometimes reflect that fact. Now before you Burke fans start sending me hate mail, let me say that I love his books. I just think his plots sometimes get away from him.

The point I want to make is, however, that when I am doing all this mental preparation I *am* writing—remember it's not just what you do sitting at the keyboard—I am just not yet putting it down on paper.

Sometimes, however, bits and pieces come so clearly into my head that I feel compelled to put them down so as not to lose them—they are ghosts, remember, mere wisps of smoke that can vanish all too quickly.

Then, although you may still not be clear on how the book is going to progress or where it is going, go ahead and start writing. It may be one scene or bits of several; a single page or fifteen or twenty—whatever it takes to transfer these ideas from mind to paper.

In this case the time comes when you will have written down all that you know. Not a book, by any means, but hopefully a part of what will become one. Of course, you want to be sure that you cannot tease out any more by trying any of the devices above.

Usually you will find that when a book is this insistent to begin, it means to be written; but not always. If, after a few days of editing, polishing, walking and ignoring, copying and everything else you can think of, nothing comes, print out your pages, put them aside, and forget them. If there really is a book there, it will come to you in time, and in the meantime there is probably something else you can work at. If on the other hand there is no book in what you've gotten down, only some notes that may give you a further idea ten or twenty years down the road (don't laugh, it happens), there's no point in wasting any more time and energy on them in the present.

Perhaps the most important thing to learn is to trust your instincts. It is hard to get used to the idea, but even when, on a conscious level, you think you are entirely at sea, the Writer within knows exactly where your boat is headed and will get you safely into port if you get out of the way and let him do his job.

III.

TIPPING THE ODDS IN YOUR FAVOR

by Charles Allen Gramlich

Author's Note: The article that follows is one of the earliest pieces on writing that I ever sold, way back in 1994. As much as anything, it was written to myself as part of the process of discovering what I truly thought about writing and publishing. I was somewhat surprised to find in rereading that I still stand by these same principles today. Although I've updated the section on marketing information, I've left the rest of it pretty much as it was. I've made the occasional modern day editorial comment in parentheses and italics.

I'LL START THIS piece by suggesting to you that I am more qualified than Dean Koontz or Clive Barker to write an article on getting published in the small press. Do you believe me? Even if you do not—and I don't always believe everything I say myself—I hope you will give me a few minutes to try and convince you that I'm right on this point.

I mention Koontz and Barker because they are among my favorite writers, and I'll admit, reluctantly, that they are better at it than I am. But, neither of the two has to think very much about getting published at the small press level anymore, and thinking about what you are doing is the key to breaking in at the smaller magazines.

Clearly, the Koontzes and Barkers know how to get published, but how many of them have to agonize over a cover letter they are sending to the editor of *Small Press Horror*? And how many of them have to worry about getting their stuff to stand out from the slush pile of manuscripts sent in by hopeful new writers? I'm not saying that their name guarantees a sale—it certainly does not—but it probably does guarantee that their stories will be read carefully.

Struggling new writers, on the other hand, like myself and like many of you reading this article, have to agonize and worry. We have to write good stories, and then we have to get an editor to notice what we've written. Even after twenty-five short story sales, as well as various articles, essays, and poems, I still have to spend my non-writing time thinking about how to get published. I have to be consciously aware of the things I try, and of whether or not those things work. So far, there's been no six-figure book deal to distract me from the small press. *(Strangely enough, that's still true today, over ten years later!)*

Given the time I've spent thinking about publication in the small press, it would be surprising if I hadn't come up with some ideas about what works and what doesn't. Those ideas are in this article. Give them a once over, compare them with your own thoughts, and then decide for yourself whether I'm really more qualified than Dean Koontz to write about small press publication. By the way, I'm better looking than he is too.

I. The Writing Itself: Tips on Making Your Stories Stand Out

1. WRITE SHORT: Small press magazines have limited space, and most would rather buy two 2,500-word stories than one 5,000-word one. The reasons are psychological. First, people who buy short stories want them short, something they can finish without investing much time. They read one on the subway, or in the twenty minutes before bed, and they can still feel the pleasant sense of having accomplished something. (Psychologists call this closure.) Second, everything else being equal, folks tend to buy the magazine or anthology with the most stories in it, even if they're getting the same number of words for their money. Having more stories often makes the reader feel as if they are getting a bonus. Editors who sell magazines and books know these kinds of things, and they want to cram as many stories as possible into their pages.

In my opinion, the best way to break into selling fiction is to write short-shorts, stories of less than 1,500 words. Four out of my first seven sales were around that magic 1,500 mark. Another was just over 2,000. In addition to the benefits of brevity indicated before, I believe that short-shorts enjoy two other advantages over longer stories. Editors can better afford to take a chance on an unknown writer's four-page story than on her twelve-page one, and short-shorts can be fitted to a magazine's space requirements more easily than longer stories. Oddly, though, you may actually have to work harder on a short-short than a short-long, but the extra effort should pay off in the greater likelihood of a sale.

2. *WRITE GENRE*: I've sold to both, but I believe it is easier to sell to genre magazines than to literary ones, particularly in the genres of fantasy, horror, and SF. It's not that the writing itself is easier, it's just that it is easier for a new genre writer to attract an editor's attention with unique ideas or a distinctive style.

Take a basic plot idea such as boy meets girl. In literary writing you are limited to realistic or at least semi-realistic interpretations of that one sentence. In genre writing, you can add such variations as boy meets monster, boy meets alien, boy meets machine, boy meets himself, boy desperately wants to meet girl, any girl. With a wider range of available twists, it's going to be easier to do something surprising. The "new" sells, and the genres give you more freedom to explore that "new." The following paragraphs illustrate what I mean in terms of ideas and style.

Unique ideas. Unique ideas are difficult to find, and most published stories are "variations on a theme," a slightly unusual way of looking at vampires, for example, or a different approach to dragons. One current trend, in genre and in mainstream fiction, is toward increasingly graphic descriptions of sex and violence. Sex and violence are not new to fiction, of course. What is new, at least to popular fiction, is the "graphic" nature of the descriptions. This marks a "variation on a theme" that has given many recent stories a feeling of newness. I'm not indicating my approval of the trend here, just stating an observation that I've made. *(This article was written when "Splatterpunk" horror was new on the scene. Although horror fiction and film have continued to push the limits of violence, most other genres have not "gored" it up. Sex, on the other hand, has become more graphically depicted almost across the board.)*

Now, how can new writers identify the variations on a theme that will give their work the shine of originality? The best way that I know is through reading—reading fiction so that I can find out what other people are doing and avoid it, and reading a wide range of nonfiction so that recent historical and scientific discoveries will inform my writing. The writing mind can only use what it has available to construct a story. That means you better feed it everything you can, and nonfiction will generally feed you better than fiction.

As examples of what I mean, in the last few years we've had the unearthing of epanterias—a carnivorous dinosaur larger and meaner than Tyrannosaurus rex—the discovery of a Roman house complete with dinner settings beneath the leaning tower of Pisa, and the melding of firefly genes with tobacco plants. *(All new discoveries in 1994.)* If you absorb enough such material, it will soon begin to percolate through your writing and add a new taste to your work, or, considering my reading habits, a new stink.

Distinctive style. Besides good ideas, another thing that can gain you favorable notice is a distinctive style. This lies not in what you say but how you say it. Compare Harlan Ellison's "I Have No Mouth, and I Must Scream" to Ray Bradbury's "Rocket Summer" if you want to see differences between unique styles. The problem is that your style must come naturally if it is to be any good. Although I believe it is possible to deliberately "craft" a style for yourself, I also think such craftings seem stilted and strained. And they often degenerate into mannerisms. You can, however, fertilize your prose in a way that will promote the growth of your own style. One way to do this is through a process called "layering."

My first step in "layering" is to write the entire story in short, declarative sentences using nouns and verbs only. Second, I go back and combine some short sentences in order to break up the staccato quality of the prose. This also involves recasting some sentences into the passive voice, and the process takes a long time because the story has to "sound" good to me when it's read out loud. Third, I put in a layer of adjectives and adverbs to modify the bare framework of my sentences, and I don't care if they're a little thick at first. Fourth, I read the story out loud to myself again, paying closest attention to the music, the cadence. To me, written style is as much sound as it is word choice and syntax. Finally, I prune the whole thing to get rid of any excess modifiers or clichés, and to clear away any dead phrasings that obscure my meaning. This also takes a long time.

Now, I certainly don't use "layering" every time I write, but I do it occasionally because it demonstrates the way in which a writer's voice is put together—from the inside out. No two people carrying out such an exercise would put their prose together in exactly the same way. That's unique style.

Finally, though, don't despair if it looks like your voice will never be a standout. You'll just have to write better stories, which is what Isaac Asimov did, and what Stephen King does. Both writers have had their prose described as undistinguished.

3. *Rewriting and Editing*: Writing well also means rewriting a piece as many times as it takes to make it good. I rewrite my stuff until I'm sick of it and have to put it away. Then I take it out later and rewrite some more. If a piece gets rejected, I rewrite (or at least re-edit) again before it goes out a second time, and I look it over

every time it comes back. For me, and I suspect for all writers, rewriting has been the key to publication. I've learned to enjoy it.

Although sometimes overlooked, a major part of rewriting should involve an effort to get the grammar and punctuation of a piece just right. Some people don't worry much about grammar. After all, isn't that what editors are for? The answer is "no" for anyone who wants to get their work published. I have over twenty books on grammar, punctuation, and usage, and I try to read a bit on the subject whenever I can. To make things easier, I extract the most important information and keep it in a computer file for quick access.

4. *RESOURCES*: Good resources are essential to helping you write well. You probably already have a dictionary—unabridged, I hope—and a thesaurus, and in the previous section we talked about a writer's need for guides on grammar and usage. You may not know, or think, however, about some of the other books that can help you. In my own writing, I use my encyclopedias almost every day, and they often take the place of the specialized references that I would like to buy but can't afford.

When I do need more detail than encyclopedias can provide, I pull out my library card and head for the nearest branch. Most city libraries will have books on the topics you're interested in, whether that be warfare, weapons, or witchcraft. University libraries are even better if you can get access. Those of you who live in rural areas or small towns, like the place where I grew up in Arkansas, may have to prepare yourself to spend more money on references than your big city colleagues. Book clubs and catalogs kept me in reading, for prices that weren't too steep, and there are always magazines, on just about any topic that you might need.

Most libraries will also carry books on the writing process itself, which can be helpful and encouraging when you're feeling isolated. Some, like this article, are collections of "tips." They give you hints and ideas to think about. Others examine more theoretical issues such as plot, voice, and character. Still others are cheerleaders. Each type can be helpful.

(If written today, the above section on "resources" would have much in it about the internet. Still, having access to hard copy physical resources has much to recommend it, and there is still a lot of information in books that is not yet available on the web. Even though I use the net frequently today, I still buy and use many reference books as well.)

II. The Magazines: Tips on Getting an Editor's Attention

5. CONTACT: If possible, make contact with editors prior to sending them stuff. This means by letter, not by phone. I'd never call an editor who I didn't know pretty well. What I do is send for "Writer's Guidelines." Most magazines have them, and they often provide information that you can't get anywhere else. I think it also makes a good impression on editors, especially when your *submission* cover letter can say something like: "Several months ago I requested your guidelines for submission, and I have now completed a story that I believe meets those guidelines." There are also "market reports" that collate guidelines, or at least the appropriate addresses, and I've included a few in the "Marketing Information" section.

Another good idea is to send for sample copies of magazines you want to submit to. I say it's a good idea, and it is, but it's not something I routinely do. The reason is money. I just can't afford it. I do buy sample copies of magazines where I hope to submit a lot of stuff, and I buy samples from magazines that offer them to writers at reduced cost. Libraries will also subscribe to some of the bigger genre magazines, but, in general, I find that the guidelines provide most of what I need. At the risk of sounding preachy, though, I do feel that writers need to support the small press as best they can. If we sell to them, then we ought to buy from them too. Small press writers and editors have to work together if either is going to survive.

(Here again, the internet has made it much easier to find writer's guidelines, and often to check out sample copies of magazines. Email is also an easy way to make contact, but most of today's editors are swamped with emails and yours isn't likely to stand out. Commenting on sample issues or on websites is one way for you to make an impression.)

Of course, the best way to make contact with editors is to meet them in person, and that usually means going to writing conferences, which can be tough if you don't live near a large city. I never attended a science fiction conference until after moving to New Orleans. There weren't any within 150 miles of my hometown. I'm hooked now, though. In just a few years, for a very small outlay of money, I've met a lot of writers and a good number of editors, including some who bought pieces from me later. I've also found out about markets that I wouldn't have heard of anywhere else. Conferences have proven to be a definite plus for me as far as making contact goes. I'd suggest you give one a try, even if it takes driving a few hours to get there.

6. *PROFESSIONALISM*: Professionalism means doing the things that make an editor's job easier, and it means doing them even when you aren't paid like a professional. The first step is to read the guidelines and follow them with care. Although each magazine is different, there are a few common courtesies that most editors will appreciate. These include a brief cover letter, which should *not* summarize the story unless you are specifically asked to do so. And don't downgrade yourself or your talent in your letter. Mention some past sales if you have any. Otherwise, just say something like: "Any consideration that you might give to the enclosed story would be appreciated.... Thanks very much for your time."

In addition to the cover letter, send a copy of your story that is easily readable, with the print as dark and clear as possible. Try reading it under fluorescent lights. If you have to squint, so will the editor, and she won't thank you for it. Also remember to put your name and address and an approximate word count on the first page of your story (Name and address at top left, word count at top right), and put a page #, a partial title, and your last name on every page. Allow ample margins (inch and a half at left, inch everywhere else) and use plain white bond paper. *(Two extra points for today's writer: 1) use Times New Roman or Courier New, in 12 point, as your font, and 2) even when emailing stories still show the same concerns for cover letters and story formatting.)*

Don't forget to enclose an SASE (self-addressed stamped envelope). Unless you send one, you probably won't hear back from a magazine, and you probably *will* irritate the editor. Editors use SASEs to send contracts to writers, or, at worst, to return their manuscripts. The writer has to make sure there is enough postage on the SASE to get a story back that's not being used. It's often cheaper to have an editor discard the story and reply on a self-addressed and stamped postcard that the writer has included. This is cheaper but I almost never do it. I like to get my stories back. *(I email most of my submissions these days, but I still occasionally find a market that wants paper submissions. That means they still want an SASE as well.)*

7. *MARKETING INFORMATION*: After you finish a story, then you have to find somewhere to send it. Some people say there aren't many markets for fiction right now. They're wrong. There are markets;

there just aren't many that pay well. Fortunately, the markets are often strong in the genres I've been talking about. Unfortunately, many of those markets are not going to be in your geographical area, and the only way to discover them is to use a "market guide." Such guides usually come in two forms, books that compile large lists of markets, and newsletters and magazines that report on fewer markets but are more frequently updated. Both types of guides often double as writing tutors, with articles on plot, setting, characterization, *etc.*

For my own writing, I started off with book guides. I now prefer to go with newsletters/magazines, because I like to get information on new markets and on changes in editors and addresses as quickly as possible. Both kinds of guides have their uses, though, and you might want to try a couple of different ones and see how you like them. Below are names and/or addresses for some of the more popular guides in each category.

Book Guides: Note: Most of these can be found in the big chain bookstores and libraries will often carry copies. *(Today, of course, most can be ordered from Amazon.com or Barnes & Noble, and there are online sites for them as well. The websites below are newly updated for this book.)*

Literary Market Place (LMP). (literarymarketplace.com). The most comprehensive annual guide available on publishers, including US and foreign publishers, as well as small press publishers. It also contains contact information for many agents, but it is expensive.

The Writer's Handbook. An annual work that lists core markets and publishers and also contains many articles and essays on writing by established professionals.

Writer's Market. An annual release that covers a huge selection of paying markets for both fiction and nonfiction. This is from *Writer's Digest Books. (Available at writersdigest.com, Amazon, or toll free at 1-800-448-0915.)*

Novel and Short Story Writer's Market. Annual, also from *Writer's Digest Books.* Covers fiction markets only, both paying and non-paying. Includes articles on fiction writing.

Newsletters/Magazines: (Again, addresses and websites are updated for this book.)

Byline Magazine. (bylinemag.com). Articles, markets, and frequent writing contests.

The Gila Queen's Guide to Markets. (gilaqueen.us). One of the most comprehensive and frequently updated market newsletters available. The editor is Kathryn Ptacek [*one of our Borgo Press authors—ed.*], who has many contacts among editors and publishers.

The Writer. (scriptmag.com). Magazine. Contains markets and articles on writing.

Writer's Digest. Magazine. Market information as well as articles and tips on writing.

III. Afterward: Tips on Surviving the Writing Roller-Coaster

8. PERSEVERANCE: You will get rejection letters, and I know they'll get you down. They do me. So wallow in self-pity a while. Gripe and growl around the house, or go to the video arcade and blow some quarters on cathartic violence. But then go back to writing. I won't give you any platitudes about "getting back on the horse." Hell, you probably don't even have a horse. What you do have is a writing tool of some sort. And you have a need to write that is big enough to have kept you reading this article. That's all I know about you. You know the rest.

9. MONEY: Forget about the cash flow for now. It's very nice to get paid for writing, and it makes you feel professional, but you aren't going to make a living at it at first. You aren't even going to make enough to pay the rent. There just isn't that much money in the small press, or in the big press for that matter, unless you write a bestseller.

What's the answer? Don't do it for the money. I've got a good job and I write weekends and nights. Any money I make, and I do make some, goes into fun things, like motorcycling or books. If you can last, and can keep getting better, the money will come. Until then, the best of luck.

IV.

WRITING IS FIGHTING THE FAMILIAR

OR,

47 YEARS IN THE WAKE OF ADELBERT AMES, JR.

by W. C. Bamberger

I ONCE HAD an exchange with Samuel R. Delany about books we had conceived of, planned, or even begun but which remain unfinished. (We were discussing his set-aside study of Donna Haraway.) For him, if I remember correctly, these were most often the result of ideas or interests turning out not to have enough depth to hold his interest, or that had simply fallen behind as newer ideas had carried him speedily forward. For me, I explained, unwritten books provide havens and connections for ideas that might otherwise simply shoot through the cloud chamber and be lost. I see them as a row of vessels, fronted by a Maxwell's Demon effortlessly sorting through incoming information.[1] (About which, more later: watch for the phrase "prognoses for future action.")

The original Maxwell's Demon was created by James Clerk Maxwell as a kind of microscopic Golem to aid in a thought experiment. (Through his steam governor, Maxwell is considered the great-grandfather of Information Theory, which tells us such things as "The more obvious the message, the less information it con-

---

[1] Thinking of writing in terms of Maxwell's Demon is certainly not original to me. Ken Kesey, for example, published a miscellany with the title *The Demon Box*, named after this same Demon—or so I'm told: I've not read it. Kesey's demons have never been mine.

veys.") This imaginary being came about as a result of Maxwell considering something familiar—how in a closed system hot and cold molecules will average out, or, to use more technically correct language, will be subject to entropy—and finding a new way to look at it. Maxwell imagined the Demon as a gatekeeper inside a sealed vessel with a wall down its middle. The Demon would open or close the gate in the wall as molecules approached, sorting the colder onto one side and the hotter onto the other, thus defeating entropy.[2]

The Demon at the doors of my own perceptions—unhindered by the laws of thermodynamics that hobbled Maxwell's creation—sorts choice bits of things I hear and see, and—especially—read, sorting the "hot" information (relevant to something I'm writing—or may write someday) from the "cold" (not relevant). The hot information goes into my mental vessels (and their stoppers, my notebooks) for such potential critical books as *George Steiner and the Gaia of Culture: A Simultaneous Diptych,* and *A Semiotics of Bizarro,* or into those for two half-finished novels, *Bi-Cameral Sonja* and *A Light Like Ida Lupino.* These, and more, exist in various stages of completion, in notes and unconnected pages, some now years old. The work my Demon does—almost nonstop—is a gift, and it's a problem.

Making this clearer will involve some Swahili.

The late 1950s were a time of accelerating evolution. The lower strata of our civilization (our basements) reveal that drab, now-extinct creatures once roamed our lands—encyclopedia salesmen, for example. Into our home some time in the mid-Fifties came the twenty volumes of the 1950-51 edition of *Collier's Encyclopedia.* At eight or nine I spent weeks going through every volume, page by page, copying out in pencil every entry on foreign languages, every isolated foreign word in any entry, onto sheets of three-hole-punched paper which I kept in a blue binder—my first, clumsily constructed physical vessel for hot intellectual molecules. One summer afternoon in this same period when I was copying out such phrases as *vi-su, vi-kali, vi-wili* (which I noted as "Swahili for 'three sharp knives'"), I was taken to *Mystery Ridge.*

The 1950s were also the Golden Age of the small-scale roadside attraction—displays of snakes in tanks, The World's Largest [You Name It], and mysteriously distorted rooms at turn-offs like *Mystery Ridge.* There were (and still are) variations on this theme in several states. The basic structure was that of a long, single room half buried

---

[2] I learned about Maxwell's Demon late, from Thomas Pynchon's *The Crying of Lot 49.*

in an artificial hill. Inside, water or golf balls would appear to run uphill, people could walk easily across floors or sit in chairs that appeared impossibly off-kilter, and children would become taller than their parents simply by moving from one side of the room to the other, or by looking through a different window frame.

    I enjoyed this, for much the same reasons as everyone else: It was mysterious, it made me laugh, I didn't understand it, and—a reason I wouldn't have quite understood then, but which later became the most central—because it was unfamiliar. And this is why my explanation involves Swahili: I was also copying out and saving languages by the page because they were unfamiliar. I and every other visitor to *Mystery Ridge* were there on vacation—that is, a willed escape from the comfortable and familiar. What none of us knew was that, for the man who had invented this distorted room, the point of it was just that: to show the viewer how completely immersed we are in the familiar, and how we need to try to escape it. And just so my Demon, for all the help it is in gathering materials in support of what I think I want to write, also weighs me down, keeps me from escaping the comfort of the ideas I've already had. It is, in very real ways, that which refuses to open the gate in the wall between the familiar and the unfamiliar and let me see through. There is, it must be admitted, in my encouragement of this hovering Unwritten Book Demon an element of desperation and clinging, of timidity: If this good idea gets away, will I ever have another as good? (Delany is certainly the wiser and the braver of the two of us.) I have always recognized this, but I have needed help to deal with it.

    Which is the main reason why, some forty-five years after my visit to *Mystery Ridge*, I decided to become Ames' intellectual biographer.

* * * * * * *

WE ARE ALL given to write what we can write, as William Eastlake pointed out. The author of the most cliché-riddled ripper is likely writing up to his potential to the same degree someone as serious as Jeanette Winterson is writing up to hers. What Eastlake didn't add was that we are also given to read what we read. Eastlake, in his seventies, was reading Faulkner and Darwin; my daughter Aja, at twelve, is reading her way through Orson Scott Card and an endless series of Manga books. Our tastes in narrative pace and language, our ideal degree of complexity, favored proportions of action to contemplation, even that great spiral of attitudes we call our "view of life" for short and look to find matched in the authors we read, all appear to be as hard-wired as our hair color. As a consequence, I am no more likely to be able to recommend a book you will like than I am to suggest a storyline you could write—so, if you're looking for specifics along that line you'll find no comfort here.

Like many who grow up to squander our lives trying to sort words and put them together in fresh and compelling orders, I've read a little something of everything, read almost continuously, for years on end. Some authors and books have become permanent parts of my intellectual DNA. Very early on, for example, I read everything by Andre Norton. She created not just alien worlds, but psychological worlds where characters mixed self-doubt with reluctant bravery—a seam Marvel Comics would mine a few years later to great effect (and my enjoyment). But her characters were exemplary in that, unlike the more old-school ethos of Marvel heroes, they didn't aspire to being triumphant *isolatos*. They looked instead to cooperation and communication, especially across divides between species—alien and animal—and between idea sets; they valued such bridges over traditional stand-alone heroics. Many shortsightedly dismiss Norton as only a Young Adult writer, an estimation with which I strongly disagree. Still, I may have stayed with her a little too long before moving on to more "adult" fiction—but then I have always come late to everything, be it intellectual, emotional, or physical. I even came late to getting my tonsils taken out—luckily so, as this led to the opening of a gate to a simplex, complex, and multiplex reading universe.

Making this clearer will involve coffee and a failed bank robbery.

My tonsillectomy was performed only a few months after my brother's skills at cutting Masonite board on a jigsaw had started me off on a course that would soon lead through a teacher named Carl Marx ("That's spelled with a C, not a K," he laughed when he introduced himself; I didn't get it), to Rimbaud, the Surrealists, Little Hat Jones, and a name that did start with a K, Kafka. I was fourteen. I shared my hospital room with a man whose now-forgotten ailment meant that he had to endure a long convalescence, but was permitted to walk the halls as he wished. I was in a great deal of pain, and my mother sat with me almost constantly over the two days I was in the hospital. Because the cafeteria was on a different floor, the man who shared my room brought my mother coffee, so he could walk and she could stay put. The morning of the second day she brought me two books. She had picked them off the rack at the drugstore because she knew I liked science fiction. One has vanished from my memory, but the other was the Ace Double of *Alpha Yes, Terra No!* by Emil Petaja, and *The Ballad of Beta-Two,* by Samuel R. Delany, someone I had never heard of. I read them, or maybe I didn't because of my discomfort, and they went home with me.

A short time later, I was reading the newspaper (unusual for me) when I noticed an item about a man being jailed for attempted robbery. I recognized his name: it was the man who had brought my mother coffee. The short article said that he had been hospitalized for a time, and so had lost his job. His money exhausted, he had attempted to rob a bank. I don't remember my emotional reaction, but my literary reaction was to go hunt up that Ace Double and reread both sides. Delany's novel was "about" (a word that should always be set off this way) the way social conditions change language, and how we can fool ourselves into thinking that because something sounds (or looks) familiar that we know what it means. This very much appealed to that part of me that had been the eight-year-old in the mystery house with Swahili in his head.

I began to seek out Delany's books, to watch for new ones to appear. The one that struck me most deeply at that time was *Empire Star.* Its many dizzying delights were tied together in part by the chanted refrain "simplex, complex, multiplex," referring to the levels of intellectual understanding and engagement the characters might achieve: "The four hundred years as gate guardian to the transport area of Rhys had leveled her mind to something nearly simplex. But multiplexity had awakened." The unfamiliar category, multiplex, was the most compelling. It referred to someone who could see things from many sides at once. The term is casually introduced by an alien life form named Jewel. Shallow as my intellectual draft was at the time, I recognized that it had most likely been given the form of a jewel because Delany wanted to suggest the word "multi-faceted" without being too heavy-handed about it. There is another, insistently multiplex, alien form called the LUMP. I aspired to being a fourteen-year-old LUMP ("Linguistic Ubiquitous Multiplex"), and only a character's assertion that "Intelligence and plexity have nothing to do with each other" gave me any hope.

Empire Star prompted a few firsts: the refrain was the first of those snippets of language which have over the years entered into my internal dialogue and remained steady compass points—phrases I hear in my head at some point in almost every day. (Others include Kenward Elmslie's "demise parody penchant," and Saul Bellow's "The usual thought suspects were rounded up.") *Empire Star* was also the first (and to this point, still the only) book I sat down and typed out, in an attempt at understanding how Delany had been able to do all the things he did here.

By way of other mixes of accident and volition, I over the years found a number of authors and individual works who struck me as strongly as had Norton and Delany. There was Milton Klonsky's essay, "Art & Life: A Mennipean Paean to the Flea, or Did Dostoevsky Kill Trotsky?"; Kenward Elmslie's poetry, and his novel *The Orchid Stories*; Sam Shepard's plays; Cynthia Ozick's stories; the novels of William Eastlake, for their dialogue; Thomas McGuane and Stanley Elkin (these last being two species of "American Mean," a sarcasm genus I favor). I was particularly taken with the works of Steve Katz, for the compelling way he combined a wholly original sense of formal invention with deeply-affecting emotion (I found this same combination in the best of Elmslie's work, as well); and with Ishmael Reed, for the syncopations of his language, for the fact that he seemed to know *everything* that no one else knew, and for his bold declaration that "Writin' is Fightin'." Thomas Pynchon's story "Low-Lands" amazed me, as did W. Watts Biggers' novel *The Man Inside*, and the Seuss-high stacks of cultural clutter in the stories of Donald Barthelme. I recognized the shortcomings of Jorge Luis Borges' claustrophobic, ticking miniatures, but still read them over and over for the intricacy of their structures. The linguistic inventions of Alexander Theroux rose like Hokusai's *Great Wave*.

I was also greatly influenced by a novel I didn't read until after years spent trying to imitate it. In Alain Robbe-Grillet's *For a New Novel*, I read about the use of repetition in Robert Pinget's *Mahu, or the Material*. I was intrigued enough to try to imitate this in several works, including *Waterwheels*, my attempt at a surrealistic novella. It prompted two repetitive chapters about dancers on a wooden dance floor that folds out of an old Chevy convertible at the push of a button—identical incident, two different approaches. It wasn't until ten years later that I finally read the Pinget in translation and discovered that I had misunderstood, but it didn't matter: the influence of what I didn't understand about a book I hadn't read lingers to this day, whereas the reading of the novel itself has had no lasting effect.

Being possessed of an excess of self-consciousness, I eventually realized that my favorites had some elements of the uncommon in common. They either didn't take place in a world I was familiar with or if they did they approached it from an unexpected, unfamiliar angle, or deliberately frustrated any expectation of "plot," or were written in language heightened, stretched or compressed, or all of the above—but they all "had something" that was something unfamiliar. This was clearly what engaged me as a reader. In contrast, to try to read Hemingway or Updike, Cheever or Beattie was to self-anaesthetize. I already knew those worlds, and even if I knew no one as rich or as poor as their characters, the actions were all too predictable, and the writing was as bare as a level concrete floor.

The works I was drawn to focused not just my own self-conscious evaluations, but those of my Demon as well. As I homed in on what interested me, it seized and sorted materials with more confidence; put them into well-thrown vessels for the fictions I hoped to write. I come to things late, so I was twenty-eight when I published my first short story. Marcel Duchamp was its hero, and the ending stuttered down the page in emulation of *Nude Descending a Staircase* and, again, that rumor of Pinget. I was thirty-two when my next story appeared: an alphabetically arranged fiction about an amnesiac, based on my own experience of being hit by a car. I published another handful of stories, most of which were soon gathered into a collection, and the urge to write more simply vanished. My short-story writing career lasted not much more than five years. And I knew very well why my interest had winked out: because I now knew how to write them. So, I resolved to become a novelist—in part, because I had never been able to write a novel manuscript that satisfied me. My Demon quickly retooled.

One afternoon, in the "Last Chance: $1" bin at a used book store in Ann Arbor, I picked up a book in the tatters of a yellow jacket. *The Morning Notes of Adelbert Ames, Jr.*, someone I had never heard of. I flipped through the book and found two grainy, washed-grey photo inserts, and in one of those photos was a room like that at *Mystery Ridge*. I laid my dollar down. I learned that Ames (1880–1955) had designed these "Distorted Rooms," now often called just "Ames Rooms," and that he had also created an entire series of related *things*: there was a chair which was really just disconnected strings; a trapezoidal window that revolved but appeared only to be swinging back and forth, and if a steel rod were suspended through one of its openings the steel would appear to bend like rubber; there were playing cards that appeared gigantic but were really only notched, cigarette packs that changed size, and many more. Reading through page after page of the intellectual lab note-style entries, repetitive analyses he'd written as his ideas struggled to break free from what he knew into unfamiliar territory, I learned that for Ames these creations were not meant simply to provide roadside amusement. They had been created to demonstrate his psychological, sociological, and philosophical ideas. The most basic of these was that what we see before us is not the simple reality of the world. Rather, everything we see is shaped by our expectations, by our tenacious need to cleave to the familiar. At the simplest level, Ames's ideas tell us that we see what we expect to see. At a more complex level they hold that what we see are "prognoses for future action"—that is, we interpret everything we see in light of how we might use it to further our goals. These goals can be as immediate as not tripping over a chair, or as abstract as an understanding of the true nature of reality.

Or as self-centered as the writing of a novel.

Ames had been a lawyer, the book's Introduction informed me, then a self-taught painter, a self-taught ophthalmologist, self-taught philosopher, and more—a living exemplar of his belief in the centrality of "becomingness." The Introduction explicitly compared Ames to Leonardo da Vinci for his range of knowledge and inventiveness, and I began to aspire to a multiplex view of Ames, the kind of view only a novel can capture in words.

I first spent a few hours at the local library skimming old reference books. Little was available on Ames, Jr., but there was a great deal about his father, a Civil War general. General Adelbert Ames, Sr., of Massachusetts, had been elected Reconstruction Governor of Mississippi, but had resigned just as the state legislature was preparing to impeach him on charges of incompetence and corruption. A familiar story: opportunist carpetbagger, corrupt politician.... General Ames had even been included in a litany of wrongdoers in John F. Kennedy's *Profiles in Courage.*

And here, I thought, is my multiplex novel: Lying politician has a son who abandons the law to develop a philosophical system (complete with askance, Dr. Caligari-like architecture) in order to remind us all that we can't believe anything we see. To repeat: We are all attracted to a given degree of complexity—and this story had mine. Or so I believed. But as I read further, I found that JFK and I had both been mistaken. It became apparent to me (and, indeed, is the consensus among modern historians) that General Ames, while no saint, was a liberal idealist who had been set-up by native politicians steamed at the carpet-bagging Governor for appointing so many blacks to his government. (The hatred of General Ames went on past his impeachment; Jesse James' famous "Northfield Minnesota Raid" was an attempt at stealing General Ames' money on deposit there.) This was still a good story, maybe even a better one, but it wasn't the multiplex novel I wanted to write. The novelization of Ames' life became a casualty of the truth.

I turned back to an idea I'd had earlier, had had so long that my Demon had filled enough vessels for two or three books—different incidents, identical approach. My idea was "about" writing a novel with almost no plot or development, one that would attempt to hold the readers' interest through sheer novelty of setting, incident, character, and use of inverted farm implements. This became my first published novel, *The Master Tanner Heads West,* set in the post-Civil War Southwest. Ames's ideas, unarticulated, dramatized in a comic vernacular, pervade the novel. The title character, Jarry Kennianc (I'd been through my obligatory Kerouac period; his name is bent versions of the names of two famous Beats) is a French-Canadian who moved to Massachusetts after his father was murdered. Jarry has read a great number of the adventure Westerns of the day, novels called Yellow Backs (which I learned of from Ishmael Reed's novel *Yellow Back Radio Broke-Down*). He relocates his family to the West to escape the unsettling, always-changing East. Once out West, Jarry again and again encounters what he initially sees as characters or situations familiar to him from his Yellow Backs. But he is always wrong. Familiar forms lead only to unfamiliar realities, frustrate rather than aid him in his attempts to reach his goals. No matter how many times this experience is repeated, Jarry never learns. Only his wife Dolley, who has no expectations, no plan, sees the West as it truly is. Barnes & Noble declined to place *The Master Tanner* on their "Featured Titles" display.

* * * * * * *

TO REPEAT AN earlier repetition: We are all drawn to given degrees of complexity. Once *Master Tanner* was finished, I was drawn back to Ames, this time with an eye to writing an intellectual biography—in part, I knew, because this was something I had no idea how to do. I had noticed during my first encounter with Ames's life that my Demon (who always has to have one hand on the door of familiarity) had offered little in the way of help. I was curious to see how this everything-connects-to-something-I-already-know part of me would conduct itself.

I found myself reading the philosophy of A. N. Whitehead (which was likely where Ames found the term "becomingness"; Whitehead was also the unfortunate role model for Ames' at times overly-dense terminology) and John Dewey (who, with Whitehead, had called Ames a genius); found myself reading equations in non-Euclidian geometry, and about how they helped a shipyard build one of Ames' most complex rooms; reading psychology and sociology texts and books on the history of aerial photography in WW I. And my Demon was silent. There was almost nothing here I knew anything about, nothing I could connect anything with. I was on my own, without that familiar part of me that thrived on familiarity.

I read Erwin Schrödinger's 1944 *What Is Life?*, the book that had inspired the men credited with discovering the structure of DNA. Ames, a lawyer turned artist turned ophthalmologist turned perceptual theorist, had read the book, which presents a physicist's theory of biology and evolution, and annotated it, making observations that were still being made by others fifty years on. I read an Ames family history, Xeroxes of letters from a brilliant niece, a history or two of Reconstruction and of the Spanish-American War, and a manual on beekeeping. All of these were subjects I'd known almost nothing about beforehand. I also returned to the late graphic prints of M. C. Escher: A very short paper written about some of Ames's research had been a direct influence on Escher's most striking later prints. I studied the prints again to see if I could see in them what I had never seen before: Ames's ideas. Expecting to, I did. And saw that Ames room and Escher's impossible stairs and ladders were very close kin, indeed.

* * * * * * *

PAPER AND PRINTER'S ink, pixel and screen enable ideas to express their complexity. But to express other aspects of their selves, ideas will at times enlist people. We can be ideas' step-down transformers; allow them to convey their simpler side.

Making this clearer will involve a little bit of brain matter out on a long cord.

Midway through my researches I contacted Ames' son, Dr. Adelbert Ames, III. Dr. Ames III graciously invited me (and my then-wife, gorgeous and queasy in her seventh month of carrying our daughter) to his Vermont farm. There he showed me a bust Ames II had made (which had been stored for years under an upturned canoe), as well as several of his paintings and drawings. In his basement, Dr. Ames patiently demonstrated one of the original Rotating Trapezoidal Windows his father had had built in the 1940s. (Built, I learned, by a local carpenter named Kimball Whipple. In the papers Ames III showed me I found a price list, complete with "Shipping weight"—Whipple sold plans and materials to those wanting to create their own Demonstrations. Anyone could have their own small monocular Distorted Room for only $225. Here was the likely source for the creation of *Mystery Ridge*....) Boxes of books from Ames II's library were carted down from the attic for me to read through (Ames II annotated books the same way I did:

the more vertical hashes in the margin, the more important the point. Here were the unmistakable tracks of Ames' own Demon); Ames III's wife shared her personal memories. But there was something more, something neither book nor reminiscence: a miniature display of—just a flash of—a gateway at the intersection of intellect and awareness of the body, the kind of gate through which Ames II's theories must have come to him.

I had been thinking of Dr. Ames just as "Ames' son," as a source of information about his father. But then I learned that Ames III had continued the family tradition of intellectual brilliance. He had become a neurologist, and, as he explained to me, he had helped solve the dilemma of how to secure a slice of brain tissue thin and intact enough to examine, when even the sharpest scalpel would damage the tissue it sliced through. In an insight of great logical and poetic beauty he realized that the retina, the nerve at the back of the eye that sends the visual signals along the optic nerve to the brain, must itself be a part of the brain; a bit of brain tissue out on a long cord like a space walker. The beauty of this, for me, lay in the fact that Ames III looked at something that had to be tediously familiar to a neurologist, the retina, and found it something other than it had always seemed. Like his father, he had looked at vision itself and found something new; he had understood the importance of trying to look at the world as unfamiliar. This very tall, dignified, and modest man, just down off his farm tractor, spoke of his revolutionary discovery as if it were the most ordinary thing in the world. For him, it seemed, what he had discovered was only a tool, and less important than the work that it enabled, research into the structure of the brain. And he didn't have much to say about that. Perhaps he knew I wouldn't understand. All of which focused something for me. It gave me, so I felt, a glimpse into what father and son had in common and, I also felt, into just a little of how they differed.

Making this clearer will involve an *overt* return to the subject of writing, and a little narrative irony.

* * * * * * *

AMES II never had a high opinion of himself as a communicator. He searched for collaborators, feeling he needed a proxy to get his ideas across. At one point there was even a project afoot to present some of his ideas in comic-strip form. Reading his writings as I wrote my book, I saw how his struggle was in large part due to his given sense of the unfamiliar. He knew that the ideas he was trying to get across were unfamiliar ones, and he tried to use precision to get them across—but what came out of the gate was an *excess* of precision—mixed with relaxed touches of folksiness, and a intermittent faith that we as readers were right there with him in what he understood:

I will not go into the optical explanation, but when we look at a solid object we use the nasal halves of our retinas so that we can look around the object as much as possible. When we look through an opening, we use our temporal halves so that we can see further out.[3]

Who knew a retina has halves?

One of the idiosyncrasies of Ames' writings is that almost every paper or note he wrote reads as if he were starting over from the ground up, with definitions of the basics getting as much page-time as the new ideas that sprang from them, the result being long blocks of repeated terms, of identical slabs of explanation that appear again and again like thick tiles in a dense mosaic. Ames' ideas are present in his writings—in fact their entire evolution is frequently present—but it is difficult in his written work to separate the gold from the surrounding material. This, I believe, is because, for Ames, there was no difference between the two.

All "good writing" (which we all define as, "I know it when I read it") is about making the familiar unfamiliar to just the right degree. To see this in fiction writing is simple enough: we say a novel or story has an original plot, or it has freshness, or even that it is an interesting variation on a classic theme. If a story is either, on the one hand, too familiar, or on the other, too distant from the world of sense as we know it, many readers will find it to be of no worth or interest, and will set it aside. It has to fall within an—within an individual reader's—acceptable middle-ground, be possessed of comfortable degrees of both familiarity and novelty. Science and technical writers sometimes think they are doing the opposite, making the unfamiliar familiar, but that's because oftentimes they don't understand where these two reside. Original ideas, however new or even revolutionary, have a familiarity for those who know the field in which they arise, those comfortable with the vocabulary and the context and the concepts, the intellectual world in which these ideas germinate and grow. Popularizers have to take these ideas and discoveries out of their familiar, original context, out of their native ecology, and put them into another. And this Ames could not do.

Ames of course knew that every idea, every discovery, is not of equal value. But for him his own discoveries, his demonstrations,

---

[3] From "Art and the Subjective Visual Sensation" (1936), unpublished manuscript at Dartmouth.

and the theories that grew out of or were reinforced by them, were all of a piece. He had come up with the theories; he had had the demonstrations built; he had formulated the implications, so for him all was one. That someone understood *how* the distorted room played with his or her preconceptions, we might think, could be seen as less important than the kind of increased mental awareness that the experience was meant to promote. But Ames' writing shows how deeply he felt that without an understanding of the mechanics of the room, there could be no true increased awareness. So, in his writings, he always felt the impulse to include every basis, ever proof, and consequence of every element of his demonstrations that went with his ideas when he wrote them up. Much of Ames' writing is choked with the kind of precision familiarity is comfortable with—"thereness," "thatness," "anaseikonic lenses"— but which the majority of us, his lay readers, are not. He often contextualized his ideas to the point where he bricked them closed. (This is true even of the notes meant only for himself and his closest associates, an extreme kind of self-consciousness that may have come from his autodidact's insecurity.) He didn't have the easy way with hierarchy I saw in Ames III. (Or, to keep Ames II theories in mind, I perhaps only believed I saw in him, because of my personal association of the New England accent with common sense and humility.) Ames II couldn't bring himself to assign overriding importance to some elements of his ideas, and relegate others to subservience.[4]

Considering the bases of his life's work, it is ironic to think that Ames's writing suffered because he knew his subject too well, that he kept it inside a self-constructed familiarity, and couldn't make himself let it come out to meet us on some common ground. But this appears to me to be the case.

* * * * * * *

THE BOOK THAT came from my years of encounters with Ames' ideas is titled *Adelbert Ames, Jr.: A Life of Vision and Becomingness*. Writing it might not have been a truly multiplex experience by any of Jewel's or the LUMP's measures, but I feel it certainly lifted me to the upper limit of complex, and I feel it is my best book. By Ames' lights, this is only natural. My experience in writing it was one of grappling almost exclusively with completely unfamiliar

---

[4] I am in the process of preparing a new edition of Ames's writings, not just the Morning Notes, but other papers he wrote, some of them unpublished. My intent is to impose a linearity and a more comfortably unfamiliar form.

ideas. I had almost no preconceptions to filter what was coming in; my Demon had to stand by helplessly. I was, happily, on completely unfamiliar ground, pulling Ames's ideas into it bit by bit through the gateway of my writing.

In working on this intellectual biography I was, in a very real sense, back on *Mystery Ridge*, walking tilted floors, in a landscape where even the simple act of sitting in a chair reading was an unsettling, off-kilter experience, and wondering why, in this one area, water could run uphill and I could be bigger than those who came before me. I was once again, without there being anything at all nostalgic about it, that eight-year-old boy in a tilted room with Swahili in his head.

And there—somewhere in the absorbing, delightful unfamiliar, hiding from my habit-forming Demon—is exactly where I want to be when I am writing. And if you write, this is where you should be as well.

V.

SLANTING CAN BE FUN AND DANGEROUS

OR,

ART VS. ALL THAT OTHER STUFF

by Charles Nuetzel

I REMEMBER reading some notes that were on a manuscript by E. Everett Evans. Ray Bradbury had run the words past his literary eyes. One statement was repeated over and over: "Trite, Trite, Trite!"

You don't argue with a master of words concerning such matters. It was quite a lesson in writing for a young budding author/fan, a wannabe who eagerly listened to anybody who was willing to teach him. And then there was another thing Ray was noted for saying to young writers: "Don't slant. Write from your guts, about what fires you." Well, words to that effect.

I have never attempted to challenge any successful writer's advice concerning their profession; and certainly not Mr. Bradbury.

My agent for many years, Forrest J Ackerman, basically grew up with a young fannish Ray. They knew each other when things were not so charmingly literary. In those early days they were struggling to discover the way to a writer's life and literary success, which would, over the years, fully realize itself for both men in their own pathway to fame.

My, even *I'm* impressed by that last paragraph.

What I want to say about Ray Bradbury is this:

He is famed for having burned the first two million words he wrote as a young, struggling writer, learning to become a master story-teller. He burned them, not as a Hitler smashing down the words of published writers for fear they might influence the masses, but for fear somebody in the future might take up these stories and bring them into print. Presenting an early Bradbury to haunt the literary master in his later years! So much of this learning period is lost, never to reach the light of public knowledge. Smart move, perhaps. Nobody can write endlessly perfect, lyrically exciting, and meaningful words all the time. Especially in their beginning years. Some, even in their later years, can't manage that. But a man of Ray Bradbury's status has a perfectly safe history, for he made sure the young, stumbling, beginning writer was muffled before being exposed to the public at large.

We all learn. Writing is a learning profession. We never learn enough; we never stop learning. The problem, in fact, can be an endless demand, command, for us to continually grow, continually do better. The past words are there to haunt us, to hammer home the flaws and our early efforts to express ideas on paper. We are a continual work in progress, attempting to not top the guy next door or down the street or in the next town, but simply top ourselves. Topping all those other fellows might be hard enough, but possible in some circumstances, but topping yourself is a plan designed to drive even the mad into fits of depressive defeat, no matter how skilled, how wonderful, how famous they may become. The better you get, the more demanding the strain to top yourself.

Writing can be growing publicly, forcing one's moments of glory to mix with horrid periods of mundane literary nonsense. Even for a Mr. Bradbury, who has managed to protect his image and his literary work by continually polishing and polishing and polishing and never slanting. Or so it would seem. I remember his reputation for having the habit of revamping a story whenever it was reprinted, never satisfied with the last end result, but continually revamping and revising and making it better as his perspective changed over the years.

I remember hearing things which implied just that. And any literary detective can easily trace such alternations by a bit of hard work. Which I'm certainly not at all interested in attempting to do here.

I'm touching on Mr. Bradbury (Ray, as most of his friends call him) because he was, believe it or not, a strong influence in my life; even if we stood on opposite poles of the writing profession.

So I remember his: "Don't slant. Write from your guts. Write what you feel passionate about."

I remember that he burned the first two million words so they would never have a chance of being published.

But I broke those rules. And I'm not bragging, not even begging for forgiveness. Just that I came from a different direction, and a different time, with a different "dream of glory" than his. We both came out of the same generalized pool of young sci-fi fans, but with different images concerning our place in the literary world.

Forry Ackerman, back in 1969, wrote this in my *Images of Tomorrow*:

"*Bradbury burned his first two million words; Nuetzel sold his. Under more pseudonyms than Henry Kuttner, he's had no less than 60 original pocketbooks published—and fully half of those translated and republished abroad.*"

Nice to be mentioned in the same paragraph with a true literary giant.

I have always suggested, in reference to that quote, *"Maybe Mr. Nuetzel should have burned his first two million words, too!"*

My tongue burns against my ragingly pulsing pink cheeks upon admitting to the above. But in fact, that is reality. I had my first million(s) published, simply by the act of slanting.

Slanting is, in effect, finding out what the publishers want, what they demand in order to pay hard cash for the right to publish an author's golden words. Then going about doing just that!

Now a writer of Ray Bradbury's status wrote from his guts and developed a style, and the end result was that he thusly defined himself as a genre. He became the slant that publishers took in order to have his name on their magazines or one of the books they released. They accepted him on his terms.

Let's be brave and brutal about this, if you will. He had to go through the learning process that went beyond bond-firing his early efforts at writing. He learned with the help of other writers. He did his kind of "slanting," which was writing for editors who required certain professional standards in order to take an author's work and put it into print. He may not have cold-bloodedly slanted, but he learned his craft under the skilled guidance of other professional writers and editors who were willing to help the young Bradbury find his way through the early creative years that developed the ground work for a literary career which will, no doubt, make him a name to remember over the coming decades and perhaps centuries. At least much longer than most writers who put words to paper during the twentieth century and beyond.

So it is it is honest to say that slanting can be dangerous.

Let me explain. Publishers have requirements which are set up to dictate what it takes to be accepted by their editors. If you want to see your words in print, best you supply what they require. If you aren't a known writer, chances are you'll have to, please forgive the word, *slant*!

And that can become a habit. For good or for bad, depending on your dedication to the word and your dreams of fame in the literary world.

Consider.

Once down a creative pathway one tends to continue along that road of least resistance. It becomes our natural style. Even if you managed to find a lot of alternative creative routes to getting published, the pressures of making a living can demand grinding out words as fast as they can be typed.

Now that doesn't sound high and mighty, nor is it, necessarily, an act of creating fine art. But we are talking about making a living at doing something you are really passionate about. Don't forget, writing is hard work, at best, and the end result is getting the words published. In such a manner the author's ideas will reach an unsuspecting audience! And communication of thoughts and ideas and dreams are all a part of the passion that drives all of us to do some of the craziest things.

Like writing.

So beware. Slanting, while many times necessary, can have its quicksand traps. It can develop a writing style that becomes a habit difficult to break.

You can get locked into a set pattern. Professionally you gain a reputation based on your end product, for better or worse. You have to feed your talent and your passion and your mouth. Yes, food is always a good thing to have around.

There were periods when I had ashtrays filled with half-smoked cigarettes, forgotten in the blaze of a creative moment. I enjoyed getting off the creative train ride by celebrating my day's work over a cocktail or two or three or more.

But food is always necessary. Plus, booze and cigarettes aren't freely handed out by your local store.

You have to pay the bills. You have to have the electricity going if you're using that to power your electric typewriter (in those days) or a computer word processor. You need to pay for the supplies involved in writing. You need to make sure your home is secure so that you don't end up out on the street with no place to sleep but the local park bench, if you're lucky enough to find one empty or unpoliced.

Hard fact of life is: no matter how you do it, ya must be self-supporting in some way or another to justify your passion for a career in a very questionable profession. A job of any sort can be more secure than awaiting the arrival of checks for your literary outflow.

Writers generally live in a world of insecure madness. No weekly check for the free-lancer. No unemployment checks offered for self-employed writers. You live in a world where checks come now and then in their own good time; but only if you happen to be one of the lucky ones.

The good part about this writing game vs. show biz (my father's passion for his son's future) is that you don't have to wait by the phone for somebody to call you offering work. You can literally create your product and aggressively send it out to the markets that are most likely to pay hard cold cash in order to print them up for their eager audience. If you are lucky enough, successful enough, to have an agent, he does all that dirty work for you, even unto "ignoring the rejection slips"! And if you are even luckier, you gain a reputation that literally lets editors call you up and offer contracts for stories and novels. Or put you on contract for a continual flow of stories. When you reach that level of madness, you can find it very difficult to turn back the clock and really start all over with a totally different set of professional connections.

If you change fields, you are startin' fresh and are an unknown to the editors involved. The only advantage you might have over non-published writers is that you can offer up a list of references: Have had X number of stories and novels published [and am interested in writing something for you]. Well, the editor might even be impressed enough to offer a little more consideration to your manuscript than that of some total wannabe unpublished writer. But that's just about it!

You bring your skills, as they were honed over the years of writing, to any one market. If they don't match the requirements, you are forced to back off and forget the whole thing or learn new writing tricks to twist your so-called skills around.

Herein is the trap. It is sometimes easier, even sounder, and simply smart to return to the field in which you have already made your connections and reputation. That other field is downright different, a totally new jungle to conquer.

You've become what you write. You have become a master of the chosen territory your words and career already conquered. You have become the slant you bent to.

The Bradbury routine sets things up differently. All literary markets are openly begging for your words.

Well. Okay. That's not quite true.

I heard that there are authors who are consistently far better storytellers than Mr. Bradbury, from the editorial point of view of some editors and publishers. I mean. Well. Everybody has their limits.

In his case those markets that find him less that perfect are easily replaced by others that can't get enough of his stories.

An author like Ray Bradbury, generally speaking, having developed his own territorial place in the literary world, will easily survive on his own two feet, which are planted firmly in the solid grounding he's created for himself, without worrying about those who are not eager to cater to his needs. And, after all, anybody who will burn two million words to keep them from getting into print will mentally have destroyed far more before letting them escape his brain! Writers edit before committing words to their stories. Each word, in fact, has been skillfully selected from a database in their creative mental files, long before being placed in line with other words to form a much-desired statement. Sure, they might be, later on, when the flush of creative passion has soothed madness to some form of sanity, but that's another story.

Writing can be rewriting, and rewriting, and rewriting. But the more skilled the artist, the easier it becomes to flash off the necessary series of words to make the most desired statement first time around. It is much like the skilled jazz singer, scatting through a melodic line of music. It is live, and no retakes can be made, and they just swim along like wild, not missing a stroke, not, at least, that most anybody (including themselves) would notice.

Writing becomes this, too, to some extent. And if a writer has a skilled editor to go through their written words, then they might not even need to revise or even look back.

Forry, the agent man, told me once that it would be smart to pay to have a professional typist retype my manuscripts, since I had better things to do with my time. And he was quite right. The time it takes to retype a manuscript is just almost the same time it takes to write a draft on a new story, assuming things work out perfectly. Even if not perfectly, it is a fact of life that there are more important things than retyping a manuscript. That kind of work can be exhausting and certainly a super drain on the creative energies best put on something new and fresh. Thus, you end up with more words to offer publishers. Instead of one manuscript retyped several times, you end up with several different manuscripts to offer for sale. Now, any reasonable person would see the logic in that.

Forry was right!

The same thing can be said for one's mental processes: it is better to do the editing before you commit words to your masterful story.

Slanting can be a dangerous thing which develops habits that won't transfer over to other writing fields, and it causes you to pre-edit in a certain manner created through long habit of…of all things: slanting.

On the other hand, it produces a wonderful way of making a living, of getting more words published.

And there is that madness of mind that keeps saying: Ya gotta do it better, can't keep saying it the same way over and over, learn, improve, do it better, find a new way to say the same ol' thing.

Plus, there is no reason to revise unless it is an improvement.

Oh. I forgot my father's advice.

"It takes two people to paint a picture. One to do the painting and the other to hit him over the head with a hammer when it is finished!"

Ah, the skill of knowing when to stop!

The song is ended, but the melody lingers on.

Sometimes we never know when the song ends. The skilled professional has that second partner in his head that brings out the creative whacker to stop the flow of words and ideas.

There's, also, a mental editor who says; "Hey, pard, that idea can be used in a different story. Remember, two stories are better than one! Don't lay all your eggs in one omelet."

Revising & rewriting, if overdone, can sometimes cripple the creative process. If you keep worrying over the opening lines of a story, you may never get to the second paragraph. I mean: you can spend all your time on that narrative hook and never even finish page one.

PAGE ONE?

Remember, you do the narrative hook and you keep the reader guessing to the final period. It is a requirement to get beyond Page One, unless, of course, that's as long as the story will be. Which makes it really rather short.

And sometimes you get to Page 12, or you might even make it all the way to 200 or longer. But in the end you will type THE END and think you've created another masterpiece.

Only if it gets published, one might say.

Which brings us to ART.

I never was quite sure what the word meant. Oh, I understand one can look the word up and get all kinds of wonderful definitions to please the mind of anybody so eager for advanced learning.

But Arty poo, as I tend to think of it, when applied to those folk who happened to be dedicated to such outpourings, can be a very dangerous method of creativity.

I have avoided that trap as much as possible. But not completely. There are stories I love, say I with a flush of red cheeks. And, sure as hell burns hot over sinner's bods, editors hated those very same stories.

Of course those editors were, after all, hacks!

I mean, up to the point where they rejected such perfect gems, they were neat, nice folk, handing out checks and offering praises and even editorial advice and tricks of the trade and all those wonderful and good things. Then suddenly they shit on your parade! They have changed from Godliness to hateful Demons from down under, horns and tails blaring hot crimson to match their suddenly evil eyes.

Reject your golden words?

If you're a hard-nosed professional with a thick skin, you scream in pain and agony and end up in some corner of your room trembling with rage and hurt feelings, and sometimes even whimpering like a spoiled child who has been denied their fav toy!

See. Even the professional is thin-skinned at some points of their anatomy.

Being a professional, you end up picking yourself up and going back to the story and filing it away, or sending it out to another editor or might even revise to their demands. Finally, though, you go on to new things.

So much for Art, say you.

But there are others who never get past that status. They never forgive. They never forget. And they simply demand that their art be saluted as ART! And they find an audience who is willing to moan and groan and clap their hands and do all the other worshiping things that satisfy the creative ego.

I'm a horrid fella. And I have this image of a group of naked teenage boys in some room together, showing off you know what, and comparing and politely admiring one another in such a manner as to suggest they really are impressed, rather than depressed, by this kind of mutual sharing.

Like I said, I'm somewhat of a nasty guy at times.

But much of that comes out of the conditioning my father gave me as a child.

You have to remember, he was a *commercial* artist, and had a natural contempt for his fellow artistic types who were less commercial and tended to go up to their garrets and paint pictures designed to please their personal artistic flaws and limits and bias and concepts, no matter how few people might salute their talents. They, instead of taming their egos, honing their skills, and using their talents to reach a mass audience, would rather do it their way and please an audience of One!

Okay. I've retold the story Dad drilled into me. What he basically claimed was that an artist should use their skills to reach a large enough audience to make a living at doing what they loved best.

He, like so many others did, through this form of "slanting," end up in a place that wasn't always pleasing to his creative soul. Sometimes he felt prostituted by the demands of putting paint down on a canvas or boards for the weekly check being paid out by Pacific Title. He wanted to do more, at times. Or, more to the point, in order to please his employer, he found it necessary to slant his skills in the necessary way in order to make a living at his chosen passion.

There was a natural price to pay, of course. And it was difficult for him at times, grinding away at a rather mundane type of creative effort. It wasn't until he retired that it was possible to do other things.

That's a story in itself, retold elsewhere, somewhere in this epic.

At one point he started doing covers for sci-fi mags, long before retiring. This turned out to be a nice extra income when he did retire, years later. In fact it was this that tangled some very exciting and interesting events into my writing career and opened some fresh and powerful doors to me that would never have otherwise been possible.

So. Becoming a commercial hack as opposed to one of those more artistically Arty folk, can have some strange results.

Both methods can be a road to fantastic success or horrendous failure.

Sometimes people will teach rather than sell out. Of course the snotty retort would be: Those who can—do; those who can't—teach." But that ain't necessarily true. There are endless ways of making use of one's creative abilities. And good teachers are those people who actually have wonderful talents in doing just that: teaching others. This is a great gift and not to be looked down upon as something of an afterthought, an alternative to failure. Sure, there are those types. But we aren't dealing with failures, but, rather, successful people doing what they were naturally talented to do and something that moves them passionately. A teacher with a passion to teach can be a wonder; a talented force that makes a major difference in society and in those lives with whom they come in contact.

What we are concerned with here is basic, and a limited and narrow pathway: how to avoid being a wannabe and become a successful published writer, slant or no slant.

Both methods work in different ways, and each writer finds their own trail through the jungle that must be tamed and channeled throughout one's life.

No matter which path one decides to struggle through, one will find it hard, demanding work, and will discover that passion must fuel the machine or nothing works at all.

When the passion runs out, the creative engine is empty and things just don't run.

I don't want to hammer home this point too hard, but at the same time, want it burned into all brains who are open to continuing on with this epic and their own possible careers at some future time.

I'm not concerned about the literary masterful artist who demands that the audience come to them, and is willing to risk life and limb to that end result. They will take care of their own survival, and either succeed, or pick up the pieces and continue on with their lives and whatever careers are offered for daily survival.

I'm talking to the general public who might be interested in what makes the difference between becoming a professional writer (commercial or art bound) and the elements necessary to find some success in that effort.

That does not mean you shouldn't dream of becoming an artist of words—classy, golden words of literary standards that all will salute. But it does suggest that in the beginning, at least, as even Ray Bradbury did, you learn by offering publishers what they need, and that involves slanting. For some writers this is the beginning, the learning phase, of a career that may someday make them not only rich but famous.

VI.

A FEW WORDS, A VERY FEW WORDS, ON WRITING

by Robert Reginald

I'M NO STEPHEN King or Terry Brooks, to name two well-known authors who have published little memoirs about their writing lives (*On Writing* and *Sometimes the Magic Works*, respectively). I'm not even Jack Dann or George Zebrowski. I don't have their reputations either as a fiction writer or as a nonfiction hack. In fact, I'm not all that well known outside of a very small group of devoted fans and curious academics.

Still, I've been writing professionally since 1968, and during those four-plus decades have sold roughly twelve or thirteen million words for a considerable chunk of extra change. It was never enough, often enough, to provide a consistently good living, and I'm rather glad at this point that I have a state pension to fall back on in my rapidly approaching (g)olden age; or perhaps I merely lacked the courage to plunge into the occupation of literature on a full-time basis.

Whatever.

I've paid my dues, have nothing left to prove, and have lost most of my ambition to the after-effects of a near-fatal heart attack (it's amazing how a near brush with death can reconfigure one's priorities). So why spout off now? Why talk about this particular topic at this particular time?

Precisely *because*....

The prospect of one's potentially imminent passing concentrates one's mind wonderfully, to paraphrase an old saying. I have a few things to say, and no one has ever been able to shut me up before.

They're not likely to start now. So bear with me, dear friends, if you please.

I've been writing since about the age of four, when I started copying the names and words off my mother's kitchen appliances in our old, two-story, rented gothic in Fairview, Massachusetts. I've been making up stories for about the same time.

I remember rising well before my parents at the initial hint of sunlight, sneaking down the stairs, and carefully opening each blind, first peering about very stealthily (of course) for all of the horrible monsters that I knew were lurking in the shadows. It wasn't really safe to play until I'd let in the light.

Then I'd create stories and serials featuring myself and Superman or one of my favorite western heroes, and play them out over days or weeks. This was oodles of fun for a little kid. It was how I entertained myself, even at that young age. Not much has changed over the years.

I write these essays—and pen my stories and novels—for much the same reason now. I haven't changed a bit in that sense: there's still a rambunctious rapscallion lurking somewhere down in my subconscious, always clamoring to be let out. Writing for me is occasionally a catharsis of sorts, and sometimes just plain hard work, but mostly (at least, *these* days), it's fun. I write because I want to, because I need to, because *not* writing would somehow represent another little death to me.

I don't care any longer about sales or markets or money or fame or any of that crap. Read my stuff or not, as ye choose. Laugh or cry with me or not, as ye choose. Agree with me or argue with me, as ye choose. Criticize my ramblings and call them crap or praise the hell out of them, as ye choose. It signifieth not, as the prophet said.

I write first to please myself, and no one else, with one caveat. If I don't also please Mary, my one true critic, then I know for certain that there's something intrinsically wrong with my story, my precious prose, my plot, my *whatever*. I do pay close attention to what she says; or, rather, I ignore what she says at my authorial peril. She's too damned bright and insightful to miss very much, and she always has my best interests at heart.

Otherwise, though, I write exactly what I please these days, without much of an eye as to where it might sell or how it might appear. I've never had any problem finding paying outlets for my stuff. Everything I've ever written of any worth whatever has been published professionally.

This doesn't mean to say, o thou would-be penpersons, that I ignore the realities of commercial publishing, or that I fail to seek contracts *first* before beginning long projects on which I would like to devote some work—or at least to have some jolly good idea of where such lengthy projects might be placed. I dislike wasting time, particularly *my* time, which has become especially precious to me in these, my latter years. And yet....

* * * * * * *

I PENNED THREE books on behalf of another, better-known writer starting in 1996, and only one of those was actually published on schedule—and that two years later than anticipated—despite numerous promises to the contrary.

Fair enough. There are very few certainties in the publishing world, any more than in life, and one takes the lumps and failures along with the successes, swallowing the pills of bitterness, and thereby learning (one hopes) from the experience. The second of the three books was completely rewritten to recast it into a different *milieu*, and was subsequently published in '04, with the third following in '05, after considerable extra effort on my part. I probably won't lend my creativity to another author in quite this way ever again.

I did, however, earn a decent trade credit and a modest financial return for my effort—and, more importantly, I learned a great deal about the craft of fiction-mongering in the process. You see, writing the original tome in the series, the guide to the writer's created universe, forced me to deconstruct that author's published works of fiction—and *that* in turn proved to be a key in unlocking my own internal creative restraints.

Why did this particular exercise make such a difference to me?

In the process of being forced to outline the other writer's novels chronologically, I inadvertently revealed their underpinnings. Suddenly, the underlying structures all became obvious to me, and I began understanding how the tales had actually been fitted together. Small flaws in transition, flow, and consistency emerged from the tangle of verbiage, tumbling into the clear, cold light of merciless day. Oh frabjous joy—the mysteries had at last been revealed unto the newest of acolytes!

There is a logical process involved in the creation of worthwhile fiction. It differs from writer to writer and often from work to work, but it's real; and those among our brethren who take the time to ponder such things, come to understand the whys and wherefores of this sometimes mysterious craft. We're fond of pronouncing to the public (usually in sonorous, somber terms, oh yea!) that there are parts of the process that are inherently indefinable (whispers of the æther whistling in the background); but the reality is that every author worth his or her salt knows what she or he is about when they put pen to paper. If they don't, they have no business calling themselves wordsmiths. Or to put it another way: if *I* don't understand what I'm doing when I'm writing a story, then who the hell else is going to care? Surely not John Q. Public!

So I began carefully examining other creative works as well—novels and stories by other writers, television episodes, motion pictures—and lo and wonderment, I suddenly acquired the ability to envision what was going to happen to a story well in advance of its conclusion. I could see what worked—and also what didn't. You see, I kept stumbling over the damned telltales.

Writers implant little hooks in their fictions, wee hints of plots to come. Sometimes they're inserted after the fact, when the story has already been completed, to strengthen whatever outcome is ultimately desired. It's easiest to glimpse such seeds in mystery novels, where there's a puzzle posed that must be solved from existing clues by the end of the narrative. The telltales will always be there, though, if the writer has the least bit of competence (if the author is really, *really* good, they won't be that obvious, however).

These blips are present in any fiction with a plotline. They're not intended to be noticed by the reader, of course. But once the faculty of recognition is switched on, it can't be turned off again—and that has consequences too.

My sudden epiphany—in effect, the loss of my literary virginity—had a very nasty little side-effect: it ruined for me the bulk of modern literature, TV, and film. I could no longer reread books that had given me much pleasure in the past. Overnight, many of them had become too transparent, too *common*, ever to be enjoyed again.

Oh, blast and be damned! Nothing comes without its price, and that was the fee that I had to pay the ferryman to cross the River Books.

Still, I won't be turning back the clock. I've sold eight novels and a story collection in the last eleven years, and I'm now working on a ninth, a long fantasy novel. I enjoy creating these worlds so very much more than the nonfiction tomes that I mostly produced in the first three decades of my career. By comparison, fictioneering seems incomparably easier to me, more pleasurable by far.

I piddle around with my own creativity, and there's no one to say yea or nay or even maybe save myself—and Mary, of course! And if someone else obtains even a modicum of enjoyment from these musings, well, so much the better. And if not, whom I have harmed, dear friends?

I write what I see.

When I'm gone, in the not-so-distant future, these words will remain behind, small signposts that I once lived, that I once thought, that I once felt, that I once fashioned all these hoary things in and of myself—and no one else did them or ever could have made them in quite the same way.

This is who I am.

In a few words, in a very few words, we wordsmiths etch pictures in the minds of other men and women just like ourselves—those currently living, those yet to be born, those inhabitants of some distantly unfathomable future civilization.

This is time travel in its truest form: I communicate directly with *you*, I talk to *you*, not just in the here and now, but for as long as these words continue to exist in some form. I give *you* my wisdom, my ideas, my self, such as they are. Take them or leave them, as *you* choose.

And some of you even talk back, although I rarely receive your responses.

You see and hear Robert Reginald and Michael Burgess and Boden Clarke and all of those other personas that I have occasionally put on and worn out as a writer. You see whatever masque I choose to display at that particular moment.

In a few words, in a very few words, *you* understand.

And that's the way it goes with Rob Reginald's prose.

VII.

WRITING WITH PURPOSE

by Charles Allen Gramlich

WHY DOES ANYONE want—or feel like they need—to learn how to write? And for this question it doesn't matter whether we're talking about fiction, nonfiction, or both. What do people hope to accomplish by the solitary, and, frankly, somewhat odd behavior of writing?

Do they want to amuse their friends with their quick wit, or perhaps amaze them with their erudition? Or do people think that good writing will help them get better grades in school or earn more money in their jobs? Could it be that some would-be writers want to get famous, maybe go on a national book tour where they sign autographs for fanatical legions of admirers, and have talk show hosts like Oprah clamoring for their attention? Maybe some folks just want to get rich and conclude that, if Stephen King can do it, then so can they.

Although some of these possibilities are more likely to occur than others, all of them are perfectly legitimate reasons for writing. In fact, there are no illegitimate reasons to write. Each writer has his or her own inner purpose, and his or her own unique way of putting information down on the page. Ernest Hemingway often wrote standing up. Truman Capote and Mark Twain preferred lying down to write, while Edgar Allan Poe liked to have his cat on his shoulder while he created. I prefer the more standard "sit at my desk and stare at the computer screen until words begin to appear," but anyone who writes will find their own path.

Given the many legitimate reasons for writing, and the many ways of going about it, is there any point in trying to identify a primary or *best* reason to write? I believe there is. I believe that we can, in fact, start by eliminating all but one reason for writing, and that is writing to communicate. This doesn't mean that other reasons are wrong or bad. It means that they are secondary to the need to transmit information, which is really basic to *all* writing. No one gets rich or famous from writing unless they can convey something interesting to a large number of people.

Some people just like the act of writing, the simple behavior of putting words down on a page and then changing them around. They care more about the process than they do about seeing the finished product in print or earning money from it. And even though I don't completely follow that model with my own writing, I honestly believe that it's the best attitude to have. It certainly helps insulate a writer against the inevitable criticisms and rejections.

But for those who need a publishable written product and cannot just enjoy the writing process, the first thing they need to learn is how to clearly communicate ideas, facts, emotions, and experiences. Of course, whole books have been written about that subject. I'm not going to cover all that territory in this short essay.

What I will say is this: to communicate effectively, whether in fiction or nonfiction, the writer has to think like both a writer and… *a reader*. The writer's primary purpose is to make the reader's work as easy as possible. At every point, with every sentence and every paragraph, writers must ask themselves: "What is my reader hearing from me?" "Am I saying exactly what I think I'm saying, exactly what I intend to say?" And unless the writer achieves this (or at least a close approximation), then no other purpose for writing will *ever* be achieved.

So how do you think like a reader? You've *been* a reader, probably for most of your life. Go back to that reading for your answer. But learn to read "critically." You've read passages in books before that confused you, scenes that you couldn't visualize, dialogue that you couldn't follow. Chances are you skipped over those passages to something clearer, or tossed the work aside. Reading critically means not skipping those passages, not tossing anything aside until it's been dissected. Ask why a scene doesn't work. Is it you? Or did the writer do something wrong? Did they leave out some critical piece of description? Did they fail to make it clear who was doing what to whom? Did they scrimp on necessary background information?

Even the passages that work must be studied critically if you want to understand writing from the viewpoint of the reader. What is it about a great scene that grabs you? Is it the characters, the concrete details, the prose itself? Most likely it's some combination of these elements, but only by careful study can you determine how much of each element is the critical amount. In this way, writing is much like chemistry. Or, maybe alchemy would be a better analogy, for writing is nothing if not taking common everyday elements like words, grammar, and punctuation and transmuting them into gold.

But you must go beyond critical reading to truly achieve clarity. Critical *writing* is also important. This doesn't mean that you must always strive for conscious awareness of everything you're doing in your prose; it means that, sometimes, you need to cut under the flesh of a story to the bones. How important is word choice, sentence length, paragraph length to producing a specific effect, such as creating suspense? What makes some dialogue sound stilted, other dialogue sound natural? How does punctuation change the flow of words? To analyze such qualities I think it's best to begin by studying the work of other writers, work that you are not so close to as your own. I'd suggest you choose writers for study who are better than you at the craft.

One effective strategy is to *retype* passages or stories from writers that you are interested in studying, not as a mere exercise but as an honest attempt to understand the process the other writer followed. Don't even allow yourself to edit the other writer's work at first—which you'll probably want to do—but faithfully reproduce it before going back and trying to make it your own. Retyping a story this way puts you in the writer's shoes, with your feet on the stones of the trail that he or she followed. Just reading a story, even if you're trying to study it, is more like driving that same trail in a Jeep. You might see the obstacles, but they won't bruise your heel. You need those heels bruised.

Once you've retyped another writer's passage and studied how he or she put it together, *then* revise the piece as if it were your own. Think about the changes you've made. Why did you recast a passive sentence as an active one? What made you add or remove an adjective? Why did you change the punctuation? Answering these questions will show you how your decisions are different from the other person's. It will make the reasons behind your writing decisions clear to you.

Good writers *do* make better grades in school and make more money in their jobs. Good writers also sell articles, stories, and novels, and they hear from people who have connected with their work and enjoyed it. Good writing pays off. But that payoff only comes to those whose ultimate purpose is clarity. The readers demand it.

VIII.

PREPARING AND WRITING

*by Charles Allen Gramlich,
Y. Du Bois Irvin, and Elliott D. Hammer*

> "The will to win is not worth a nickel unless you have the will to practice."
> —Unknown

PART OF THE writing process is so visceral as to defy any simple "how to" explanation. How do you begin? Where do you begin? And, most importantly, how do you continue through the hard work of building a paper? Though there are no simple answers to these questions, this chapter offers some points to consider and some suggestions on how to proceed. These have been gleaned from your authors' own experiences, and from those of other professional writers. Give them a listen and try to see if they can work for you. For now, there are three topics we'll be covering in this chapter, 1) time management, 2) the personal aspect of writing professionally, and 3) getting words down and keeping them flowing.

Time Management

WE TALKED ABOUT "Time Management" briefly in Chapter 1, but we need to revisit the topic more completely here. We do so because no one can write a word unless they have time, but our lives are busy and finding time is arduous.

Making time is much easier. Think about when you wanted to do some fun activity so badly your hair hurt. Weren't you busy then too? Yet, you made time for the fun. And without adding a physical minute to the day. *Time* is there if you know how to manage the hours already available.

Deciding how to best manage your time is a process of self-discovery that can even be fun. It begins with a realistic look at your daily schedule. Create a worksheet (NOTE: there's one included in Appendix A in the volume [*Writing in Psychology*] from which this essay is reprinted—ed.), and make as many copies as needed. Also, pick up a calendar on which to mark important dates. On the worksheet, put down those items that must have a place in a day's activities (*e.g.*, sleeping, eating, showering, dressing, classes, chores, transportation, and walking the dog). Be realistic in your estimates. Time yourself. Use a stopwatch if you have one. Next, enter the activities that you engage in every day but which are more flexible, such as studying (about two hours for every hour spent in class), reading, talking to friends, napping, watching television, *etc.* Here you might include listening to music or playing with the cat.

Repeat this exercise over several days (a full week with weekends included would be best), remembering to add in those tasks such as shopping for food or emptying the trash that aren't done *every* day. Then sit down to see where and how your time is spent. Every hour is probably filled with some activity, but we'll bet that not all of those activities are critical. We'll bet there's plenty of "wasted" time.

Do you really need to watch that *Simpsons* rerun for the third time? How often do you have to check email? Will your best friend actually get mad if you don't "text" her every hour? Cut back on TV, computer games, surfing the 'net, and other non-essential activities, and this will free up time to use for writing (or for other important things). And for goodness sake, is it absolutely necessary to call someone on the phone every time you have a free moment? Think about it.

Once time has been identified that can be focused toward writing, take out that calendar we suggested and mark off important dates, such as holidays, test days, and paper deadlines. Match the deadlines with your daily schedule and see how much time will be available for each task. During the early part of the semester, plan to spend three to four hours a week doing research for each paper that you have. Allow more time toward the end, and set a definite date for when everything will be finished. Make that date at least a couple of days before the assignment is due so that you can fine-tune and proofread at a leisurely pace.

The reason why more work time is needed at the end of the semester is because that's when you really begin to integrate your research and your own creative thoughts about a topic. This is the critical juncture. Think of it as that point in cooking a gourmet meal when all the ingredients have been carefully assembled and laid out delicately on the counter. Now it becomes crucial that you blend, stir, mold, and peel with great precision and refined perception. That's where those extra hours will be helpful.

If you follow a writing schedule faithfully, the results will more than compensate for a few lost phone conversations or for missing that TV show, which, of course, you recorded anyway. (Isn't technology grand?) Time management takes self-discipline and requires self-honesty, but in return it offers a sense of direction and a pleasant feeling of having imposed at least some order on chaos.

Here's a last little hint about managing writing time. Build rewards into your schedule from the beginning. After finishing a section of the paper, go watch a favorite TV show or get an ice cream bar. And after a week of hard work, you deserve to see that new movie that just opened. Reward yourself for doing good work and you won't burn out.

The Personal Aspect of Writing Professionally

IN ADDITION TO time management skills, you need to find ways to get involved emotionally in writing a paper. No matter what the topic is, no matter whether you are writing a term paper, a research report, or an essay for some other kind of project, your own interest and excitement needs to shine through if you are going to produce the best finished product.

For example, a psychology instructor might assign a term paper on Delusional Disorder. A simple clinical description of symptoms, predisposing factors, essential and associated features, age of onset, course, and complications of the disorder can be harvested from the *Diagnostic and Statistical Manual of Mental Disorders IV* (DSM-IV-TR; American Psychiatric Association, 2000). Pretty much anyone can do this. The problem is that such a paper won't have anything uniquely *you* in it. Your personal perspective and personal passion will be missing, and that's what an instructor wants.

Please remember that teachers don't want just to be fed dry facts that they've already eaten and digested. (One teacher described it, memorably, as like swallowing "intellectual vomit.") So, how can you complete an assignment without making this common, and grade-lowering, error? Pay close attention to the human element. Use case studies to enliven the discussion of the topic, and make your report personal. Can you imagine what it is like to suffer from

Delusional Disorder? Can you imagine how others would think and act toward you? The data that you're reporting will be the main course of the paper. You'll add the flavoring, the gravy, the side dishes of salad and sweet dessert. These will come from your experiences and imagination. Take the facts, mix them with your own empathy, and put the results down on paper using your own unique language and expressions, not paraphrases of someone else's.

Even when writing a research report or research proposal, where the rules are stricter on what you should and should not say, your personal passion needs to show through. *Why* are you asking the questions that you claim to be asking? What is the importance of this research? Why do you care? Why should anyone? Tell us why, in simple, straightforward language that reveals your personal commitment to the topic.

Teachers don't expect undergraduate students to be perfect in grammar, syntax, and scientific expression. Of course, they want to see your best in those areas, but they also want to experience the world, and issues such as Delusional Disorder, through your eyes. This does not mean that scientific writing is based on opinion or on subjective emotions, but there *is* an important place for individual perception. It is *your* understanding, and *your* writing, that professors want to see.

Getting Words Down and Keeping Them Flowing

INTERRUPTIONS ARE the writer's worst enemy. Just when you're ready to work, with your thoughts focused on the topic, the phone rings or someone knocks on the door. Or, even worse, you're already writing and in the flow of the piece when the interruption comes. You lose track of where you were, and suddenly your thoughts are eddies where before they were a swiftly moving stream. Take steps *before* you write to make sure this doesn't happen.

Interruptions come from two places, outside of you and inside of you. But you can arrange the writing environment to avoid, or at least minimize, both. To avoid external interruptions, set up phones to take messages instead of answering them, and then find a physical location to write where people are unlikely to discover you. Many libraries, for example, have small study rooms called carrels that are available to students. These usually have lights, a desk, a chair, and a place to plug in a laptop. Not much distraction there. (One of your authors routinely uses library carrels for his own work and highly recommends them.)

Now, what about the internal interruptions? I'm talking about those things that writers do to break their own concentrations, such as deciding that they "really need a soda," or they "forgot to get a pen," or they "ought to check their email one more time." These are more difficult to deal with, but a little self-discipline can work wonders.

If you like a sip of water now and then while writing, make sure to have water on your desk *before* starting work. If you like to listen to music, set up the stereo ahead of time and pre-select the songs to listen to. Put a dictionary, thesaurus, the APA manual, and a grammar guide within easy reach so you won't have to "fetch" them. Spread notes and references out in some logical order. (Remember back in Chapter 3 when we suggested organizing your notes by putting them in file folders? Here's where that will pay off.) Shut down email and all other web pages that you aren't actually using for the project. Make sure there's a pen and notepaper handy, and prepare whatever idiosyncratic items that you might want, such as soft lighting or hard candy.

Now you're ready to begin. Writing time has been scheduled and you haven't waited until the last minute to start. You're feeling confident in your ability to complete the project because you've checked with the instructor about anything that was confusing. You've arranged the environment to help rather than hinder you, and you have the physical tools you need (pen and paper, computer, whatever).

The first thing you'll write will be the title. Follow that with the headings developed in your outline. Already the threatening blankness of the page is broken. But where to next? Well, what about a definition of the topic? This will tell the reader up front what *specific* issue you are addressing.

Some writers block on the first sentence because they insist that it be brilliant and creative, that it suck the reader in. Brilliant and creative are great, but you can't wait weeks for inspiration to strike. Get a textbook, find a definition of the topic, and put it down as the first line under the title, properly citing the author of the definition, of course. Starting with a definition is always a safe way to begin, and you can change that first line later when the brilliantly perfect phrase hits you.

Once the definition is down, work with it to make it clear to your readers. Say the paper is on schizophrenia, for example, and the definition contains something like "a psychotic disorder accompanied by hallucinations and delusions." Well, after the definition you should probably explain what "psychotic" means, and what "hallucinations and delusions" are. Then you may want to give an example, so describe a case study. By now, half of the first page is filled and the paper is well underway. What next? History of schizophrenia? Symptoms? You decide.

As the paper gets underway, don't worry too much initially about correcting errors, especially in grammar, spelling, and punctuation. As we suggested earlier in this book, if the sentences sound terrible at first, leave them anyway and go on. If you can't find the perfect word or remember the scientific name for a concept immediately, type in a ___ and keep rolling. Like most kinds of work, writing can develop its own momentum as you practice it. Once the barrier of the empty page is broken, the words should start to flow more easily. They may not be great words perfectly organized and polished, but that's to be expected. All first drafts are awkward, but this one you'll reshape into a final masterpiece (or at least into an "A" paper).

Remember that you've set some limits on how much time you'll spend or how much work you'll accomplish in each writing session. Adhere to that. Again, as we've said before, a good paper cannot be finished in one sitting. Pace yourself.

So, how long *should* you work? How much *should* you do? The answers to these questions are different for each writer, and you'll find your own answers through experience. To begin with, we might suggest to try writing for an hour each day, or until you finish one good page. Of course, you may find that you can't manage quite that much, or that you're comfortable doing two hours or two pages, or more. Adjust your schedule as you begin to learn your limits, but remember to *always* put down words in every writing session, even if they don't seem to be any good. Keep making progress and you can reach any goal. One of your authors (the best-looking one) has the goal of finishing *at least* one good paragraph every day, no matter the distractions. That's not much, but there are only three to four paragraphs on an average page. One paragraph a day means ten finished pages in a month, and, of course, he often writes more than his minimum.

As you finish each writing session, remember to jot some quick notes at the end as a guide toward the next session's work. Begin each new day of writing by reading over and correcting (if necessary) the previous day's work. This helps you get "warmed up" and will ensure continuity within the paper. Stephen King does this. Ernest Hemingway did it. Hemingway always stopped writing before he got tired, when he was still interested in finding out what happened next. This helped him leap right into his work the next day.

Finally, adhere to your writing schedule and commitment without exception (short of family tragedy). This is a repetition of what we've already said, but it may be the most important of all the hints and suggestions that we've given. In doing this, you should quickly find that the *unusual* task of writing has become the ordinary, just another part of your everyday activities, and you will also have begun a remarkable odyssey into your own mind. From there comes the "stuff" that makes any writer's work unique.

IX.

IMAGES

by Damien Broderick

WHAT MAKES A particular work of fiction appeal to us? Indeed, what is it about the storytelling we call fiction that readers find so satisfying, even compulsive? Many elements, clearly, as well as the gestalt the words build, the imaginary peopled world constructed from words and memories, the images (as we say glibly) that these evoke in our awareness: these half-dreamed pseudo-experiences we live as we read invented lives in invented worlds. But what are these "images"? How do they operate inside us? Let's edge into this.

* * * * * * *

WHAT SORT OF fiction appeals to the largest number of adult readers, and how does it work? I decided to read some Dan Brown. In *Angels and Demons*, aside from one strikingly effective speech, where the late Pope's charismatic administrator or camerlengo denounces modernity and godless science (378-83), the Dan Brown method turned out to be quite incredibly crude, as many critics had reported disdainfully. It alarmed me to think that Brown might have researched hundreds of best sellers and factored down to the kind of sentence structure most people approve because it is nothing more demanding than a string of concrete labels. These bluntly convey knowingness and wealth, sex or terror, and dialogue that often seems drawn from those pulps once enormously popular among the barely literate. "Tonight we change the world" (9). "As you probably know, Vittoria, human beings normally use only a very small percentage of their brain power" (484). Surely that couldn't be all that was in play.

Brown assumes that the reader is a know-nothing simpleton. Aside from the bald infodumping (although he does a lot of that), he has Robert Langdon explain to a genius wheelchair-bound Stephen Hawking look-alike who Galileo is and what his crime was, who the Illuminati were, who the Masons were. But Langdon, world-famous Harvard symbologist, is sometimes conveniently doltish. At a key crisis in the narrative, Langdon studies a still-hot iron brand used to burn into a human chest an Illuminati ambigram. It's gibberish, a random metallic scrawl. Many minutes later, the obvious dawns on him: "He had also forgotten that iron brands, just like rubber stamps, never looked like their imprints. They were in reverse. Langdon had been looking at the brand's *negative*" (472). No doubt this revelation is intended as a thematic masterstroke, since the plot revolves around symmetries, inversions, reversals, light and dark, faith and science, matter and antimatter. And this device proved so attractive that in *The Lost Symbol* Langdon stares perplexed at a graphic starting IIIX. "The Roman numeral I-I-I-X doesn't exist," the expert symbologist explains (97); it takes him a while to think of looking at it upside down. You can see why people who get all their information from TV sound bites would warm to such handholding.

Some of Brown's immense success is no doubt an accident of timing, plus the big dollar publicity push on a selected candidate, but plainly that's not all. It's easy to identify the elements—strange ancient mysteries, dark conspiracies of church or state, and the usual blockbuster "expertise" of a grotesquely itemizing kind ("He slipped into his Slashnburn 450-GT hybrid manufactured in Uppchuck Sweden, of which only five had ever been handcrafted for the Kings of Siam, careful of the crease in his Fortum & Freemason grey twill pantaloons hand stitched by the leading Gnome of Zürich, Herr Frogleg Sauerkraut"), *etc.* For many readers, evidently, this is the very hallmark of compulsively readable fiction. To a smaller number, it constitutes an assault, like a tone-deaf drunk braying "Danny Boy" after midnight. It is almost unreadable.

* * * * * * *

THERE ARE AT least two ways to understand "readability". Make that three: after all, books written in Mandarin or French are unreadable by some of us, due to our ignorance of those languages; not knowing the codes of English epic poetry or the references to mythology and history embedded through it can make those works unreadable as well, or at least not readable in the way we like to enjoy entertainments that are "transparent" to us.

Leaving aside that basic competence: there's "unreadable" because a text repeatedly insults our intelligence. Much of the time, Dan Brown does just this—with baby talk, repetition, and his absurd datadumps masquerading as conversation or reflections: "Since the beginning of history," Langdon explains to the director of CERN in Geneva, one of the premier scientists in the world, "a deep rift has existed between science and religion. Outspoken scientists like Copernicus—" (*Angels and Demons*, 31).

And at the farthest extreme a text can be "unreadable" because we just can't make out what the hell it is saying, not at all, so it's easier and more comforting to suppose it is incoherent word-salad than to question our own skill or patience.

Then again, one can admit that a text is beyond one's grasp and ruefully put it down again, wishing one were smarter, or better educated, or had more endurance. That's largely my reaction to *Finnegans Wake*, but I don't immediately feel a blustering urge to denounce Joyce as a wanker and a phony. Perhaps, some will surmise, this only proves I've been cowed by mandarins (fakers all, so we're often told, engaged in a conspiracy of bullshitting for their own advancement; I mean, a three year-old could paint like that). Maybe, but partly it's because I once lived with a psychiatric nurse who looked after retarded people who loved to wear bunches of useless keys on their belts and whose favorite slight was, poignantly, "You're stupid! That's stupid!"

Better, then, to recall Vladimir Nabokov's reply on the question of how the writer (figured as male, since in some measure he spoke of himself and his work) relates to the reader: he "clashes with readerdom because he is his own ideal reader and those other readers are so very often mere lip-moving ghosts and amnesiacs. On the other hand, a good reader is bound to make fierce efforts when wrestling with a difficult author, but those efforts can be most rewarding after the bright dust has settled"(Nabokov, *Strong Opinions*, 183).

How does bestselling Dan Brown elicit images in the reader's mind? Not through luscious, sensorily-rich evocations, it's fair to suppose. Consider several typical passages from *The Lost Symbol* (2009):

> The Capitol Visitor Center had been a costly and controversial project. Described as an underground city to rival parts of Disney World, this subterranean space reportedly provided over a half-million square feet of space for exhibits, restaurants and meeting halls. (24)

Chapter 4 opens with this leaden recitation:

> The U.S. Capitol Building stands regally at the eastern end of the National Mall, on a raised plateau that city designer Pierre L'Enfant described as a "a pedestal waiting for a monument." The Capitol's massive footprint measures more than 750 feet in length and 350 feet deep. Housing more than sixteen acres of floor space, it contains an astonishing 541 rooms. (18)

Can you form an image from these drab statistics? We learn that

> Robert Langdon...was sitting all alone in the enormous cabin of a Falcon 2000EX corporate jet as it bounced its way through turbulence. In the background, the dual Pratt & Whitney engines hummed evenly. (6)

Oh, *that* model of corporate jet! Does this parade of catalogue entries ignite the scenes in your mind's eye? It doesn't do a thing for me. But then, in my case that's not unusual, and not the responsibility of Mr. Brown. I don't *do* visual images, even when it's Nabokov singing hauntingly in my ear in the closing stanzas of his most famous novel, *Lolita*:

> After coughing myself inside out, I rested a while on a boulder, and then, thinking the sweet air might do me good, walked a little way toward a low stone parapet on the precipice side of the highway. Small grasshoppers spurted out of the withered roadside weeds. A very light cloud was opening its arms and moving toward a slightly more substantial one belonging to another, more sluggish, heavenlogged system. As I approached the friendly abyss, I grew aware of a melodious unity of sounds rising like vapor from a small mining town that lay at my feet, in a fold of the valley. One could make out the geometry of the streets between blocks of red and gray roofs, and green puffs of trees, and a serpentine stream, and the rich, ore-like glitter of the city dump, and beyond the town, roads crisscrossing the crazy quilt of dark and pale fields, and behind it all, great timbered mountains. (299)

Nope, not a thing. Just the words, the words.

* * * * * * *

HERE IS ONE of my recurrent obsessions: I believe most people take it for granted that everyone else in the world uses roughly the same kind of mental imagery protocols. We all know enough to distinguish extroverts from shy nerds, and the strutting jocks from the willowy sensitive types, and the inarticulate from the freely babbling; but since the early 1960s, when I had an epiphany about all this, I have been informally polling people about their visual imagery. Many people tell me they can form some kind of red triangle in imagination, turn it green, then yellow, and rotate it to the left, then to the right, and go on to make a picture of their dear old Momma, check the color of her eyes, and so on. Some are exceptionally good at this stunt, making elaborate flowcharts and tracking through them without moving a muscle (or maybe they twitch in sympathy). Others can "see" whole movies as they read a novel.

I have *zero* visual imagery, at least when I am awake.

The brain module is simply not there, apparently, or is shunted offline during consciousness. Presumably this is one reason I was regarded as a slow child in primary and most of secondary school. I could not spell very well, because I could not inwardly *see* the words. Eventually I managed to recognize words on the page, but answering "spelling bee" questions was utterly hopeless. Even though I soon knew several times as many words as everyone else, and more or less how to use them, I could not spell them aloud because I could not *see them inwardly* (whatever that is like).

The same thing happened with simple arithmetic and algebra, let alone geometry. It was hopeless. Scribble, scribble, tongue out the corner of my mouth, maybe by brute force I could work out what the teachers were babbling about. So much of the routine instruction was automatically pitched in the visualization mode that I was repeatedly stranded.

As a result, and to my intense regret, I never became a scientist. I met obstacles as a philosopher, too, once the notation went up on the blackboard. I need to turn everything into narrative, run compression algorithms on the word chunks, then fool around with those. This can be amazingly powerful, and many poststructuralists do just this, which is why they sound like poseurs—and I suspect many of them must share my cognitive defect. Not all, though, now that movies and visual art and TV are such a major part of the postmodern agenda.

This skew has a very strange effect on my writing. Since I write a fair bit of fiction, often set in places where the settings are unfamiliar, I need to provide the cues and codes that switch on my readers' visual imagery machinery. Since that stuff does not work with me, from the inside, I am in roughly the position of a deaf person learning to grunt out unheard sounds painfully associated with meanings, with hardly any immediate feedback. It is a weird way to live, I assure you.

I conjecture that a lot of those smart people who never quite "achieved their potential" might share the same unorthodox imagery structures as mine, or maybe other kinds that are equally alien. I do use a kind of ancillary kinesthetic imagery in the place of the "inner eye," with portions of my body image *feeling* as if they are rotated in space. So I can score fairly well on those rotate-the-gadget-and-say-which-one-is-next tests in IQ trials, by turning myself into one, and dancing. I almost immediately knew the answer to one famous question about tetrahedra, cited in an Arthur C. Clarke novel, that only geniuses are supposed to get. But I am damned if I can *picture* a tetrahedron in my head....

Oh, and I have no depth perception (stereopsis), either. This might not be a coincidence, although it was caused by an eye defect and then became neurally hardwired in infancy.

* * * * * * *

I WAS AT THE end of my first year of an English literature degree when I suddenly realized, with an immense sickening shock, why people kept talking about *imagery* in poems (a medium largely obscure to me, although I liked the rhythms and sounds and compressed density of some verse). "Images"—like, like, um, like...*pictures*, you mean? Those words about rain and roses and swaying daffodils and running lions and golden light glinting from the blade *make pictures in your head*?

I wanted my money back!

Despite this defect, people often tell me they enjoy the visual density of my writing (although others, like critic Bruce Gillespie, now know what they have sensed was absent in it.) Here's a sample, from my novel *Quipu* (2009):

> *the first photograph*
>
> This oblique monochrome portrait is grainy, somber, regretful, bursting with a droning darkness despite the abundance of light, the reverberations of the afternoon sun. All the low swell and ripple of the sea traps shadows like crushed foil in its looping lacy brightness. Caroline is captured lightly askew, her expression as passive and

> warm as a Fra Filippo Lippi madonna. Eroded tussocky cliffs blur in the background, gnawed by this sea and wind, made by mere brute elements into a gothic construct in a land too new for Gothic ruins. Foreground to this remote menace, Caroline's long pale heavy hair is blown by the sea's wind, and the angled sun makes shadows on her face like faint healing wounds. She watches nothing particularly, simply standing in the rough sand with hands in the deep pockets of her leather coat, the denim of her jeans pressing the tibia bones of her braced legs. (1-2)

So what does it mean that people can assume I have a rich visual imagination, since my fiction has given them such striking pictures? It is mostly their own work, that's what; I'm just providing the wiring instructions. But then, so is every writer; it is just that I'm doing it at two removes.

And it helps explain why my fiction is so adjective- and adverb-clotted. Other people (or so I surmise) use descriptors sparingly because they are notating their inner visions. Sometimes most descriptive elements are actually absent (as in Hemingway, famously), since it is assumed readers will fill in the blanks (literally). Since all I *have*, visually, is blanks, I code up my text with heaps and lashings of modifiers. But there is usually some kind of musical riffing that a mainly visual reader probably misses, being keyed to another coding modality.... (To put it in my favored abstract-densified fashion.) Luckily, I can at least respond to Nabokov's evocation of sounds, achieved *through* soundless sounds in the words that run on from my previous *Lolita* citation:

> But even brighter than those quietly rejoicing colors—for there are colors and shades that seem to enjoy themselves in good company—both brighter and dreamier to the ear than they were to the eye, was that vapory vibration of accumulated sounds that never ceased for a moment, as it rose to the lip of granite where I stood wiping my foul mouth. And soon I realized that all these sounds were of one nature, that no other sounds but these came from the streets of the transparent town, with the women at home and the men away. Reader! What I heard was but the melody of children at play, nothing but that, and so limpid was the air that within this vapor of blended voices, majestic and minute, remote and magically near, frank and divinely enigmatic—one could hear now and then, as if released, an almost articulate spurt of vivid laughter, or the crack of a bat, or the clatter of a toy wagon, but it was all

really too far for the eye to distinguish any movement in the lightly etched streets. (299-300)

The saddest aspect of this visual defect or variant I share with so many others is *not being able to activate the inner movie* for myself, but only its sound track! In *The White Abacus*, an sf-warped version of Shakespeare's *Hamlet* that goes sideways fast at the end, all the "word-pictures" were my own.... No actual Denmark scenery, a rather hi-tech ghost, no swords as such. And my Ophelia was smarter and prettier and a damned sight tougher. I certainly tried to make it a visual treat, borrowing from some excellent space art (acknowledged in the afterword), but making my own wide-screen baroque from it, *etc.* I yearn to see it in my mind....

I am waiting sullenly for the plug-in cognitive module. Yet, strangely enough, I do enjoy (and sometimes suffer) vivid visual dreams. Obviously people like me do possess those basic visual processing modules that allow us to transform retinal activation patterns into an experienced world (a flat one, in my case, with depth guessed from inferential cues, as one does in a movie). So when our waking consciousness switches down and off, in sleep, and the brain starts generating specious imagery out of scraps of the day's events, imagined connections, *etc.*, that whole machinery is presumably fully available to build up a pseudo-world with a certain sensory richness. When we dream, the standard visual parts of the cortex light up on brain scanners. When I am awake, though, presumably a different set of dominant cognitive pathways or hierarchies gets activated.

I have sometimes wondered if I could learn to switch into the dreamvision mode with lots of practice. But then, reading novels is exactly that kind of practice, you'd imagine, and it has not happened. I am left, like Hamlet, with words, words, words.

BOOKS REFERENCED

Broderick, Damien, *The White Abacus*, New York, Avon, 1997.
----- *Quipu*, New York, E-Reads, 2009.
Brown, Dan, *Angels and Demons*, New York, Atria Books, 2003.
----- *The Lost Symbol*, New York, Doubleday, 2009.
Nabokov, Vladimir, *Strong Opinions*, New York, McGraw-Hill, 1973.
Nabokov, Vladimir, and Alfred Appel, Jr., *The Annotated Lolita: Revised and Updated*, New York, Vintage Books, 1991.

X.

EMOTION AND INTELLECT IN POETRY

by Michael R. Collings

FOR A FEW pages, I would like to re-don my professorial cap (you know, the square one with the tassel), and posit two poles from which poetry may start: emotion and intellect. There are, of course, many other ways to discuss poetics, but these two seem at the moment most relevant. But before the discussion, two assertions:

Neither approach is right.

Neither approach is wrong.

Most poetry would in fact fit nicely on a continuum between extremes, and it is perhaps impossible to write a piece that emanates exclusively from one or the other. But for the purposes of discussion, let's begin there.

POETRY OF EMOTION draws most strongly, obviously, from the depths of the poet's emotions: love, fear, loneliness, hatred. Such poetry has as a primary intention recreating that emotion, in many cases privately and personally; readers become in essence adjuncts to the process, at times even irrelevant to it. The poem is directed inward, to the poet's core. It becomes a means of emotional adjustment, a way to extract a particular emotional state and express it directly.

Such poetry relies little on poetic conventions and greatly on experience. The poet speaks directly, often in first person, often alluding to private experiences readers are neither expected nor invited to share. In some instances, a specific, single reader might serve as audience—particularly in poems of love or loss—but more commonly even that reader is peripheral to the expression of deep and often painful emotion.

Such basics of written communication as grammar, syntax, spelling, punctuation, and sentence structure rank low on the poet's scale of priorities, sometimes even perceived as hindering the "honest" expression of emotion. Revision becomes antithetical to the purposes of the poem; to hold the poem up to scrutiny, to alter its white-hot rhythms and diction, would be to diminish the authenticity of its emotional content. Such poeticisms as image, simile, metaphor, or symbol occur only tangentially, as it were, as byproducts of the poet's need to allow the emotion to surface.

POETRY OF INTELLECT, on the other hand, relies, equally obviously, on intellect; not on reason or rationality *per se*, but on the conscious manipulation of them. The poem becomes a puzzle to create and to interpret. The poet becomes distanced in the sense that words become means to an end, tools by which to create a preconceived artifact.

Poetic conventions become the driving force behind the construct. Image and simile may occur, but more usually the more rigidly logical, objective tropes predominate: metaphor, with its conscious awareness and manipulation of similarities and differences between unexpectedly juxtaposed objects; and symbol, with its equal if not greater requirement of cerebral engagement to state effectively an idea not in fact present in the poem.

Such poems exploit the possibilities of form to the utmost, either traditional forms, including requirements of meter and rhyme, word or syllable count; or nonce forms in which free-verse lines express preconceived structures. Language similarly becomes a tool for puzzle-making and -solving, with acrostics, anagrams, palindromes, and other related techniques at times subordinating sense and meaning.

Again, I'm considering here extreme polarities possible in poetry. Most, if not all poetry, lies on the continuum between extremes; and much of the greatest poetry clusters near the center.

However, there is a point to be made by discussing these polarities. Much of the apparent discord that arises between poets and respondents, between poets and poets, may result from individuals not differentiating between two essentially antithetical purposes for writing.

I tend toward intellectual poetry, for example; it bothers me, and for me detracts substantially from a poem's effectiveness, to see misspellings, grammatical infelicities, awkward or strained syntax (particularly in service of an equally awkward or strained rhyme). Form frequently seems preferable to free verse, since it automatically creates an intellectual challenge that I appreciate—how to communicate specific ideas, images, and, yes, even emotions, within the constraints of pre-existing line or stanzaic expectations. At the same time it provides relatively objective criteria for assessing poems: how well do they perform within those expectations. My own work tends to be formal…and at times it tends to be dispassionate, distanced, cold.

ON POETRY AS A FAÇADE
BEHIND WHICH THE ESSENCE LURKS

> Meter comes easily. English tends to
> Shift and swirl in rhythmic fall-then-rise.
> Syllables allow themselves (almost) no
> Hesitance. Sounds link in subtle ways
> But can be tracked and traced across crisp lines,
> Arrows drawn if needed to make clear
> How "m" persists, or "l," what strengths it gains
> By repetition. What remains to mar
> The texture of a piece, to hinder
> Transformation from mere craft to art
> (If one can hope for such in fonder
> Thoughts) is that oblique, intrinsic part,
> That revelatory, quintessential goal:
> The power and the passion and the soul.

Others poets, however, equally if not more proficient and imaginative poets, tend toward emotional poetry. For them free verse is often preferable to form since it allows for, if not invites openly, overt expression of emotion. Niceties of grammatical conventions can be overlooked in favor of intensity, authenticity, excitement, and directness. Evaluating such poems becomes itself an act of emotion, of subjectivity: Do I like this poem? At the most distant extreme, that question might frequently supersede a more difficult question: Why do I like this poem?

There may be, as noted in the beginning of this consideration, many other ways to discuss poetry. But regardless of other options, it may be helpful to keep a couple of questions in mind when we approach a poem. What does the poet's choice to write a sonnet, or a haiku, or meter and rhyme, or stripped-down free-verse suggest about why the poet wrote this particular poem? And what can we therefore legitimately expect to encounter when we enter it? Taking a moment to identify a poem as essentially emotion-oriented or intellect-oriented may make the experience of reading poems more beneficial, more constructive, and ultimately more enjoyable.

XI.

MAKING THINGS HAPPEN

by Ardath Mayhar

IN ORDER TO write action that grips the reader and makes him live the thing that is happening in the story, you have to learn to write about action as if you were involved in it yourself. That is the only way, for someone who stands off at a distance and describes what is going on is going to lose his reader's interest very quickly.

The method I have found that works best for me is really very similar to method acting. I go inside the protagonist most involved in the scene, and then I act and react within his skin, feeling his emotions and pains and triumphs. See the contrast between the following scenes:

> John walked into the garden. It was cold, and he shivered as he hid behind a bush and waited to hear the signal. The danger that faced him was very real, and he might not come out of this formal garden alive, he knew quite well.

Now how about this:

> John waited for a moment, listening for any sound in the chill formality of the garden. The wind, catching his coat collar, made his earlobes ache, as he found a hidden spot behind a camellia bush, now frost-touched and stiff, and settled to wait. He wondered when the signal would come...and if he would survive this contact and return tonight to Jennifer's warm room and comforting presence.

Watch what happened there. I went into that garden with him. I felt that gust of wind. I heard the camellia bush rustle. I longed, with him, for the warmth of his girl and the safety of her room, and I dreaded, with him, the signal that would take him out into danger.

This is not a difficult thing to learn to do. And once you do learn it, the very act of becoming your character will provide a great deal of detail, of emotion, of inner depth that otherwise you would never know was there. And now let's see what happened to John, there in that garden.

> The whistle, when it came, was shrill and hurt his ears. He sighed and straightened, still cautious, to peer from behind his bush. Even as he moved to leave its shelter, hard hands caught at him from the other side of the low hedge.
>
> "Got him!" said a strangled voice. "Here, haul him over!"
>
> He felt the stiff twigs of the hedge scraping his skin, tearing along the rough weave of his trousers and coat, as he was jerked unceremoniously from his position to the other side of the stubbly growth. He went limply, as if caught off guard, but when his feet touched the ground, he exploded like some delayed action bomb. His right fist sank into an unprotected belly, as his left hand tangled in a beard and yanked a face down to meet his lowered skull. A nose broke audibly against his head. His feet were busy, too, and a suppressed shriek told him he had connected with someone's groin. He heaved backward, away from the now less enthusiastic hands, and in an instant he was over the hedge again and out of the garden, leaving whoever had betrayed him to sort out the catastrophe without him.

You have to get into that fight yourself. You have to know something about hurting and being hurt in a hand-to-hand situation. Having a younger brother, as I did, helped me with that a great deal.

You have to choreograph the action so that you won't have someone doing something physically impossible or going in two directions at once, or simply going about what he's doing all wrong. That will lose you a reader in a hurry.

A battle that is described in fiction must be handled in much the same way. You need to figure out just what parts of it are crucial to your story. You need to put one or more characters into important engagements and then to follow them through their parts, linking each together by transition or "reports" in order to make the shape of the battle conform to your needs.

The difference between this technique and the long distance one can be seen if you will read any history textbook account of an historic battle, and then will go and find personal accounts of that same battle, such as those that Bruce Catton used in his wonderful Civil War books. The difference between the immediate and personal and the distant and impersonal is the difference between the interesting and the dull.

An important part of action, as well as every other aspect of a story, is the feelings that the characters have and that the reader finds affecting him. A person with no emotions is not a real one, and you must, as with the action writing, make the characters' emotions your own.

Grief, anger, fear, pleasure, triumph, joy, anticipation—all the range of human emotional response is at your command. Few writers, or anyone else, can go through a life without knowing all those and more. Take your own feelings and pour them into your characters. You will get a surprise. Your crotchety old grandfather character will not deal with sudden anger in the same way that his fearful young granddaughter will. Suddenly, your own feelings will assume a wide range of differences, each suitable to the person who is involved in the emotional situation.

Make your reader feel for and with the characters.

Watch:

> She sat, limp and unmoving, on the shore, staring out at the spot where her child had gone down. Tears had not come.
> Grief had not come...not yet.
> She felt drained, exhausted, cold as the bare-branched oak trees that leaned over the river. It would have been such a relief to cry, to shout, to rage at God and nature and her own weakness, and yet she could not.
> She felt as if cold mud filled her, throat to belly, and she would never move or speak again. One huge pain, she would sit here in the damp forever, staring at the water that had taken her son.

And now for another:

> Clarence almost danced along the stone-flagged walk. His black-gloved fingers grasped the gift tightly,

and he had to loose them consciously, for fear of crushing the delicate filigree of the brooch.

Cynthia would be so delighted, so proud—she would know that he had saved for a year to buy this special gift, and she would, perhaps, smile that wide, warm smile that welcomed him home to more than four walls and a dinner.

It is useful to write small exercises like the ones above, just to hone your ability to evoke action and emotion, not to mention imagery and characterization. A pianist or a violinist must practice. There is not a thing wrong with a writer's taking a leaf from the musicians' book and practicing as well.

XII.

PLOTTING A SCIENCE FICTION STORY

by Brian Stableford

THE OVER-ELABORATE attention that most teachers of writing give to characterization is usually complemented by a marked indifference to plotting. It is almost as if the business of constructing a plot were considered too vulgar to warrant consideration by the truly literary, although it does seem to be the case that the majority of readers are more interested in the plots of the stories which they read than in any other aspect of them.

One objection that teachers of creative writing have to the business of plotting is that it is something that can be summarized very easily. A description of how an author goes about the business of characterization might be longer than the story, but an account of the plot is always shorter. Worse still, plots are very often conventional, reducible to formulas. Thus, the plot of very many detective stories can be summed up as: somebody gets murdered; the detective gathers all the evidence and uses ingenious powers of logical deduction to determine who did it. The plot of most romances is just as simple: nice girl meets ruggedly handsome man; their attitudes and circumstances seem bound to keep them apart, but they eventually get together, realizing at last that this is the one thing which will make their lives worthwhile.

The fact that one can reduce whole genres of fiction to fairly simple formulas seems to most literary critics to be a blanket certificate of worthlessness. After all, one of the qualities that great works of literature are supposed to possess is originality, and the kind of originality that simply produces endless variations on a single theme seems substandard. Would-be writers, however, might care to bear in mind the fact that formularistic plots do work. In spite of their predictability, they command the attention and the affection of many readers. People who do not care for them often speak scornfully of the kind of romances published by firms like Mills & Boon or Harlequin, mocking the rigid formula to which they are produced, but that derision does not prevent the millions of people who value the experience of reading them from buying and enjoying them.

At first glance, science fiction appears to be much less formularistic than most genres. Science fiction has many different settings, and the range of potential happenings in a science fiction story is much greater than in any other kind of fiction. Nevertheless, its plots do often follow familiar patterns, and there are good reasons for this. It is action and suspense that make stories attractive and exciting to the great majority of readers, and action and suspense are generated by plots. The plot is, in a way, the skeleton of a story, upon which the literary flesh is built. It may be the literary flesh that is responsible for making a story distinctive and beautiful, just as it is actual flesh that makes people distinctive and beautiful, but it is the skeleton that gives the story structure, strength, and power of movement; and if it is to do that, it needs to be built according to a certain set plan. Plots vary, just as the skeletons of birds, fish, and mammals vary, but their variations are variations on a theme.

I would advise would-be writers not to despise plot formulas, and to make what productive use of them they can. Some of the best-known science fiction writers in America worked for the Scott Meredith Literary Agency at a time when the agency advised would-be pulp writers ambitious to become its clients to use a standard formula. The formula ran along the following lines: begin by establishing a sympathetic lead character who is faced with an urgent problem, then show how his (or her) preliminary attempts to cope with the problem make things worse, before he ultimately contrives by his own efforts to bring about a solution.

It is certainly true that there have been countless good stories written that do not fit this formula, but there is no doubt that it is a useful item of equipment, which is capable of generating lots of good stories. It is arguable that nothing in the formula is absolutely necessary to the production of an effective story, but each element does serve a purpose. If your lead character is not sympathetic, you may alienate some readers; if there is no urgency about what he has to do, your story is likely to lack pace and suspense; if he is not at first frustrated, the story may seem too facile; if a solution is not obtained as a result of his own efforts, the reader identifying with him will get less satisfaction out of the climax.

Writers should never become slaves to formulas of this kind, but they can be invaluable crutches, especially for beginners, and they deserve to be taken seriously. They do not undermine or seek to take over the processes of creativity; what we mean by an "original" plot is not one that avoids the formula, but one that sets up a particularly ingenious or unusual problem for which the characters will ultimately discover a particularly elegant or ironic solution. The capacity that science fiction offers for unexpected happenings certainly opens up much more space for surprising events and surprising endings, but if these do not become part of the hero's frustrations and achievements as mapped out by the Scott Meredith plot formula, the reader may simply feel cheated—a story where the central problem is solved by dragging in some entirely new factor (what the jargon calls a *deus ex machina*) usually does not work very well.

What I have seen of the first efforts of would-be science fiction writers (and it is certainly supported by my own early experiences) suggests to me that it is regrettably easy to get carried away by a particular image or idea, so that one writes down a description of a bizarre event or a strange environment without paying any attention at all to the question of what kind of plot would make the best use of the idea. It is true that a science fiction story usually has an idea rather than a character as its focal point, but that does not mean that the idea can support a narrative on its own. The lens that brings the idea into focus is the plot of the story, and the hardest work a writer has to do—far harder than actually thinking up ideas to use—is in shaping his story to display his idea to best advantage. Providing an effective plot is the most fundamental aspect of that shaping.

Some writers do tend to be dismissive about the work of plotting, observing that there are only a handful of "basic plots." Robert A. Heinlein wrote a celebrated article offering advice to would-be science fiction writers, in which he claimed that there were only three: "Boy Meets Girl," "The Little Tailor," and "The Man Who Learned Better." It needs only a slight adjustment of perspective to recognize that all three are variants of a single theme: the Success Story. The first features success in love, the second success in a career, the third success in coming to terms with the way of the world. One might add that there are other kinds of success story: "Who-Done-It?" features puzzle-solving success; "How The Hell Do I Get Out of This Mess?" is the escaped-threat success story (which features very prominently in horror fiction). One might also point out that each of these plots has a corresponding "anti-plot"—or "tragic variant"—in which success is not attained.

Reduction of this kind should not, however, be interpreted as a dismissal of the problems of plotting as something unimportant or facile; it is really a matter of pointing out what we mean by the word "plot." What this kind of argument says is that the plot of a story relates to the projects that the characters in a story have, and to whether those projects will come to a successful conclusion or not. There are exactly as many "basic plots" as there are basic needs of human existence: the elementary factors involved in surviving and thriving. That is why a useful method of trying to find a plot that will display an idea to good advantage is to ask who might get hurt if the world were changed in the way that the idea imagines.

What plot formulas tend to leave out, curiously, is the reason why plots are capable of gripping the attention of readers and getting them "involved" in the story—which is perhaps the main reason why such a thing as fiction exists at all. What both the Scott Meredith formula and the Heinlein account of basic plots fail to mention, although it is in a sense the very essence of plotting, is the notion of moral order.

The world in which we live appears to have no inbuilt moral order. As St. Matthew and everyone else has observed, rain falls on the just and the unjust alike. The wicked are no more likely to get struck down by lightning or by cancer than those who live like saints. This conflicts with our moral sensibilities; we feel that the wicked deserve to suffer misfortune and that the good deserve to be rewarded. It is because the real world perversely fails to punish the wicked and tragically fails to reward the good that people have always speculated about an afterlife in which this failure will be decisively rectified.

The world of a story, however, differs from the real world in that the writer is there to guide the hand of providence. He has the power to reward his good characters and punish his wicked ones, and if he does not do so it is because he has chosen not to do so. Chance plays no role in fiction—or, if it does (if, for instance, a writer were to decide to let the outcome of his story depend on the throw of a dice), it is only because the writer deliberately refuses to exercise his power of choice.

What happens in a story, therefore, cannot help but have some kind of moral significance. This is why the success of the hero of a story is uplifting: that success is the reward for all his cleverness and virtue. Readers love to see the villain of a story come unstuck and perish horribly, not because they are sadistic, but because they recognize the moral propriety of his extinction.

This is why people are not only willing but eager to read what is, in essence, the same plot over and over again—it is a ritual assertion of moral principle. This is also why most people prefer "upbeat" (morally proper) endings to "downbeat" ones (where the good do not receive the full measure of their apparent entitlement, and/or evil goes unpunished). Downbeat stories—tragedies—are intended to make us uncomfortable, by sharpening our awareness of the failings of the world we live in, and many people feel that they are all too sharply aware of that already.

The plots of science fiction stories cannot help but be similar in kind to the plots of other kinds of fiction. The characters with whom we identify, whether they be human or unhuman, may have projects which are distinctive in detail—boldly going where no man has gone before—but they inevitably have the same kind of moral weight as the projects adopted by characters in Greek drama, Shakespearean tragedy, western films, and romantic novels. It is true that our notions of what ought to count as good and what ought to count as evil are subject to negotiation, varying from society to society and over time, but the nature of moral questions does not alter, and there is a substantial cross-cultural consensus about the fundamentals of good and evil.

Having said this, though, it must also be said that there are some particular moral issues that are addressed more easily and more frequently by science fiction than by any other kind of fiction—and this is the main reason why I believe that science fiction is an interesting, worthwhile, and important species of fiction. There are two issues that seem to me to be of cardinal importance.

One moral issue that science fiction writers often address in their plotting, but which writers in other genres rarely touch, is the question of how we should actually constitute a "moral community"? To what kind of entities do we owe moral consideration? In the real world, and hence in mundane fiction, this is an easy issue to evade, the simplest move being to say that we owe moral consideration only to other people—this still leaves room for painful disputes about animal rights and the rights of embryos, but it narrows down the discussion to a point where we often do not inquire deeply into the underlying logic of our decisions. Only in science fiction can we produce moral dramas asking whether an animal with augmented intelligence, or an alien, or a sentient machine, is worthy of moral consideration. By asking such hypothetical questions, we can actually get to the heart of the question of what it is about an entity which entitles it to be the object of moral concern. There are some science fiction stories, like Robert A. Heinlein's "Jerry was a Man" and Vercors's novel *Borderline*, in which the case is actually argued out in a hypothetical court of law.

A second issue that is implicit in the plots of very many science fiction stories, but much less obvious outside science fiction, is the question of what constitutes "progress." It is not only individual people who have projects in which they may succeed or fail; people band together into groups, ranging from families and clubs to professions and nations, and these groups take on projects of their own in order to serve the needs and interests of the individuals within them. It makes sense to ask whether the whole human race ought to have a project, what that project should be, and what the chances of succeeding in it might be. These are the questions that are involved in the concept of progress; they are questions that surface explicitly in many science fiction stories, and which are tacitly at stake in many others.

The resolution of a plot in a science fiction story is almost always concerned with more than the fates of the characters who appear in it; the story usually requires that its resolution bears upon the fate of the hypothetical world—which is, in a sense, the true "hero" of the story. Science fiction is not just about good and bad people who may or may not get their just desserts; it is about worlds that might be better or worse than ours, and the prospects of changing them.

It is possible to make a career as a science fiction writer by writing costume drama, in which the only things at stake in your plots will be whether or not the protagonist makes a fortune, gets his own back on the bad guys, and marries the prettiest girl around. There is a lot of that kind of costume drama in fantasy, too, although it should be pointed out that the best fantasy also has a particular moral significance of its own—indeed, the chief attraction of Secondary World fantasy is that it can bring moral issues into much sharper focus than fiction about the real world usually permits, often with a literalized conflict between Good and Evil. I think that science fiction's handling of the moral issues with which it is most often concerned entitles it to much more serious consideration from literary historians and literary critics than it has so far received. It is interesting to note that science fiction plots and situations have come to play a significant part in modern philosophical arguments that try to grapple with such questions as how we ought to define a moral community.

Science-fictional costume drama, which employs the Scott Meredith plot formula in its crudest form, and is concerned only with the fate of the particular characters in the story, can be exciting to write and to read. I would say to all would-be science fiction writers, though, that if you want to produce real science fiction, then you must bear in mind while you are designing your plots that larger issues—up to and including the fate of the human race—can and should be a matter for consideration. The fate of a hypothetical society transformed by its adoption of a particular technology is something that you might require your readers to care about as much as, and perhaps more than, the fate of the particular individuals who figure in your story. All the best science fiction possesses this grander moral vision, although doctrinaire literary critics sometimes do not recognize it as a virtue, and sometimes regard it as a poor substitute for "good characterization."

In my own fiction, especially with respect to plotting, I have always tried to incorporate these larger issues in my work, even in the crudest of my works. The stories that I have written of which I am most proud—which include "And He Not Busy Being Born...," "Sexual Chemistry," "The Growth of the House of Usher," *The Empire of Fear*, and *Prelude to Eternity*—are all consciously and directly addressed to the question of what would count as a better world than the one we now live in; and I made every effort to be clever, original, and provocative in formulating their plots around that question.

Although critics have sometimes claimed that I have a rather downbeat view of things (which I deny), I think that I am on safe ground in claiming that my story "Sexual Chemistry" not only has a happy ending, but that it has the only truly happy ending to which a science fiction story should aspire. At the risk of spoiling the surprise for readers who have yet to encounter it, the last two lines of the story are:

They lived happily ever after.
And so did everybody else.

XIII.

SAYING MUCH WITH LITTLE

SOME PRACTICAL SUGGESTIONS FOR TIGHTENING BULKY LINES IN POETRY

by Michael R. Collings

CHARACTERISTICALLY, poems tend toward compression. One hallmark of great poetry is that it communicates much more than the total of its words. Diction, image, metaphor, symbol—all combine to give poetry the sense of a flower unfolding, revealing more and more meaning the deeper we examine it. For that reason, for example, it usually takes far more words in prose to express the meaning of a poem than the poem itself used, and frequently, even after our best attempts, the poem still evades absolute explication.

Compression—the art of saying much with little—is fundamental to effective poetry. From haiku, which consciously avoids unnecessary words and concentrate on every sound and syllable, to longer, more expansive pieces, poetry struggles to expand beyond mere word count. And one of the most common difficulties a poem encounters is the sense on the reader's part that it is wordy, bulky, flabby.

As a matter of practical application, there are two large divisions of words in English: structure words and lexical words. *Structure* words function primarily as adjuncts of syntax and grammar. They do not carry significant meaning in themselves, but instead provide important signals as to how other words relate to each other and to meaning. They are notoriously difficult to define specifically; most often, definitions tend toward the abstract. The simple preposition *for*, for example, can mean "with the object or purpose of," "intended to belong to or used in conjunction with," "in place of," "to the amount of or extent of," and literally dozens of other possibilities; its specific meaning in a given phrase depends entirely on the meanings of the words that surround it. In general, structure words include prepositions, articles (*a, an, the*), and the copular verbs (*is, seems, becomes, etc.*).

Lexical words, on the other hand, can be defined. They relate to specific things, actions, movements, qualities. Their meanings usually refer to image-making constructs: *walk, run, touch, tree, fence, boulder*. In most cases, these words are nouns, verbs, adjectives, and adverbs.

[CAVEAT: At this point it is important to emphasize that there is nothing inherently **wrong** with structure words, or with using them within poetry; nor does the presence of lexical words automatically make for tight, lean, effective lines. Structure words do, however, frequently occur unnecessarily and add bulk, a sense of the prosaic, and a rhythmical flatness when not used carefully and consciously, just as lexical words can create a sense of vividness, imagery, action, and specificity.]

* * * * * * *

LET'S BEGIN BY looking at the most notorious of the structure words: prepositions.

One on-line dictionary defines *preposition* as "any member of a class of words found in many languages that are used before nouns, pronouns, or other substantives to form phrases functioning as modifiers of verbs, nouns, or adjectives, and that typically express a spatial, temporal, or other relationship, as in, on, by, to, since." The definition is long, abstract, and cumbersome, particularly since the words being categorized tend to be remarkably short and direct. For practical purposes, however, perhaps the best definition of a preposition is "anything a rabbit can do to a hill": in the hill, on the hill, by the hill, around the hill, through the hill. Only a limited number of words function as prepositions in English, yet at the same time they are among the most difficult class of words to use idiomatically and "correctly." In spite of all this, they are essential to creating meaning in English.

In terms of compression, however, prepositions almost always add words, often unnecessary words. By definition, a *pre*-position comes before something; therefore prepositions, when functioning as such, always have objects, words that function as nouns. These, in turn, are frequently prefaced by articles (*a, an, the*) which in essence simply announce "Watch out! Noun coming."

Three words. Only one carrying meaning.

Let's look at an example from one of my earliest poems, an elegy to my uncle:

> For in the soothing sounds of waters' whisperings
> As they turn a moss-encrusted wheel,
> He is present.

Ignoring other problems for the moment, look at the first two lines. Fifteen words—three prepositions (*for, in, of*), two articles (*the, a*), a vague pronoun (*they*), and a wasted adverb (*as*). Nearly half of the total devoted to telling readers how words—substantive, meaningful words—fit together or relate to each other. And the poor reader has to make it to the fourth word before anything is actually said. An overly long, bulky, uninteresting set of lines.

To revise for compression and energy, let's first look for a verb. The sentence, as written, has one, of course: *is*, the weakest verb in English (more about that in Part III). In addition, it comes so late in the lines that the reader has to perform a juggling act just to keep all of the intervening parts straight.

If we look for an active verb—or a word that could become an active verb—a couple of things emerge. First, words such as *soothe, sound, whisperings*, and *turn* could easily become verbs. And second, the sentence as it stands makes no sense; stripped of verbiage, the opening clause actually reads, "sounds turn a wheel"—not at all what I was trying for. Wordiness, precipitated by incessant prepositions, gets in the way of meaning.

So…in that opening clause, where is our true verb? Probably the most likely is the noun *whisperings*—rather artificially nominal, since if we remove the noun-making endings, we get a strong verb: *whisper*. What whispers? *Water*. Where? *Through a moss-encrusted wheel*. And we have a sentence: "Water whispers through a moss-encrusted wheel."

But we have more than that. What happened to "sounds?" In its noun form, *whisper* is a sound; the earlier, more abstract, more general (how many kinds of sound are there?) word is redundant. What about "soothing"? Don't whispers usually soothe unless otherwise described, especially in an elegy? And if water whispers through a waterwheel, doesn't it turn the wheel?

In essence "Water whispers through a moss-encrusted wheel" says everything implicit in the first two lines, using seven words instead of fifteen, one preposition instead of three, and eliminating "they" and "the."

What, then, to do with line three, which asserts bluntly the point of the image: "he is present." Again, *is* the weakest of verbs, followed by *present*—vague, abstract, generalized, non-imagistic, boring. The only word truly working here is *he*, which in the context points specifically to an individual: my uncle. Three more words (bringing the total to eighteen); only one carries significance for the lines.

This brings us back to an earlier problem: what do these lines want to say? When I wrote them, I was standing beside a waterwheel my uncle had built perhaps forty years earlier, moss-encrusted as the line says, still functioning. Just seeing it, hearing it, brought him forcibly back to memory. So what should the subject of these lines be? *Water*, which seems at this point tangential; or *he*? Let's go with the latter. If we move *water* to a different place in the line, and replace *a* with *his*, we get:

> He whispers through his moss-encrusted waterwheel.

More imagistic, metaphorical, possibly symbolic, certainly more interesting—in seven words, fewer than half of the original count, but saying more clearly what I intended.

Are we finished? Perhaps. A judicious break might transform the line into creditable free verse:

> He whispers through
> His moss-encrusted waterwheel.

Or we could keep going, transforming and re-structuring:

> His moss-encrusted waterwheel whispers...*him*.

Possibly simply:

> His moss-encrusted waterwheel whispers....

Or transform it into a haiku-like sequence:

> moss-encrusted
> waterwheel—
> his ghost whispers

Or any number of other possibilities, none readily apparent in the first version.

Of all the parts of speech, then, prepositions (and their accompanying nominal phrases) most often work against tightness, compression, and clarity in poetry. Lines needn't be stripped down as far as I have taken this one, but on almost every level, particularly in early drafts, finding prepositions and prepositional phrases, identifying the underlying verb, defining the actor performing that action, and restructuring accordingly may at least present new alternatives for expression.

XIV.

THE TWO-HEADED AUTHOR

THE CHALLENGES, RISKS, AND REWARDS OF COLLABORATION

by John Howard Weeks

MY FRIEND AND I decided a long time ago that we wanted to write a book together. We spent thirty years talking about it, then one year doing it.

The result is the novel *Window Beyond the World* (2006) by John Howard Weeks and William S. Thomas, which even today, several years after publication, is holding firmly in the list of top three million sellers at Amazon.com.

OK, so it's not a bestseller. It never was. But it's a hell of a good book, and the story of how it came to be written may prove informative, or at least entertaining, to other authors who are considering a collaborative writing venture.

Let me say at the outset that Bill and I found the experience to be delightful in every way, and we are obnoxiously pleased with the result. And we still are friends. Other collaborators may tell cautionary tales wracked with pain, suffering, disappointment, ruined friendship, and regret. That's their story, not ours.

Perhaps people who find that they cannot get along with one another, productively, should not be writing books together.

I can tell you, with the wisdom of hindsight, that my list of arguments against collaborative writing is a very short one indeed.

There's only one item on it, and here it is:

You have to split your profits!

Fortunately, Bill and I found this to be far less painful than we expected, as the profits always have been quite manageably low. If we had made millions, there may have been problems. We'll never know.

My list of arguments in favor of collaborative writing is a much more lengthy one, and it contains several items. Two-headed authors work more quickly than one-headed authors, at least the two-headed authors who are doing it properly, because they goad and motivate each other.

They also produce a cleaner, sharper manuscript, because they constantly edit each other as they go along. They also have more fun, because they surprise and impress and excite each other in ways that one-headed authors cannot possible manage unless they happen to be bipolar.

Two-headed authors also enjoy a unique indemnity, even immunity, from criticism that is not available to one-headed authors, who must take reproof entirely upon themselves. Two-headed authors, on the other hand, when confronted with condemnation, can blame the other guy.

It's like a free pass.

Finally, and most importantly, two-headed authors end up with a book that is wonderfully different than the book they thought they were going to write. And quite likely more wonderful, period.

Bill and I worked at the same newspaper, a Southern California daily, for a good chunk of the 1970s. We quickly developed a mutual respect for each other's talents and skills, and we became friends to boot.

It didn't take long for Bill to get the itch to write a book with me. He never tired of reminding me of how a gaggle of reporters and editors at another newspaper had made a fortune when the racy novel they patched together as an office joke, *Naked Came the Stranger*, became a fluke bestseller.

It was his opinion that if they could it, we could do it, too.

To the best of my recollection, he never tried to build a large team of colleagues to replicate the success of *Naked Came the Stranger*.

Perhaps he didn't want to split the proceeds too many ways. No, he only nagged me. And he nagged me constantly.

And he never stopped. Even when he took another job, in another city, and we no longer worked or lived in proximity to one another, he often would call me, and always the first words out of his mouth would be, "So when are we going to write that book?"

Years later, when the Internet came along, he would email me and call me both, and ask the same question, again and again.

I always was too involved in my own solo book projects to take up the challenge. Ultimately, though, as the years passed, it dawned upon me that, while my solo book projects were yielding a large number of outstanding manuscripts, they weren't resulting in a single published book.

Ironically, as it turned out, my first published book would be the book that Bill and I finally wrote together. That says something, right there, about the benefits of collaborative writing. At least it says something to me.

Yes, I probably should have acted sooner. I shouldn't have waited so long to take Bill up on his challenge. But I will say this about those thirty years of constant nagging and badgering and wearing me down.

When I was ready, I was ready.

I had conceived an idea for a novel, a ghost story set in the mountains of Southern California. At the time, I had a second home in Lake Arrowhead in the San Bernardino Mountains. Bill had lived at one time in nearby Wrightwood in the adjoining San Gabriel Mountains. We both were stirred by the call of high places. I thought it was a story we could do together.

I decided to write the first chapter, along with a plot outline, and surprise him with it.

Yes, I know what you are thinking. Is this the best way to begin a collaboration, by blindsiding your collaborator, initiating a project with no mutual planning or discussion? No collaboration, in other words?

You may have a point. But this is the way it happened, in our case, and it worked out very well in the end.

I think there may be certain collaborative writing projects, especially of a scholarly or scientific nature, where the partners must work shoulder-to-shoulder from the beginning. In those cases, that is the way it must be done.

It was not the way I wanted to do it, for any number of reasons. For one thing, it would have been physically impossible. Bill and I lived 200 miles apart at the time.

Secondly, I prefer to write in solitude and silence, which I know must sound strange coming from the lips of a proponent of collaborative writing. But it's true. I want no distractions, at least during the first-draft composition stage, and I can think of no greater distraction than the immediate presence of another person directly interested in what I am writing. I couldn't write a word under such circumstances.

Thirdly, Bill previously had attempted a collaboration of the shoulder-to-shoulder kind, working with another newspaper colleague on a work of non-fiction. Nothing ever had come of it, though, in the way of a published book, and Bill had told me enough horror stories about the frustrations of writing in this way, that I was quite certain it was not the method he and I should choose.

So, like I said, I blindsided him. And despite my best intention to write only the first chapter, and surprise him with it, I ended up writing the first eight chapters, and surprising him with those. What can I say? The story took hold, and I got carried away.

In retrospect, I probably wasn't thinking like a true collaborator yet. I wasn't thinking of the book as "our" book. I was thinking of it as "my" book. Bill would be my "helper."

Very quickly, though, Bill converted me to a better way of thinking, and I'll tell you how he did it.

You see, I not only emailed him the first eight chapters, but I also added a longwinded set of directions for how I thought he should advance the story. I was making it easy for him, I thought. It would be like filling in the blanks for him.

His response, which unfolded in many stages over the next several weeks, still makes me laugh when I think of it. It makes me laugh at myself.

He responded, first, with great joy and enthusiasm at the prospect of undertaking the project. He loved the novel's premise, he said. He thought the rough plot outline was great. He was ready to go.

During the course of the next few weeks he reported often, and breathlessly, that things were going very well indeed on his end.

Then, in far less time than I expected, he emailed me the book's next eight chapters. And I swiftly discovered, as I read them, that he had gleefully ignored every word of my painstaking instructions.

A smile of rueful bemusement turned into a beaming smile of admiration, however, as I read page after page. He had adopted my characters as if they were his own children, and he had developed them and moved them forward in just the right way, but he had taken them completely off script into a plot twist of his own invention.

And it was a plot twist that worked wonderfully. I loved him for his insolence.

I had envisioned a story that would stay local, with the action rooted in Southern California. My collaborator, being the hotshot world traveler and adventurer that he is, immediately whisked the whole company of main characters off to Africa, on a safari adventure that proved to be profoundly consequential for each of them.

Bill had taken "my" book and made it "our" book. He not only had added his own chapters, full of his own lively vision for our story, but he had gone back through my chapters, editing and correcting and suggesting changes here and there.

And thus the pattern was set for the way we would create this book, our book, together.

I proceeded to write my next batch of chapters, and I also went through the chapters he had written, making minor edits and suggestions. Then I sent the whole lot back to him, this time without a set of directions for what I thought he should do next. I trusted him now. I knew the story was safe in his hands. And he did not disappoint me. Nor did he fail to surprise me again.

This time he snatched our narrative off to Rio de Janeiro, in Brazil, another place he knew well from his extensive travels. And again it proved to be an exciting backdrop for propitious developments that dynamically advanced our story and evolved our characters. Then it was my turn again.

And this is how we proceeded, each of us writing our own chapters, and editing each other's, incorporating all the agreed-upon edits as we went along, talking occasionally on the telephone, communicating more often by email, cheering and egging each other on, until our first draft was finished. It happened in less than a year, and the draft was fairly sound because it already had been vetted, in effect, many times.

Since we respected each other, as editors as well as writers, there was very little quarreling between us. Generally we were content with the changes we made to each other's copy. Alternatively, we usually allowed each other to win whatever small arguments might pop up.

There was one lengthy paragraph of his, in which he described with an historian's detail a military battle of some importance in the life of one of our secondary characters. I kept taking it out, every time the manuscript came my way. And he kept putting it back in, every time the manuscript fell back into his hands. In my opinion, the paragraph violated our rule, established at the beginning, that we would forswear descriptive, decorative writing as much as possible, allowing the narrative to hurtle forward with breakneck speed. Hell, I think we even took an oath against using metaphors. And, by the way, if there is a book of English literature with fewer metaphors than ours, I offer my obeisance to it (once the claim is proven).

I felt the disputed paragraph slowed the story, however briefly. Bill thought it provided fascinating context. I found it less fascinating than he did. We played cat-and-mouse for months with that damn paragraph, me taking it out and him putting it back in. In the finished book, I think you will find that it is there, in all its fascinating glory. Bill wore me down.

Honestly, both of us were willing to concede minor points to one another, because we both believed that the other brought so much to the book in all the major ways that count the most.

My chapters inspired his chapters and his chapters inspired mine.

Here's what it says on the back cover of our novel:

> Lance Segundo's midlife crisis takes a bizarre twist when a long-dead loved one shows up seeking help. And offering help. The two embark on a journey of mutual self-discovery that takes them around the world—and beyond the world.
>
> Nothing you ever have read will prepare you for "Window Beyond the World." It's a transforming novel that will change the way you look at life and death, because it takes you to the strange, wonderful meeting place between the two.

It's only because we wrote the book together that it can be described in this way. If I had written it by myself, the first two sentences of that back-cover copy might still have been applicable, but none of the rest of it. It was Bill who stretched the boundaries and took the story from local to global; and the fact that he did so gave me the courage, gave us the courage, to take the story even farther than global, into an other-worldly realm where the story reaches a conclusion that neither of us envisioned when we began, a conclusion that everyone who reads the book agrees is astonishing.

That's all the bragging I will do.

Bill and I met in the same room only once during the creation of *Window Beyond the World*. When our first draft was completed, we celebrated with an all-day meeting at his home in Santa Barbara. We accomplished a number of important things during that meeting. We agreed on our next step, which would be to edit the whole thing again, separately, then share our revisions and discuss them.

We also aired our trepidation over the small but potent amount of R-rated material in the book. OK, X-rated. *Window Beyond the World* is a story of redemption, a story of how tarnished humans can rise into fantastic light from places of fathomless darkness. We had agreed from the beginning that we needed to depict the darkness fully and frankly—which certainly was the right choice, artistically.

Still, we literally worried about what our mothers would think. Yes, our sweet, delicate mothers.

And all the other sweet, delicate people out there.

We agreed that Bill, in talking to his mom or anyone else who might express dismay, would blame all the naughty bits on me. And I, if similarly challenged, would blame him. Remember what I said earlier about the wonderful immunity that is available to the two-headed author? I can tell you, it works like a charm.

Also, in our face-to-face meeting in Santa Barbara, we debated the title of our novel. Originally we had wanted to call it *Uncertain Death* or *Dead Again* or some other cool title with the word "dead" or "death" in it. Trouble is, all those titles seem to be taken.

Window Beyond the World became our working title, as we wrote, and it is a reasonable one, I suppose, given the fact that it is the name of the portal between the temporal and spirit worlds that appears frequently in our story.

Later, though, the agent with whom we eventually signed a contract suggested that we change the title to *The Window*. And we did, for awhile. But then, shortly before publication, Bill wanted to change it back to *Window Beyond the World*. I agreed, even though today I must admit, in retrospect, that I don't care for it. It sounds to my ear, now, like the title of a daytime television soap opera. "*Window Beyond the World* will resume right after these words from Tide detergent!"

It makes me cringe.

Personally, I wish we had stuck with *The Window*. We ended up dumping the agent who suggested it, but I think, now, that he was the voice of reason on that one point.

Mostly, during that all-day meeting in Santa Barbara, Bill and I discussed what we were going to do with all the money we would make when our novel hit the stands. This substantial part of our conversation may have come after the depletion of a bottle (or two) of celebratory champagne.

It is my firm belief that this remains the sole example, during the entire collaboration, of our excellent two-headed author talking utter nonsense.

XV.

LOVE, ANYONE?

OR,

HOW TO WRITE SEX SCENES

by William Maltese

HOW SERIOUS, THEN, THE SEX?

YOU AND I KNOW some pretty funny things can happen when any two people get together for a little loving. So if you are *positive* you can write "funny"—not just *think* you can write funny; not someone merely having *once* told you that you can write funny—then, by all means, write funny! There's a big demand in any area of the publishing business for anyone who can put across life's wittier moments, including those that happen in the bedroom.

That said, my advice for most writers is to steer clear of the humorous side of sex, because too few of us have the genuine knack to pull it off. Ill-handled, it can turn genre-romance or erotic sex truly ludicrous. Most readers aren't out for laughs, anyway. They have enough unintentional laughs in their own bedrooms. What genre-romance and erotica readers want from you is something to get their juices flowing. Too often, an injection of humor equals embarrassment for characters *and* for the reader, and that's a turn-off for all concerned.

"If you have to ask about the advisability of putting humor in any written sex act, I'd say don't make the attempt," a genre-romance editor once warned. "It's very difficult to mix humor and sex and still maintain intimacy. Best to forget the laughs and concentrate on life's sensuous but serious moments as you know them."

YES, BUT DO YOU PERSONALLY *HAVE* TO EXPERIENCE THE SEX YOU WRITE ABOUT?

WELL, FOR SURE, most readers haven't a clue as regards how many hours we writers sit on our getting-fatter asses in front of computer screens with so little time for anything else *but* writing, including for sex.

"If you don't slow down your fucking, young man," a well-intentioned fan once warned me, "you'll burn yourself out before you're thirty." I was thirty-three at the time.

* * * * * * *

"There!" Tom said and pointed through the thick tree branches toward the sapphire splotch of Blue Lake made bluer by the parenthesizing greens of thick forest. "Didn't I tell you it was worth the climb?"

The scenery *was* stupendous, but it wasn't what made Priscilla's first climb of a tree since her tomboy days so worth the effort. Better than scenery was study Tom Wonlin and what she proposed doing with and to him on their perch high above the ground. Her cunt was deliciously moist and slippery in her silk panties. There was something about muscular Tom, in his blue-checkered flannel shirt open to his navel, his chiseled chest and scalloped abdominals veneered with a thin film of sweat from the climb, which really got Priscilla hot and bothered. The thick meatiness of his cock, ill-concealed by the stretch of his faded jean crotch, was a big turn-on, too. So was the aphrodisiacal scent of fresh and heady pine.

She scooted back and forth on the thick limb she'd straddled upon first reaching their observation point. The roughness of pitchy bark against her Levi's-and-silk-sheathed pussy produced an exciting itch that made her more anxious for Tom's lovemaking.

"I want you to fuck me, Tommy Boy," she said, having mapped out the terrain enough to know it could be done. Three close-growing tree limbs extended nearby and could amply support her and the weight Tom would put on and in her.

"Fuck you, here?" Tom asked, all innocence. She couldn't believe he *hadn't* had sex in mind when he'd cajoled her up this tree in the first place. Tom was the type to think of fucking in an eagle's nest and, then, let his date think it was her idea.

"Yeah, right here," she affirmed, unbuttoning her shirt and peeling its red flannel free of the ivory smoothness of her non-brassiered tits. Her creamy, alabaster breasts jiggled enticingly as she hung her shirt on a higher limb. She unsnapped the top button of her Levi's, excited as hell by the lust sparking Tom's dark eyes. He'd coaxed her up here for a fuck all right. "You going to get that big blue-veined prick of yours out for action, or what?" she invited, detouring her attention to her shoes, since her pants would have to come off over them.

"We're liable to break our damned necks," he warned, but he didn't sound overly concerned, and he had his tennis shoes off before she could remove hers. He tied together a lace from each of his shoes and draped the result over a tree limb. Damned right, he knew what he was doing, and Priscilla followed suit, luxuriating in the roughness of pitch-smelling pine against the soles of her feet.

"Our ancestors fucked in trees," she reminded, "and with all our airs of civilization, it isn't going to take us but a second to revert to the primitive."

"Think so?" Tom asked; his shirt was off, and the top button of his jeans was open to reveal the curls of his dark pubic hair. When he unzipped, more wiry curls came to view, as well as the thick base of his cock swollen downward along his left thigh. The bastard already had a hard-on and was wearing no underpants to boot. He was up that tree to fuck her; there was no doubt about that. Well, she was going to give him no argument. There was nothing she wanted more than the push of Tom's limb-sized meatiness inside her bole-hole pussy.

She balanced expertly on one leg and then on the other as she removed her Levi's, readily believing the knack for fucking in treetops was imprinted on her genes. Stripped to her silk-panties-gone-wet-at-their-crotch, she took a good look at Tom who was naked as a jay.

His cum-bloated testicles hung halfway to his knees, suspended in a hairy sac of crinkly skin that moved sexily under its own steam. His wrist-thick cock had sprung from his pants like a catapult, slapping his hard belly and scattering glistening drops of preseminal moisture into the black hair haloing his deep navel.

"You want me to fuck you through those pink panties?" he asked. "I've a cock hot enough to burn right through."

"You know how much silk panties cost nowadays, especially when they're monogrammed?" she asked, suggestively caressing her embossed initials on her panty leg. She pinched the elastic leg-band and pulled it so he got a good look at her fleecy blonde curls until then no more than a *V*-shaped shadow beneath sex-wet silk. "They cost so much, a ruined pair would probably not make even a fuck by you worth it," she added teasingly. "So—" She hooked the waistband of her panties and slipped it down around her round hips, balancing first on one foot and then the other as she stepped out of the silk. Her sensitive bare butt scratched pine-smelling bark. "—I guess I'd better put these safely to one side," she said, stuffing them into the pocket of her Levi's now hung over the same limb as her shoes.

"If we could get you laid on those limbs," he said, pointing, "we might get the ball rolling."

"Maybe we can even get *your* balls rolling, do you think?" She held to a limb with one hand, and she cupped his cum-bloated balls with her other hand. Goddamn, he had tennis-ball balls! There was no other way to describe her handful of his scrotum-made-fuzzy-by-thick-black-hair. She rolled his cum containers and made them collide within her playful fingers until Tom gave a low, guttural groan, and his cock oozed clear lubricating juices. With his copious leaking and her thoroughly buttered cunt, they would have no trouble getting every last bloated inch of his monster erection stuffed inside her. Good thing, too, because, high above the forest floor, neither of them needed complications.

She should have been a circus performer, the way she laid down and jiggled seductively to wedge tree limb lengthwise between the perky cheeks of her ass. It wasn't the most comfortable bed for fucking, but there was something more exciting about it than lying spread-eagled on silk sheets. She was so balanced, she didn't need to hold on, but there were limbs on all sides if she felt the urge.

It wasn't at all scary looking up at fragrantly green pine needles, glossy with splattering sunlight and moving in a breeze that Priscilla sensed but didn't feel.

"I didn't bring Vaseline," Tom said, one massive hand wrapping as much of his cock as it could. "Shall I use pitch?" he joked, milking his blood-bloated erection until it turned even more golden with leaked natural moisture.

"I've plenty of wet waiting for you in here," Priscilla said; she pulled on the outer lips of her cunt so he could see the layers of her pink-to-red petals that were dewed with cuntal honey. "So, what are you waiting for?"

"Nothing!" he said and moved with a quick dexterity that betrayed the fact that she wasn't the only Jane this forest-Tarzan had enticed into this treetop for fucking. He knew just the right limbs on which to stand—limbs that were attached to the trunk just below the three limbs on which Priscilla was laid out. He knew where to hold so he was suspended in a convenient push-up position over Priscilla, needing only his cock inside of her to anchor him more completely and allow him to begin fucking in earnest. In the next instant, his long, thick, and meaty prick became sandwiched between the rippled hardness of his stomach and the yielding softness of her belly.

"Want to do the honors of positioning my dick?" he asked. "I'd hate to lose my balance and climax by breaking my neck, especially when I've a far better climax in mind." He raised his hips; she reached down and took firm hold of his dick, prying its bulk toward the position he'd requested. "Don't break it off at its base," he said, bragging hardness hardly diminished since his teens.

She put his cock head to her steamy cleft and played it there for several long and delicious seconds, enjoying the tease of his pulpy phallic fist against the sensitive outer folds of her pussy. She was as anxious as he, though, to have all of his cock inside her where it would feel one helluva lot better than where it was now.

"I'm going to fuck you, baby," he forewarned, nuzzling his cock head more securely into her steamy cleft. "I'm going to fuck you like you've never been fucked before."

"That's what we're in this tree for, isn't it?" she invited willingly.

With savagely delicious swiftness, he poked his blue-veined stiffness from its bloated tip to its burgeoning base, his black pubic hair meeting and mingling with her blonde pubic hair as he sensuously ground his muscled belly against her vulnerable softness.

****

I'VE NEVER FUCKED in a tree. I've never fucked atop a pyramid (I did climb to the top of the largest at Giza, but that exhausted me too much for sex), nor screwed on horseback. I've never raped a schoolteacher (or anyone else for that matter), nor whipped a woman with a cat-o'-nine-tails. I've never performed self-fellatio (I tried twice, spraining my back both times), nor made love in a coal mine. I've never peed on my girlfriend (I can hardly manage in a urinal when there's someone else in the room), nor deflowered a virgin. Yet, I've successfully written about those and more. I've never been in love, nor asked anyone to marry me, yet my genre romances and erotic novels do exceptionally well in the U.S. and abroad, thank you very much!

For the record, I'm not six-foot-four, not all muscled pectorals and washboard abdominals, not hung like a horse, nor am I a nonstop sex machine, and I apologize to those whoever went to bed with me thinking—from misinterpretation of my books—that I ever was.

HOW *DO* YOU GET INFORMATION FOR WRITING REALISTIC SEX, THEN?

1. You get *some* from personal experience. I was given a blow-job by a Korean prostitute. She spit my cum in a brass bowl. I remember mother-of-pearl streamers floating in pale water.

2. You get some from hearsay. I haven't screwed a dog, but Gregory has. He says, "Do it from behind, because they've really bad breath, to a one. They growl and get nasty if you try to stop before they're finished."

3. You read it in someone else's novel. No author can copyright a sexual position, *only the way he writes it.*

4. You can buy an illustrated sex manual. I can't get into some of those pretzel-like positions, but that's never prevented my characters from being limber. Sex manuals are good, too, for making sure you know the human anatomy. Get it wrong, and you can count upon being found out. I once knew a writer of erotica who had his heroine's clitoris in the wrong place. His readers went ballistic.

NEVER MAKE YOUR CHARACTERS RIDICULOUS

Tandy started laughing. She couldn't help it. Her uninterrupted gales of merriment pealed from her like tones from a bell whose cord was pulled by some fat monk in a monastery. She dared any woman to contain her mirth in the face of this joke.

He was pathetically funny, looking more like a beached walrus than a man. His fish-grey skin hung in descending folds, beginning at his chins and getting progressively larger until ending in one final and massive overflow that completely draped and hid his penis.

That is if the pitifully little wee-wee that Tandy had to bend to see could even be called *a penis*. She couldn't tell if his needle-sized prick was even erect, so hidden was it within the salt-and-pepper-colored bush of pubic hair that grew damp and lank in its triangular patch on his lower belly.

"You have to be kidding!" she said between giggles. "I mean, *really*, you've *got* to be! How do you find your cock to pee, let alone expect to round it up for sticking into me?"

God, but this was too much to keep to herself. It deserved sharing. Too bad she couldn't buy time on national TV. She went to the door and swung it wide, sticking her head into the hallway. "Girls!"

she shouted in invitation. "Get your asses down here and take a look at this! I've seen bigger pricks on a guppy!"

YOUR READERS associate with your characters and don't want to think that the author is secretly laughing at those characters, or at those who are interested in reading about them.

NEVER MAKE SEX UNPLEASANT OR UNSATISFACTORY

Damn, but he did stink! She'd bet good money he hadn't bathed or wiped his shitty ass in a month of Sundays. Sure as hell, his black and crooked teeth were rotting in his ugly face. His nose ran coagulating snot, and his mouth drooled brown-tinged spit. His cock was coated with so much rancid smegma that it drooped under the weight.

Oh, well, who was she to complain? She wasn't the freshest fuck after having taken on four Saint Bernard's and a jackass during the sex show, the jackass's monster cock leaving her bleeding at the cunt. She scratched her crotch which was additionally irritated by the stubble of red pubic hair she would have shaved during the day if she hadn't had too much of a hangover to bother. She still had in her mouth the bitter-sour taste of yesterday's liquor and morning vomit.

"Okay, buster, it's your ten minutes!" she proclaimed, plopping down on the edge of the bed. She parenthesized her cunt with her filthy hands and sorted out a couple of fleas while she was down there; they perished with lurid pops between her fingernails black with encrusted grime.

She laid back, opened her legs and yawned.

He hopped on and shoved home a cock that didn't do much for her. God knew, it was big, but it wasn't big enough for a cunt stretched to barn-size by years of overuse. Still, he didn't seem to mind, pumping away until he was sweating like a boxer. When she ran her palms along his back, she squeegeed perspiration that flowed like rivers and smelled like sewage.

"Kiss me, bitch, kiss me!" he demanded. So, she kissed him, her mouth exchanging her liquor-and-vomit spit for his chewing-tobacco-browned saliva.

THERE ARE TOO many distasteful things likely going on in your readers' lives without inflicting more of the same into their fantasies.

THERE'S NO SUCH THING AS AN IMPOTENT MAN—

"I'm sorry," Carl apologized. "Really, I am, but I told you this wouldn't work."

"Relax," Mave told him. "I haven't seen a soft cock I couldn't get hard."

She pushed him back on the bed and climbed between his legs, eyeing his limp prick like a Mexican eagle eyeing succulent rattler. Goddamn, she wanted to see what happened to his coil of soft manmeat once she breathed life into it! Something told her it would get bigger and better when it stiffened, even though it was usually the smaller cocks that made the most impressive gains in erection. Her husband's cock was big when soft, but it didn't get any bigger when standing tall. This one, though, would be different. She felt that from the purse of her ruby lips to the depths of her rosy-hued snatch.

His limp prick was sensuously heavy against the curve of her palm. She liked fat cocks and couldn't get her fingers around his even when it was limp. This made her more determined to see it hard.

It was circumcised, its head a pulpy bulb with a deep mouth dry of piss or lubricating wet. She preferred a cock that leaked, because they tasted more interesting, but she'd make do.

She kissed its tip and executed suction to draw all of Carl's luscious-but-limp inches inside her mouth. Her lips clamped hard around the base of his prick, her nose burying in the masculine-smelling pubic hair that V'd his lower belly; her chin propped against the pillow made by his sac of big balls. Her face pulled upward; his cock stretched and flattened between her pressing lips before she let it slip free. When her ovaled mouth locked in the groove beneath the flaring of his heart-shaped corona, she sucked again, once more dropping into the heady male smells originating at his crotch.

Hell, she'd sucked her husband's cock to hardness after he'd screwed her ten times running. If she could put the starch back into that prick, this one didn't stand the chance of a snowball in hell of holding out against her.

She gave it more of a workout, calling into play all the little tricks she'd learned since first sucking her brother Bob's big cock when she was the ripe old age of fifteen. There'd been a lot of male meat in her mouth since then. Some bigger than this (not many), some smaller (a good deal), and she'd done good by them all.

She used her lips, her teeth, and her tongue, fluttering her cheeks and making vibrating sounds deep in her throat. Her mouth pulled and yanked the cock, her hands twisting and corkscrewing it, her tongue lapping and teasing.

All to no avail.

—UNLESS THERE'S A WOMAN TO CURE HIM

Mave, though, wasn't giving up. She hadn't gotten to be the best cocksucker in the whole United States by taking no for an answer, and she kept right on working. Until—

"Jesus, God!" Carl exclaimed, feeling his cock give an unfamiliar twitch inside Mave's hot mouth.

By heaven, yes, she had him on the rise! He'd lucked out this time, and so had Mave. She was going to have a really appreciative stud on her hands once she delivered what he'd never figured to see again.

She worked even harder, not about to lose her advantage. His cock kept growing, but it wasn't hard enough yet to storm the doors of her pussy. It might have been forcibly manhandled into a cunt as big as a barn, but her steamy cleft was tight-as-a-vise and took a firm bit of hardness to squeeze on through.

"Suck it, yes, oh, sweet baby, yes, suck it!" Carl begged, and Mave could tell he was hyper excited. She didn't blame him. To have her swinging on his cock for his first erection in years had to be some special experience. Wait until he pushed through the luscious gates of her cunt, and he'd really be in seventh heaven!

He was working to help her now, his butt bouncing on the bed, his hands on her head, guiding her to faster speed. He knew a resurrection in the works when he saw and felt one, and he was exhilarating in the wonder of the miracle.

Mave was right in thinking she'd suck Carl to complete hardness. She was right in thinking his cock would get bigger as it got harder. Its crown socked the very back of her throat every time her face pushed deep into his crotch, and it even started leaking tasty juices which she savored on her appreciative taste buds.

"Fuck your face, fuck it!" Carl chanted, getting really carried away. If she'd let him, he'd fuck to creaming inside her mouth, but she wasn't going to let him do that. She hadn't worked him to stiffness and to fever pitch to waste his yummy cum in her mouth.

With a well-timed twist of her head, she jerked loose of his cock and his handholds on her head. He groaned in loud and frustrated disappointment, his cock slapping hard against his belly and splattering her spit and his juices. Now Mave had a good look at the results of her efforts, and she was impressed. She'd known his cock would get bigger but, goddamn, if it wasn't a certifiable monster!

She hopped to a squatting position that dangled her leaky pussy over his jerking erection. She lifted his pulsing prick and poked its fat head into the steamy slot of her eager cunt; she sat down hard and fast, taking every hard-worked inch of his prick deep, deep, deep inside her.

"Goddamn!" he bellowed, too long without a cum to keep from this one. He shot luscious wads of pearly spunk, his stiff cock a fountain that didn't seem to want to stop.

THERE'S NO SUCH THING AS A FRIGID WOMAN—

Grace would endure this only because she loved Craig, and she continued to feel guilty she didn't give him all a wife was supposed to give her husband. Oh, she'd tried her best to fake orgasm, and it had worked for a time, but he'd finally grown wise, and all her assurances it wasn't his fault had fallen on deaf ears. He'd continued to get off inside her, never turning to other women until she'd told him he should. Even then, he'd resisted, because he loved her. There was never any doubt in his mind or hers that she loved him.

Finally, he'd gone to bed with Sheila. Grace had been happy, not only because Sheila gave Craig the genuine response a man liked from a woman he was fucking, but because Sheila was a happily married woman who'd asked her husband's permission before she'd fucked with Craig. This left Grace still feeling secure in her own marriage.

Everything had been perfect until this happened to ruin it. *This* was Sheila and Paul's penchant for wife swapping. Since Sheila and Craig got it off so well together, everyone was sure Grace would like Paul. She *did* like him, but not the way everyone hoped and wanted.

Granted, Paul was handsome. An aircraft executive; he took regular advantage of the management-only gym at his company. His physique was still a fair semblance to the one he'd boasted when he'd captained the varsity gymnastics team in college. He had only the faintest trace of a paunch, a well-developed chest and fantastic arm muscles. His cock was neither large nor small but pleasantly in between; it was clean-cut, flattened along its erect front and back and attractively bowed. In short, there was nothing wrong with Paul Pontry, or his dick; any normal woman should have looked forward to what they could both do for her in bed.

Grace, though, wasn't normal. If all she required for orgasm was a handsome man with a great body and an attractive cock, she'd have been blasting off beneath her husband all along.

Going to bed with Paul was a dead-end street but, if it gave Craig continued access to Sheila, Grace would put up a good show.

"There! There!" Sheila bellowed from the other bedroom. She and Craig had wasted less time in getting their part of the show on the road. "A little higher, to the right!" Sheila instructed loudly, punctuating with a high-pitched squeal. "Right there! Oh, yes! Just keep running your hard cock back and forth over *my* stiff...stiff... clit."

Grace envied Sheila. Grace envied any woman who could get it off with only a cock inside her and a few pumps of that cock thrown in for good measure.

"Why don't we get more comfortable?" Paul suggested. He was kind and considerate, but Craig was kind and considerate, too. This...wasn't...going...to work!

Nevertheless, Grace went to the bed and laid down on it, opening her legs and waiting for Paul to climb on. He seemed in no hurry. If the frantic moans and groans of his wife, suddenly orgasming beneath Craig's sweat-glossed body in the other room, was something he found sexually exciting, he was keeping it pretty much in control. Except, of course, for his hard cock which had poked through his robe when he'd greeted her at the front door and which hadn't drooped since.

"What would you like me to do to, or for you, honey?" he asked, surprising her with a request she didn't know what to do with.

"Make love to me," she said, wondering if she were blushing. She'd had strict upbringing as a girl and could still get flustered talking about *it*.

"Yes, but *how*?" Paul asked.

"How?" she echoed, wishing he'd just put his prick in and cut the small talk.

"Let me count the ways," he said with a wide smile. He had very white teeth and a dimple in his left cheek that made his attractive features even more attractive. "I can finger-fuck you, get you off with a dildo, eat your cunt and/or ass, screw your asshole, or put my cock in your cunt any one of a thousand different ways. I await your command."

Did he know how much he was embarrassing her?

"Or, perhaps, you'd like to jack me off, suck me off, take a hand-vibrator to my prick, or stick your finger or a dildo up my asshole," he suggested.

He didn't *sound, act,* or *look* as if he were purposely out to make fun of her.

"Masks, whips, and handcuffs are in the closet," he offered as additional alternatives. "Ropes, too."

"Ropes and handcuffs?" Grace asked, a shiver cascading the length of her spine.

"We've all the toys," Paul assured, flashing another smile "Anyway, most of them," he amended. "Sheila and I have never really been into enemas. However, if you're interested, I could find a rubber hose somewhere with which to improvise."

"God, no!' Grace insisted, laughing nervously.

"There's no need to feel uneasy about your needs, whatever they are," Paul encouraged kindly, sitting on the edge of the bed. Ever so lightly, he trailed his hand up one of her legs and down the other, only briefly feathering her fleecy pubic curls as he passed his fingers over them. "You'll find me liberal and accommodating. I very much doubt—" He gave another smile that showed her the attractive dimpling of his left cheek. "—that you could suggest *anything* to me to which I wouldn't respond favorably at this moment. You need only ask."

Grace didn't know what to say. "Do you really have handcuffs and ropes in the closet?" she asked, at a loss for anything else. Immediately, she realized how that might be misinterpreted. It was.

"Shall we see?" Paul asked, standing.

"No!" she said, quickly reaching for his arm and taking hold.

"There'd be little harm in looking," he reminded but didn't leave the bedside.

"No need, though," she assured, experiencing more thrills. There was something about Paul that *was* different from other men she'd known. Could he be the one to take her where she'd never gone before? God, if that were only possible! "I just want you inside me," she said, surprising herself. She'd never been that blunt with her husband or any other man. A deliciously wicked thrill sparked through her and lingered.

In the other room, Craig and Sheila were at it again, louder and wilder than ever. Their moans, groans, grunts and sighs were less distracting for Grace than they had been. There was a definite wetness between her legs, but that wasn't unusual. She didn't malfunction on all levels, only where it counted.

"You want me to fuck you in plain, old, ordinary, everyday-type missionary style?" he asked with tender amusement. She nodded. "Nah!" he disagreed. "I'm here to put a little spice in your life, remember?"

"Sex doesn't have to be different to be good," she said. "Does it?" What did *she* know?

"Of course it doesn't," he agreed. "I sometimes forget there's something damned exciting and satisfying about two people fucking face to face without accompaniment of toys."

"Yes," she said, licking her lips, wondering if it would be different for her with him. "And that's how I want it. With you. Now." She opened her arms and legs in invitation, and he lowered his chest against her breasts, his stomach against her belly.

From the other room, Sheila bellowed: "Deeper up my asshole, bastard! Deeper…aghhhh…deeper!"

Grace had let Craig butt-fuck her, too. The experience had been no more or less satisfying than when he pumped himself to climax up her cunt.

"I'll fuck you missionary style or any other way you want," Paul said, his nipples hard against her breasts, the head of his cock deceptively velvety against the lips of her vagina.

He entered her in one easy slide, Grace breathlessly anticipating chimes, bells, and fireworks that didn't materialize. What she felt was pleasurable but no more so than when Craig's cock was inside her. Being fucked by Paul or Craig was less pleasurable than when she played with herself.

Paul supported his raised torso on his forearms, his biceps impressively bulged. He brushed a stray strand of her hair from her cheek and kissed her gently. His breath was minty-fresh, his body smelling pleasantly of soap and lime-based cologne. He brought all the right sexual ingredients into the bedroom, just as her husband always did, so what was missing inside her to keep the magic from happening?

"How is it so far?" he asked, his buttocks dimpling as he stirred his cock inside her, and then slowly pulled it out to its head.

"Wonderful," she said as his cock returned to full submersion inside her cunt. A lie! God, she wished it wasn't.

He cupped her face tenderly between his hands, his thumbs tracing the full curves of her lips, his hips rising and lowering in a smooth and easy cadence that Grace was positive should be driving her wild. Why wasn't it? What, when, why, where, and how had it all gone wrong for her?

He stopped, his cock locked inside of her. She avoided his eyes, because she would read in them what he must intuitively know. No more than Craig could Paul conjure for her the pleasures that both he and she wanted him to.

"It's not good, is it, Grace?" Paul asked intuitively. He was more experienced than Craig, and it had taken him far less time to pick up on her true response beneath her it's-great facade. She could lie again, but he would know she was lying.

She sighed. "No," she admitted. "It's not you, though, Paul," she hurriedly added. She doubted he was the type who took every failure in bed as a direct reflection on his manhood, but she wanted no question as to whom was at fault here. "It's *never* good for me."

"Not even with Craig?" he asked; she shook her head. "How about with women?" he asked. It wasn't a snide, cutting, or bitter question. It was something asked by a man who seemed genuinely anxious to please if he only knew how. Grace had no doubt he would willingly step aside to be replaced by Sheila if Sheila was what Grace wanted and/or needed.

"It's no good with women, either," she said, tears filling her eyes. "It's no good for me with anyone."

—UNLESS THERE'S A MAN TO CURE HER

Paul pulled free, his cock made harder by what had to be pure frustration. How he must see himself shortchanged by this deal, what with his wife and Grace's husband continuing their loud sexual marathon in the other bedroom. God, Grace was sorry, but she could have told him it wouldn't work. Maybe she should have been fair and told him from the start how hopeless it was for her, but she hadn't wanted to spoil what Craig had going with Sheila. Damn, she'd been thinking of herself, too, hoping Paul would be the one to work the elusive miracle.

She sat up, preparing to get dressed and chock off the whole experience as another failure in a long line of failures.

"Don't leave," Paul said. "Not yet."

"I think it would be best," she said, all her hopes gone, dashed to nothing. Sheila's mewls and lascivious grunts, as her rubbery asshole wrapped Craig's fucking cock, were becoming too much for Grace to bear.

"Don't I get a chance to strike out three times?" Paul asked, walking to the mirrored closet door. "Come on, play fair!" He slid open the door, and there were the ropes and handcuffs he'd told her would be there. There were the whips, the chains, the thousand little sex toys, many of whose purpose Grace couldn't begin to guess. There was an assortment of head gear—a hard hat, cowboy hat, yachtsman cap, sailor hat, military hat, even an Indian headdress. There were boots—cowboy boots, construction-worker boots, policeman boots, motorcycle-rider boots, moccasins. And clothes—rather, costumes—hung so closely she couldn't tell all of them apart, only singling out the leather fringe of buckskin, the sergeant stripes of an army blouse, the insignia of the California Highway Patrol, and a National Park Service uniform.

"I think not," Grace said, trying to define her feelings as Paul selected four lengths of rope and showed them to her. "Really, Paul, I...." She was brought up short by the sudden flush of lubricating oils into her pussy.

"Do it for me," Paul said, pulling the four ropes taut between his hands. "Not that you owe me anything..."

She knew she should give him the same courtesy she gave her husband: the chance to get off inside her. That was only fair, and she was more than willing to lie back on the bed and let him take up where he'd left off. But he was suggesting something else.

"Do what?" she asked. She thought she knew, but she wanted it spelled out in black and white. Something told her to run, get as far away from Paul and his ropes as possible. Something else kept her rooted to the spot.

"Let me tie you to the bed and fuck you," he said. She shuddered, not unpleasantly, at the mere contemplation of her bound and helpless body.

"I don't think so," she said. Tempted?

"You know you can trust me, don't you, Grace?" he reassured. "Don't you?"

It was a good question. He was a good friend and neighbor. He was considerate, kind, and caring. What, though, might be his hidden nature revealed once he had her tied down and completely helpless?

"It's not a matter of trusting," she said. God, what a stupid thing to say! He'd now ask what *did* matter, and what could she tell him? It *was* a matter of whether she trusted him enough to give him carte blanche to do with her whatever he pleased, held in check only by his—not her—sense of propriety. She'd never even given Craig *that* much power over her. Even the thought of surrendering so much made her giddy and weak in the knees. Her cunt oozed more lubricating honey that overflowed to bead amber droplets within the fleecy pubic hair fanned over the tightly closed lips of her vagina.

"It's not as if we're here alone," Paul reminded. "Craig is in the other room with Sheila."

Yes, and by the sounds, Craig was too far gone to hear his wife's yells for help. Even if he did hear, would he come, or would he only hope the miracle they both wanted had finally happened?

"Craig wouldn't let me hurt you," Paul said, sounding so logical, so persuasive, so *I-wouldn't-hurt-a-fly-let-alone-you-Grace.*

He could stuff her mouth with a gag once she was tied. She'd do no screaming if that happened. Hell, he could use one of those fancy contraptions (ball-gags?) in his closet that looked specifically designed to keep silent a victim's screams.

"It's your decision, Grace," Paul said, as if he were proposing something as innocent as a stroll in the park. "But I've this feeling you should try a few more options before you cross yourself off as a lost cause."

She'd sucked her first cock with the idea it might be the wanted breakthrough. She'd bumped pussies with Joanna in college to explore that same possibility. She'd let Craig fuck her in the ass, and she'd agreed to go to bed with Paul, all with false hopes. Nothing had worked, and more variations on the same theme were a waste of time. Except, she couldn't know that for sure without trying.

If Paul tied her to the bed, if he went too far, if he did horrible things to her, Craig would make him pay. Paul surely wouldn't risk something so far out there'd be the complications of a doctor and/or the police. That he had ropes in the closet, with so much else, told her she wasn't the first woman he'd ever tied down. Had there been trouble with the others, the police would have cleaned everything out by now to use as evidence. Paul would be in jail, or in some mental institution.

Was he crazy for asking if she'd be tied to the bed, or was she crazy for considering it?

"You want to tie me to the bed?" she asked, as if the reality had only then dawned on her.

"And fuck you," he said, his cock jerking to slap its pulpy head against his belly. She saw the splatter marks of clear juices jolted from the deep gash in his cock corona. "Fuck you long, fuck you slow, and fuck you easy," he said. "Make it good for you. Make it better for you than it's ever been before. Maybe even make it so good that...."

He let the promise go unspoken. He must know how much she wanted the miracle of an orgasm, but he couldn't guarantee this would do the trick. She couldn't guarantee it, either. Yet, it was something untried. How marvelous if it *was* the key to make her writhe in ecstasy beneath fucking cock.

"It probably won't work," she said pessimistically.

"Maybe not," he admitted with a shrug. "But *I'll* like it."

Yes, Grace thought, *she did owe him a good time.* If she couldn't be as obliging as Sheila to Craig—the squeals of another orgasm were even then erupting from the cock-impaled woman in the other room—at least she could go one better than making Paul play with himself after she'd gone. She thought of how many times that evening Sheila's mouth, butt, and cunt had milked Craig's fucking erection, and here Paul was, still toting the same hard-on and full balls he'd sported upon Craig and Grace's arrival. His scrotum was a large, compact, hair-covered sac, and anchored securely to the thick base of his cock. Would it sag appreciatively once its stockpile of creamy cum was jettisoned?

Grace leaned back on the bed, saying neither yes nor no to Paul's proposal but insinuating by her actions that she might go a few steps farther.

He moved slowly and gracefully, his exquisite lines in no way made less so by the glaring extension his cock made up and out from his body. He first tied one of her ankles to the footboard of the bed, then tied her other ankle to it. He tied one of her wrists to the headboard; then, he sat on the edge of the bed with the last piece of rope in his hand. Grace's free arm was thrown protectively over her breasts and anchored there by sheer determination. Granted, she probably had come so far that he could easily overpower her but, as long as she had her one arm free, she could *pretend* she was still in control; one hand was all she needed to undo all the knots he'd so expertly tied.

"You needn't be scared," he said, his voice softly soothing and reassuring. "I've done this many, many times, and it's nothing more than a game. Everyone enjoys a game on occasion, don't they?"

Sheila and Craig were enjoying games in the next room, Sheila announcing her nearness to yet another orgasm. Craig wouldn't hear Grace's cries for help over the racket Sheila was making and would be making.

Paul didn't try forcing Grace to volunteer her unbound wrist, content to sit there and drag the last piece of rope back and forth over her naked body. He paused to tweak her nipples to hardness; then, he soaked his fingertips in the lubricating honey drooling from the slightly pouted lips of her pussy. Grace marveled at his control. Foster Crain, a jock she'd dated in college, hadn't lasted nearly as long before he'd whined and complained she'd given him a terminal case of "blue balls". When she'd finally let Foster's short, fat cock near her cunt, it had creamed on contact, without even having achieved a partial entry.

"I suppose I've come too far to turn back now," she said, lifting her arm above her head. She'd made her decision, and she would have to live with it. Wherever he was taking her—probably nowhere—she was committed.

"It's never too late to turn back," he assured. By not immediately affixing the last rope to her positioned free arm, he was saying he'd untie her if that's what she wanted.

"I don't want to turn back," she said, verbally making the commitment her brain had already accepted.

He loosely tied her last wrist to the headboard and crawled up on the bed between her legs, plunging his beautifully throbbing prick through the fleecy curls and fleshy lips of her naturally lubricated pussy.

There was something about the entrance of his cock that jolted Grace like no other cock before it. Strange, because her husband's cock was longer, fatter, and had plowed the same territory plenty of times before without this effect. This same cock had fucked her only minutes before, and…

"What?" Grace questioned, hardly knowing she said anything. Paul's butt elevated, his cock dragging from her suctioning cunt and then sliding slippery inches back inside. "What?" she repeated as more new and unique sensations grew to life within her.

"Feel good?" Paul asked, rolling his hips on a down stroke, his cock stirring inside her sizzling cleft like a pestle turning within a tightly fitting mortar.

"Yes, God, yes!" she answered, unable to believe what was happening to her. Was there really so much magic in putting total trust in another human being?

"Let's try to make it even better," he said, expertly pulling and pushing his cock at different angles so he explored new territory with each flex of his hips. "You tell me where you like it best. There? There? There?"

"Jesus, there!" Grace gasped, shocked by the rolling wave of exquisite ecstasy pounding through her.

She struggled against the ropes, but not to be free of them. God, no! Her jerks were automatic responses to whatever it was taking hold of her.

"That where you like it?" Paul asked, twisting his cock expertly inside her. "That where my cock makes it feel so…so…so…fucking…good?"

"Yes!" she exclaimed breathlessly, her head rocking, her fists clenching and unclenching, her legs flopping and straining as she tried unsuccessfully to whip her thighs up around Paul's luxuriously fucking body. "God…good…good!"

Fireworks went off inside her, more marvelous because she'd never sensed even a hint of them before now. If she thought that was all there was to it, she was mistaken. Paul's hard cock still pumped fast and strong. When he finally got around to filling her with his overdue shots of thick, ropy cum, she began her wildest roller-coaster ride of all time. His sperm sloshed inside her, filled her, overflowed the red lips of her cunt to bead like baroque pearls in her pubic hair and in his crotch hair, before being ground to creamy paste by their undulating, sweaty bellies.

THERE ARE NO CRABS, GONORRHEA, HEPATITIS, SYPHILIS, HERPES, AIDS, UNWANTED PREGNANCIES…

Betty watched from the bed as he undressed, her heart thrilling with excitement, her heartbeat so audible she thought for sure he could hear it.

He proceeded slowly, as if realizing correctly, that part of her pleasure was watching the sensuous emergence of his nakedness from his clothes.

How handsome he was! So much so, she hardly believed he was hers and that he loved her. Roger Weston, who had played the field with so many glamorous, exotic, and wealthy women—the Vogue model, the English baroness, the French-perfume heiress, the American playgirl—was here with her, Betty Freestep from Seattle, Washington.

He smiled, showing white teeth, blue eyes, black hair, deep dimples, square jaw, cleft chin, and the attractive laugh lines that had graced the glossy pages of a thousand international magazines and newspapers.

She trembled at the muscled magnificence of his naked chest, his shirt discarded to a nearby chair. Two nipple-punctuated rectangles of muscle faced each other across a deep and serrated pectoral groove that opened onto the scalloped plain of his stomach. A brief fanning of black hair across the top of his chest V'd into a descending line that divided his stomach into muscled mirrored halves that haloed his attractively knotted navel and continued to disappearance beneath the hugging waistband of his pants.

His skin glowed in the light of the lone lamp, his arms smoothly curved by well-developed biceps and triceps that rippled as his large hands worked at the button holding his pants together above his still-locked zipper.

When the button came free, his pants fly peeled back in a *V* that would widen even farther once his zipper was released. There was evidence of more wiry black hair on his lower belly, and she yearned to comb her fingers through those tightly curled strands.

She'd waited a long time, weighing the pros and cons of this moment before finally deciding there could be a chance for happiness in the joining of one mildly successful portrait painter from a middle-class background with an industrialist who'd been rich since the day he was born.

Her intake of breath was audible as his zipper opened all of the way, revealing grey cotton under shorts. His pants dropped around his feet; he stepped out of them and out his sandals.

The only things separating her and her wildest dreams were a pair of grey underpants, the few steps it would take Roger to reach her, and the sheet she kept modestly pulled to her chin. There were even fewer barriers when he hooked the waistband of his bikini underwear with his large hands and dropped the material down over his slim hips and magnificently sculptured buttocks.

Suddenly, he was naked, nothing hidden. Walking gracefully toward her and the love she wanted so desperately to share with him, he presented her with his wondrous arousal marred only by the syphilitic canker sore halfway down his powerfully uplifted cock shaft.

IF IT'S NEGATIVE and not a positive reflection on the joys of sex, leave it out.

CHARACTERS CAN USUALLY ORGASM TIME AFTER TIME...

WHERE YOU AND I, in real life, might be laid out flat in the aisles from exhaustion, after multiple orgasms, characters in genre-romance and, especially, in erotica, celebrate nonstop sex in a

Never-Never Land wherein sperm ducts never fail to deliver, cunts never cease to be hungry, cocks hardly ever go soft, men are *real* men and women are *real* women. Vaginas are always wet, never dry, never sore, and always ready for one more of whatever men are so always ready, willing, and able to provide on a 24/7/365 basis.

"...cumming!   AAAAGGRUNNGGGH...CUMMMM-MING!" Mark bellowed for this third time that evening, his streamers of creamy sperm splattering Peg's cunt walls and drooling white curtains in vivid contrast to the glistening reds of her pussy membranes.

He withdrew his blue-veined stiffness from Peg's cock-hungry snatch that was greedy for repeats. He had starch left in his prick, but he wasn't about to re-plow familiar terrain with all the sexual smorgasbord waiting to be sampled.

Peg reached for his cock, wanting it returned to her cum-glued hole, but Mark was already crawling for sexy May Toller. May saw him coming and met him halfway, grabbing his cock before somebody else could latch onto it. By its feel, it had plenty of starch left in it to satisfy her and a few of the other cock-hungry broads in the room.

"Want it, do you, hot cunt?" Mark asked; he was eager to take her on. Before the night was over, he'd have his dick dipped in every last one of these horny bitches.

"That's why we're here, stud," May confirmed, keeping hold of his slippery dick and going dog-style before it. She guided its cum-slippery tip to the rosy-red opening of her vagina.

"Let me do the putting-it-in, Honey-cunt," Mark said, his bulky prick coming free of her grip with a lurid plop. "You just stay where you are, and I'll give you the ride of your life."

May looked over her shoulder, jiggling her ass and slime-slicked pussy in eager invitation.

Mark fanned one hand across her ass, his other hand playing his cock tip coyly at the outer lips of her cunt which he had no intentions of plugging. Not that he was giving up May for someone else, because he wasn't going to let her go without one helluva sample of his abundant goodness. His cock was well enough greased with pussy juice from its three previous fucks to make it slide easily up the tempting hole centering May's cheeky buttocks.

"Ready?" he asked her.

"Shove it in, Big-cock!" May commanded, mistakenly anticipating the ecstasy of his throbbing hardness up her naked, cuntal sheath.

With some pretty fast wrist action, perfected from long years of practice at orgies like this one, Mark detoured his cock from her cunt to her rubbery asshole. He didn't wait for her to figure out what was happening, either. With well-coordinated dexterity, he pumped his hips forward, taking hold of her ass with both hands to pull her asshole over his thick cock that was simultaneously thrusting forward.

"My God!" May shrieked in surprise. As many cocks as she'd had plowed up her butt, her rubbery rectum was still tight enough to be jolted by the sudden sodomistic assault of this really big one.

"Love it, don't you, May, baby!" Mark said, and it wasn't a question. He'd yet to plug an asshole with his big cock that didn't leave its female owner begging for more. May wasn't going to be any damned exception. He kept right on pushing his cock and pulling her ass, watching how her rubbery pucker sank round the circumference of his entering meaty erection. His belly finally contacted her ass with a resounding whack, and he quickly followed with a series of small staccato bucks that made his gut and her cheeky buttocks collide and separate with the sounds of machine-gun fire.

May wasn't long in catching her breath, nor short in her determination to milk this wise-ass bastard's balls of so much cum that he wouldn't have a drop left for the other eager ladies in the room. If she would have preferred using her experienced cuntal muscles to do the milking, everyone to his own thing; Mark evidently got off on browning his big prick up her asshole. All fine and dandy!

In feverish frenzy, May gyrated her cheeky buttocks against his hairy crotch. She would have corkscrewed his damned cock off at its base if she could have mastered a bit more torque.

"You tight in the saddle?" she asked, feeling Mark's bushy pubic hair scratching her tender ass cheeks. "I wouldn't want you falling off before the buzzer."

He pulled his cock out to its bulbous tip and fed her every last seven inches of his prick once again. His low-hanging scrotum swung forward and upward, colliding his two nuts against the overhanging curve of her buttocks almost as far as her pussy. For him, the resulting sensation was more pleasurable than painful, so much so that he did the same thing again.

May narrowed the circumference of her rubbery rectum with a practiced contraction, farther strangling the lengthy stiffness Mark was pumping like sixty. She thanked God his big cock was lubed from earlier workouts, or his hearty strokes would have turned her anus inside out in no time.

"Yes, baby, yes!" Mark grunted, giving her ass a few slaps with his hands and enjoying the way her rectum responded by squeezing tighter with each blow.

May was pumping her ass back and forth like a swing on some old granddad's house porch. Mark got hotter seeing his thick meatiness appear and disappear in the space between his crotch and her creamy ass cheeks.

Damn, he enjoyed fucking a woman's ass, and Mary's rubbery rectum was one talented number.

"Easy, baby, easy," he warned, but May only increased her efforts. "Now! Now! Jesus, now!" he announced, socking his cock all the way home and keeping it there while it pulsed thick creaminess to whitewash her spasming brown asshole.

His hands clawed her ass cheeks, and he was still pumping his load when May gave a quick swing of her ass that pulled it free of his exploding erection and his handholds. The last of Mark's rich cream plastered the outside of her buttocks with a cobweb design, like the cum-shot in a fucking stag film.

"Holy shit!" Mark protested, frustrated he hadn't planted each and every last drop of his exploded cum up her clutching hole.

May didn't stick around to hear his bitching, though. She'd pulled loose prematurely, because she'd spotted John Wenton finally finishing with Melody LaFrank; no one fucked better than John did.

Besides, Mark wouldn't be left distraught for long. Sandra Metclin had been drinking the last of the cream from Slim Timon's anything-but-slim dick when Mark's prick left May's rubbery asshole. Sandra gave Slim's stiff meatiness a final farewell lick; hungry for the exotic flavors May's butt hole had smeared on Mark's erection, Sandra went for them.

"Looks like your blue-veined hunk of meat could use a good washing," she told Mark as soon as she reached him. He was still a little uncertain what had happened to May's vanishing asshole that had left him, in the end, fucking thin air.

"You want it, it's yours," he said magnanimously, recognizing Sandra as someone he'd had his eye on. He would have preferred her ass or her cunt to her mouth, but he was as much for variety as the next guy. From what he'd heard, she had an educated tongue, and there was usually fire when there was that much smoke around.

Sandra didn't waste time. She bent her lovely face over his crotch and executed a mighty suck that gave her all his hard cock and, then, threatened to uproot it.

"Jesus!" Mark moaned appreciatively.

She lathered her mouthful with spit, swallowing a combination of residual flavors from natural cock, three different pussies, and an asshole. Tastes from the latter weren't as overpoweringly delicious as they might have been, because hygienic-minded May always took an enema before these kinds of group fuck sessions.

"Goddamned greedy little bitch, aren't you?" Mark said, undeniably impressed by Sandra's sucking technique. His wife had a tendency to bite whenever she went down on him, and it was always a treat to fuck the face of a pro. Speaking of his wife, where in the hell was she? Ah, yes, spread-eagled under Calvin West's humping body. She'd been hot for that jock's hard inches ever since she'd first met him.

Mark returned his attention to Sandra, her head bouncing on his great cock like a horse gone wild on a merry-go-round. She sounded like his cock was a straw, his balls an empty glass. Well, she was going to get one helluva milkshake any damned minute now.

Her tongue busily wrapped his cock, whipped it, curled against and around it. She sucked only the pulpy knob of it, both of her hands gripping its thick shaft and beating it rhythmically.

Mark liked it when she sucked his cock, jerked it, and fondled his nuts, all at the same time. He really enjoyed it when she snaked a finger behind his balls and up into the crack of his ass. He had no doubt where her finger would be when he blew his wad, and his ass pucker contracted in eager anticipation.

"I'm about there, baby," he told her, wanting her to have plenty of time to prepare. He didn't want her mouth pulling any fast tricks like May's vanishing ass had managed.

Sandra didn't disappoint him. Even before he could bellow, "Now, Jesus, now!" her finger was up his butt, and he was creaming…Jesus…creaming…in her wet-warm mouth. She swallowed in heaving gulps, the force of which stretched his exploding cock to half again its normal length and vacuumed his cum all of the way from the copious reservoirs in his balls. When her finger up his butt crooked and jabbed his prostate a good one, he let out a resulting grunt and fed her a bit of extra cum for juicy dessert.

"Honey, you can give me head any time," he congratulated while she lingered in cleanup.

She finally came up for air, flashed him a bright smile and licked her lips suggestively. "How about my diving for immediate repeats?" she suggested.

He checked the room for better alternatives, but Sandra took full advantage of his hesitation and was back down his blue-veined meatiness in no time. She anchored her yawned mouth around the base of his cock and, one by one, poked his fat nuts into her mouth with his stiff joint.

"Baby," he moaned. "Baby…."

THAT SAID, ROMANCE-GENRE CHARACTERS ARE NEVER SATYRS OR NYMPHOS, ALTHOUGH EROTICA CHARACTERS CAN BE BOTH

IN ROMANCE-GENRE books, as opposed to erotica, heroes and heroines usually remain monogamous, even if—sex becoming more and more acceptable—neither is a virgin at first meet-up.

* * * * * * *

"I want to make love with you, Clara," he said, his voice a whisper against her ear that warmed all of the way to her toes.

"Yes," she consented simply, no longer arguing as in the past.

"Yes?" he asked, obviously surprised. "My God, *yes*?" His delight was rare and wonderful. He genuinely looked as if he'd been given some exotic and glorious gift he'd never really expected.

Clara thrilled at his never having taken her for granted. She'd been as free to say no as yes, and he would have honored her decision. But she'd said no enough times and, if she remained less than one-hundred percent sure he loved her, she loved him. Yes, she'd finally admitted to herself that she loved him. Maybe because he was leaving tomorrow and, despite all his assurances, might not come back. His ex-wife's legal machinations might keep him in Paris, and Clara would never forgive herself for not taking full advantage of this possibly last night together.

"Yes," she repeated, confirming to herself and to him that her love made their upcoming lovemaking as natural as night following day.

"Do you know how happy that makes me?" he asked; a strong arm collapsed her legs behind her as he lifted her and carried her to the bed.

She hoped his happiness was that of a man who loved a woman, and not that of a man made cocky by final conquest. If she still had doubts that his emotions were genuine, she'd cast them from her mind for the evening. She'd sort out all her lingering doubts later, before he returned from Paris—if he ever *did* return. Now, she would cater to desires boiling uncontrolled within her.

He laid her on the bed, standing beside and over her, looking as if he couldn't believe he'd gotten her that far and could go farther, all with her consent.

It hadn't been easy for her to say yes. She had more doubts about him than she'd ever had about Walter. She shut her eyes, trying to analyze why she was having thoughts of Walter at this key time in her life. She was pleased she handled them with no sense of guilt. For the first time since Walter's death, Clara knew he would understand and approve of what was happening. So many times he'd told her, "Clara, if anything happens to me, go on with living *and* loving. After all, I could be hit by a car tomorrow. So, I want you to...." Of course, she'd always kept him from finishing. Her love for him had been so deep, so real, so strong, she couldn't have fathomed life without him. Well, he'd known life must go on, and she'd finally discovered what he'd been trying to tell her.

Not that her love for Russ lessened her love for Walter. Her love for Walter had merely shifted to another plain. It would always be special, because he was her first man, and a woman's first was usually special. Walter, though, had been more than *just* her first. He'd been her husband, her friend, her lover, and there'd been no man in her life since him—until Russ. Not because she condemned others who hopped nightly into a different bed. God, no! She wouldn't knock any kind of shared closeness between people. It just happened that promiscuity had never been right for her. She wasn't sure why, except it might have had something to do with her father's parents celebrating sixty years of marriage the previous January, or with her mother's father so heartbroken over his wife's death that he'd died less than two hours after she had. Maybe it was her parents sticking together through thick and thin, still kissing and caressing lovingly at unexpected moments. Maybe it was Clara's enduring fantasies of just one loving Prince Charming, instead of a whole room full of horny knights.

How lucky to have found Walter and loved him. How lucky to find Russ and love him.

"I love you," she said as his deft fingers peeled back the terry cloth of her robe to bare her body. She lifted to slip her arms out of sleeves and then collapsed back against the bedspread.

How long it had been since she'd been naked and awaiting a man's nakedness to meld with hers. Marvelously, she'd never missed the anticipation—until Russ whom she'd wanted naked atop her from the very first moment he'd turned up on her doorstep with intentions of winning her stock proxies in the battle for control of Linlan Electronics. How long ago that seemed, while simultaneously seeming only yesterday.

God, she was happy! So happy she was afraid fate might strike her down for the overabundant bliss she'd squeezed into her short lifetime. Granted, there were heartaches, too. There was no denying the nights she'd laid awake only with those in attendance, but the joy and wondrousness of living and loving had outbalanced the negative, leaving her only fearful that there might well be a piper to pay somewhere down the line. It was painfully conceivable that Paris and Mariana were enticements to take Russ away. She knew his driving ambition, because it had brought him from poverty to success in a few short years. She knew the attraction Mariana offered by dangling her block of stocks that could sew up control of Linlan for him. If Mariana's asking price was Russ's marriage to her for a second time....

Clara cast out those bad and worrisome thoughts. This was the now. Yesterday was yesterday. Tomorrow was tomorrow. If she had no other future with this man she so loved, she would still have this evening. So many people went through life without loving, without experiencing the ultimate joy of intimate sharing. She may have only the one night, but she would have the memory of this one night forever.

She didn't need memories of ten men, or twenty, or even three to make her life full and meaningful. Two were enough. Two were more than enough. Counting on a third, after Russ, would be to expect another miracle. If she never loved, or made love to another man, this was adequate compensation. She knew it was enough, even before he joined her, even as he stood there with his white bikini underpants still separating her from the wonderment he brought her. She wouldn't be disappointed for saying yes, because her love made this the right time, the right place, the right circumstances. Her love made Russ the right man, the *only* man with whose burgeoning manhood she could presently feel guiltless.

He hooked the waistband of his shorts; she watched clinging white cotton peeled down his slender hips and over the unyielding curves of his muscled buttocks. She experienced uncontrollable yearning from the fullness of her heart to the honey-coated warmth between her legs.

"I love you," he said, standing by the bed like a Greek god. Whether he loved her or not, she was glad he said it. His undeniable arousal wasn't necessarily evidence of love, because an erection was too easily stimulated by mere lust. He might lie, words even easier to come by than lust, but she believed him. She *had* to believe, because of her commitment already irrevocably made. If he didn't love her, at least not enough to resist what Mariana was offering him in Paris, that didn't negate Clara's feelings. It was acceptance of her love for him, more than his assurances that he loved her, which put her willingly on that bed as his nakedness dropped gracefully to join her.

She wrapped her arms around his neck, her flesh goosebumping as his muscled chest mashed her breasts, his hard stomach resting atop the yielding softness of her belly. Her lips found his, discovering sweetness that was more than *just* his minty mouthwash.

She no longer compared his kisses to Walter's. She was released, too, of all compulsion to compare his lovemaking with that of her one-time husband. Some illuminating revelation had sparked the realization that no two men were quite the same, nor were the responses of any one woman to them. There was no comparing ruby to emerald, except to say each was valuable in its own right. Gems occupied separate niches, as did her memories of Walter, as did the reality of Russ.

Her hands ran from his head of silky blue-black hair to the sensuous play of muscles on his back. She reveled in the slow and easy way he caressed her, controlling his passion until he could be sure she was prepared and ready to take him insider her.

There was no need for such lengthy foreplay, because her arrival at this moment, after so many days of questioning her feelings, emotions, and motivations, had been all the lead-in she needed. She was ready for him, mentally and physically, and each second he didn't claim her was more and more unbearable for her.

"Love me," she whispered against the striated muscles cording his neck. "Love me now."

Her nipples were hard tacks against his chest, and there was velvety wetness between her legs now lifted in pronounced parenthesis around his lower body.

He claimed her yearning body in smooth, easy, unhurried, and overpowering sensuousness.

"Clara, I love you," he mumbled low and sexy against her cheek, his buttocks dimpling as he locked her with a closeness she'd known with only one other man.

"Yes," she said, her hips undulating between him and the bed. He did love her, and she did know it. There could be no denying his love as part of what was happening. His love was a major part of the total radiance that filled her.

Such magic, love given and returned! What infinite joy, the pleasure of him atop her, his arousal the key to unlock all the wonder and passionate enchantment yearning to be free after so horribly long in confinement.

She held to him, fearful the tidal waves of joy that swept her would tear her from him and toss her frustrated on some distant and lonely shore. She didn't want him to leave but, if he did choose Paris and Mariana in the morning, then one night of loving would have to be forever enough.

She groaned in response to the marvelous sensations he was conjuring. She wondered how she could have lived so long without them. It had taken Russ, and only Russ, to resurrect life and love dead since Walter's death.

"Russ, Russ...," she chanted, just to enjoy the aphrodisiac his name became upon her tongue.

He propped himself on his forearms, his hips not missing a beat. He looked into her blue eyes, his black ones smoldering with intensity that fired hot sparks. He cupped her head with his large hands, his thumbs gently tracing her pink-pink lips.

She flattened her hands over his hard nipples whose swollenness provided sharp points against her palms. She tented her fingers; her fingertips captured those burgeoning buds, squeezed them and twisted them, first one way and then the other.

He groaned, and she exhilarated in the joy she gave him in return for the joy flooding her. Her world telescoped to nothing but her and him. Time stopped within their cocoon of love. Pleasure, loosened inside her, swelled closer and closer to unavoidable detonation.

Suddenly, the fireworks went off. She shut her eyes and saw explosions. She opened her eyes and became lost in Russ's dilated black pupils.

She surrendered breathlessly to his kiss, their mouths one as his tongue entered her as thoroughly and as deeply as that other glorious part of him pulsing new life into her body. His weight was full upon her, their sweat and passion the glue that kept them bound.

Waves of sensuality washed her, one after another after another, until he quieted atop her, his heartbeat echoing hers through their joyously joined flesh.

She buried her hand in the blue-black strands of his hair, rearranging sweaty curls across his forehead.

"Do you know just how wonderful that was for me after four years?" he asked.

"Four years?" she echoed, her response automatic. "Wasn't there the beauty queen, the copper heiress, the movie actress?"

"I dated those women, sure," Russ admitted, "but, despite all the rumors, and opportunities presented, I've never felt it necessary to indulge each and every time. I've never had the great need to prove my masculinity to myself or to anyone else, and I didn't get where I am today by settling for second best in business or in love."

Four years without? He'd been divorced from Mariana for over three. Clara experienced a new flooding of pleasure that left her tingling. Russ hadn't hopped indiscriminately into bed on each of the innumerable opportunities with which he'd admittedly been presented, then, having waited four years before choosing Clara; that had to be proof-positive of his commitment to her. Wasn't it?

She could tell him her doubts were no longer as great as they had been…that she was less fearful of the outcome of his meeting with Mariana in Paris…and she did just that with a kiss. She wrapped his strong neck with her arms and held on for dear life. They would work out everything. Mariana's selfish refusal to surrender him…his ex-wife's plot to buy back his body if not his affection…the control Russ wanted of Linlan Electronics. Their love would prevail! It had to! She'd lost Walter, and that was God's will, but she had something to say about Mariana's plotting, and she was determined to fight tooth and nail for the man she loved.

OFTEN, THOUGH, AS IN EROTICA, ONCE ISN'T ENOUGH EVEN IN GENRE-ROMANCE

THESE DAYS, BECAUSE genre-romance readers are demanding more sex in their reading material, and because an immediate repeat sexual performance by the book's hero says an awfully lot about his degree of emotional commitment to the book's heroine, you'll be able to get away with even more sex in, say, a Harlequin than was once the case.

* * * * * * *

Clara groaned against his lips when his shifting weight affirmed the wonder of his continued arousal.

"I'll never have enough of you, my love," he whispered, lifting his hips but not breaking contact, lowering and stirring new wonderment and excitement inside her.

"So much pleasure," she said, her voice catching in her throat as his buttocks dimpled deeply and attractively.

Would she survive? Sometimes, there could be too much of a good thing, and she had been close to unconsciousness when the full impact of ecstasy struck her a few minutes before. She'd hung on to consciousness only because she'd been greedy, not wanting to miss one single moment of the magic. To explore those same dizzying heights, those same excruciatingly pleasurable falls, those same moments of buffeting ecstasy, was perhaps too much to ask. Except, she was totally addicted, and there was no way she could tell him to stop.

If all she would have was this one night, she had to fill it to capacity. She had to risk sanity in the madness of passion.

"Yes, my love, yes," she encouraged, his muscles shifting beneath his velvety skin.

"God, what you do to me!" he said, his voice a hot whisper against the pulse spot on her throat. "I've never met anyone who gets me so excited."

Clara was shook by a resurgence of pleasure. Her head pressed deep into the bed, her neck arching beneath Russ's kisses, her hips undulating in sensuous fury. Her fingernails dug into his hard muscle.

"Ahhhhhhh," she sighed breathlessly, another shudder passing through her, a new washing of ecstasy propelling her to a higher sexual plain.

God, what he was doing to her, this man she loved! He was turning loose sensations so long dormant she'd forgotten they existed—if, in fact, they ever had. It had been her early suspicions of just this very wonder that had kept her so long from giving in to him. She had resented his power over her, feared his ability to manipulate her according to his game plan and not her rational judgment.

"I'm yours!" he whispered, his hard nipples chafing hers as he danced so enticingly upon her.

Was he lying, or did he mean it? Was he hers, in body and soul, forever and ever, amen, or was he hers only until his pride and ambition opted for the corporate power Mariana offered in Paris?

Clara welcomed new pulsings of ecstasy that brought her suddenly to the edge of swooning, forcing her back from pondering unpleasant possibilities. No one ever said life was easy, nor had she ever found that it was. Even for her and Russ to get this far had called for great effort, self-examination and hard work. That was how it should be, because the best-savored victories were the hard-won ones. Obstacles were there to be overcome. Having surmounted so many, real and imagined, they would win and keep on winning. Mariana didn't stand a chance!

He was breathing hard and fast, his gasps hot and exciting. Her fingers ran into his hair, taking hold of silky strands. Her body automatically responded to his, complementing his speedy fuck-rhythm with a fast-and-furious cadence of her own.

Pleasure battered her, this way and that, coiling tighter and tighter. Their bodies were one, their pleasure one, their love one. God, they were unbeatable!

She held his face against her cheek, her breathing hot and ragged in his ear. "Yes, yes, yes," she begged, consumed by the basest of urges.

Her dilated eyes blurred with passion. Her moans became more frequent and more guttural. Her body glossed with perspiration; his body went even more golden with sweat.

Oh, dear God, where was he taking her? She was higher than she'd ever been and was going even higher: above the mountains, above the clouds, into the euphoric rarified atmosphere where only lovers flew.

He collapsed with a resounding shudder against her, pushing her deeply into the cushioning mattress of the bed. He filled her with molten lava that burned swiftly to her very core and flared, there, in glorious, ultimate brilliance.

"Love me!" she screamed, forgetting a tomorrow that included Mariana, Paris, and Linlan Electronics.

WHEN, THOUGH, IS ENOUGH—*ENOUGH?*

WELL, IN EROTIC novels, you begin sentence one, page one, with hot and heavy sex, no lengthy lead-in required—yes, please, and thank-you—and go nonstop from there.

"Fuck me, you bastard! Push your blue-veined meaty cock so deeply up my sucking cunt that I can feel its pulpy head stuck through my belly and into the base of my throat!" would be a typical beginning.

That get-to-the-fucking-fast attitude, and the nonstop sex that follows until book's end, is the direct result of there being so little need for anyone—writer, editor, characters, or reader—to be overly concerned with plot or other such distractions.

"If you can't give me your erotic-book's plot in one sentence, it's too damned convoluted!" says one prominent publisher of erotica. There wouldn't be plots at all if threads of some kind weren't needed to string one sex scene to another, AND if erotica publishers and writers weren't still constantly paranoid about crossing through the grey area that separates acceptable erotica from unacceptable hard-core pornography.

Sex in genre-romances is more governed by the author having to deal with a helluva lot more than just fucking. You have plot, subplots, and conflicts. This is why some of the best writers of erotica often can't make the transition to genre romance. My outlines for Harlequin Superromances ran to as many as twenty-five pages, *sans* sex. While romance publishers *talk* recreational sex (*à la* erotica) and experiment with publishing it (on very rare occasions), most genre-romance heroines still must feel something more from the hero than plain, unadulterated lust before hopping into bed with him. That *something* must constantly be called to the reader's attention, and further elaborated upon each and every time there's even the possibility of sexual intercourse.

In genre-romance novels, you don't begin with sex, either.

"Who's he?" Tammy would likely ask her dear friend and restaurant hostess. "He looks familiar."

When genre-romance sex *does* occur, it's apt to be a kiss on page twenty, a more pronounced bit of caressing on page fifty, and, maybe, actual consummation of the act by page one hundred—if then.

XVI.

WRITING FOR THE STAGE

by Francis Jarman

DRAMATISTS ARE not like other writers. Not for playwrights the lonely anguish of the poet, or the long brutal hours of brooding and rewriting that create the novel. You are never really alone if you write for the stage, although, especially at the very beginning, there will have to be moments of deep concentration, probably somewhere where you are on your own and will be undisturbed. It need not be in a quiet room. Two of my own plays were first conceived, and the plot and the main characters outlined in my imagination, as I walked along the beach in Corfu, Greece (on separate occasions, several years apart). The beach wasn't very clean, and on both days it was cold and windy. How and why the ideas came I have never understood.

Some of your thinking and writing may actually be done in noisy, crowded places. The first really effective dramatic scene that I ever wrote, one that, years later, I am still proud of, was jotted down on a notepad in a slow train, trundling between Koblenz and Frankfurt in Germany, as I returned from an academic conference. Sitting opposite me was a fat lady with a tiny, hyperactive dog, which (with no discouragement from its owner) repeatedly scrabbled onto the table and over my notepad, smearing the writing from my ballpoint pen.

Even if you are in a quiet room, though, with your pen poised (or your fingers twitching over the keyboard) and the empty piece of paper (or the blank screen) in front of you, you will not be alone. A number of different spirits will be hovering just behind your shoulder—less metaphorically: at the outer edges of your consciousness—jostling to make their contribution to the creative process.

First of all, whether playwright, poet, or novelist, you will at some point be inspired by your *muse*.

The successful film *Shakespeare in Love* has been responsible for encouraging a whole range of popular misconceptions—of theatre in general, of Late Elizabethan theatre more specifically, of Shakespeare, and of the way in which writers work—one of them being that once a suitably exciting love object has flashed onto the playwright's emotional radar screen, the inspiration will flow and flow: light will break through windows, nightingales and larks will go for it with a vengeance, and there will be much inappropriate use of balconies, *etc*. Unfortunately, it isn't quite like that, otherwise writers wouldn't need to do much more than stagger about with their tongues hanging out, looking for The One, rather like Ginsberg's Walt Whitman in the supermarket in California, "poking among the meats in the refrigerator and eyeing the grocery boys. [...] Are you my Angel?"[5]

(By the way, I've just broken one of the cardinal rules for writers, which is that you never, ever, however indirectly, compare yourself with Shakespeare. In a moment, I'm going to break the rule again.)

Muses are probably an essential, in the sense that when you write you are normally writing not only for your own critical intelligence but for someone else too, either a real someone or a someone in your mind's eye: to impress them, to restore their good opinion of you, to make up for past rejections or humiliations, and not necessarily just to get your muse into bed. The muse can be your mother or father, your ex-girlfriend, your former schoolmates (all those jocks who used to push you around), or friends and family who have long marked you down as a loser. Well, then, you say, look at my smash hit, my literary prize, my rave reviews, my fancy publication, *and show some respect!* The writer may have internalized this, and not be aware of the origins of his motivation. Not that I exclude the idea of a writer Doing It for the Good of Literature. (Unfairly, perhaps, I visualize at this point someone who looks more like a bank manager, a T. S. Eliot clone, maybe.) However, the peculiar, strenuous and (for the most part) extrinsically unrewarding nature of literary writing would seem to suggest that there has to be a strong personal reason why anyone should choose to indulge in it.

Lorca, the Spanish poet and playwright, was less than enthusiastic about the muse, who "dictates and sometimes prompts", but "can

---

[5] From Allen Ginsberg, "A Supermarket in California". In: *Howl and Other Poems*. San Francisco: City Lights, 1956, p. 23.

do relatively little, for she is distant." She "awakens the intelligence", but comes "from outside us." There is also the *angel*, who "dazzles, [...] shedding his grace," giving "lights," just as the muse gives "forms".[6] The third and most interesting member of Lorca's trinity of artistic inspiration is the *duende*, a dark, sudden, Dionysiac inspiration that rises up from sources too deep to be grasped logically. When the *duende* rides you, there is magic and danger, and—for a true artist of course—no possibility of compromise. The *duende* will not approach at all, declares Lorca, "unless he sees that death is possible. [...] the duende enjoys fighting the creator on the very rim of the well. Angel and muse escape with violin, meter and compass; the duende wounds."[7] Put more prosaically, the *duende* is there at those creative moments where everything is risked. Non-writers don't understand this, nor do writers who always have a safety net, but poets know it, and great performers know it best of all:

> All arts are capable of duende, but where it finds greatest range, naturally, is in music, dance, and spoken poetry, for these arts require a living body to interpret them, being forms that are born, die, and open their contours against an exact present.
> Often the duende of the composer passes into the duende of the interpreter [...][8]

This is incomparably true of theatre, too (but not of film). Words and movements conceived in thoughtfulness, perhaps with just an inkling of their potential magic, are transformed by fine acting into passion and heartbreak. Film can merely fossilize this, recording it as a memory—Brando in the "I coulda been a contender" scene in *On the Waterfront*; Helena Bonham Carter in *A Room with a View*, teetering on a hillside outside Florence, trapped between joy and panic; Halle Berry in *Monster's Ball*—everyone will have their own personal list—but the actors onstage can not only hold the audience in their grip, they can thrust the knife in (and turn it, too), and they can do it differently every time. The audience waits for such moments, and there is a communion, an event of shared excitement. For all its beauty, the same scene in a film is just a dead thing. This

---

[6] Federico García Lorca, "Play and Theory of the Duende" (1933). Translated by Christopher Maurer. In: F. García Lorca, *In Search of Duende*. New York: New Directions, 1998, pp. 50, 51.
[7] *Op. cit.*, p. 58.
[8] *Op. cit.*, p. 54.

is why so many great film actors return again and again to the stage, despite the financial sacrifices that this entails, because of the magic that theatre can create. For the playwright, there comes a tipping-point in rehearsal when the actors stop reading or reciting their lines and slip into the characters that he conceived months or even years earlier. That moment is deeply thrilling, as is the "birth" of the play on the stage (either in dress rehearsal or on the opening night, and sometimes on both occasions). There is nothing like this for the novelist—holding the first copy of your new novel is also a fine moment, but it's not magical. On the other hand, it is sad to write a play and never see it performed. I can't agree with Dr. Samuel Johnson's dictum, in the Preface to his 1765 edition of Shakespeare's plays, that "A play read affects the mind like a play acted."[9] However beautiful or witty it may be, a play that has never been staged is like an airplane that has never flown.

I shall never forget moments of *duende* that I have experienced in the theatre, beginning with the treacherous killing of Hector in Shakespeare's *Troilus and Cressida* in a London production that I went to see as a schoolboy in the Sixties. Achilles enters swiftly with his team of killers. Catching Hector unarmed, he gloats over his enemy's helplessness:

> *Achilles.* Look, Hector, how the sun begins to set,
> How ugly night comes breathing at his heels.
> Even with the vail and dark'ning of the sun,
> To close the day up, Hector's life is done.[10]

It was terrifying, and the temperature in the theatre seemed to plummet. What made it so exciting? The way the actors moved, the lighting, the intonation of the lines—and the text, of course.

I remember, too, the scene in a fine production of Schiller's *Maria Stuart* where the author, with a cavalier disregard for the historical facts but with psychological acumen, brings together the two rival queens, Elizabeth of England and Mary Queen of Scots: Elizabeth patronizes and sneers at the captive Mary, until Mary can stand it no longer:

> *Mary.* The throne of England's sullied with a bastard.
> The noble-hearted British [*sic*] are betrayed,

---

[9] *Dr. Johnson on Shakespeare.* Edited by W. K. Wimsatt (1960). Harmondsworth: Penguin, 1969, p. 72.
[10] William Shakespeare, *Troilus and Cressida*, Act V, Scene 8, 5-8.

> By a sly trickster.
> — If right prevailed, *you* would lie here before me,
> Here in the dust, for *I'm* the rightful Queen![11]

"Bastard" was not merely an insult. In the eyes of Mary's Catholic adherents, she was indeed the rightful Queen of England: Henry VIII's marriage to Catherine of Aragon had never been legally dissolved, and so Elizabeth, daughter of the interloper Ann Boleyn, was illegitimate and thereby without proper claim to the English throne. On this issue, Elizabeth was insecure and vulnerable, as Mary well knew. Schiller's imagined cat-fight between the two queens is a gift for actresses, and in this production they gave it everything, with thrilling effect.

The most frightening final scene of any major drama is probably that of *Ghosts*, Ibsen's notorious play about family guilt, hypocrisy, and the horrors of syphilis. Osvald Alving has inherited the disease from his father, Captain Alving. Nursed by his mother, he is waiting for the return of the terrible symptoms. There is a powerful night-time scene between mother and son, in which Osvald reveals his dread of the inevitable coming regression into infantilism and the "softening of the brain." He shows his mother some tablets he has secreted, and begs her to give him "a helping hand" when the time comes. Mrs. Alving tries to comfort him, but she is unwilling to face up to the situation. For the moment, though, the crisis seems to be over. Then the dawn breaks:

> *[She goes to the table and puts out the lamp. The sun rises; the glaciers and the peaks in the distance glow in the morning light.]*
>
> Osvald *[sitting in the armchair with his back to the view, suddenly speaks without moving].* Mother, give me the sun.[12]

The actor's timing was perfect—and I was not the only person in the audience whose blood ran cold.

When I turned my own hand to playwriting, the first play that I wrote, *A Star Fell* (1998), contained a considerable amount of vio-

---

[11] Friedrich Schiller, *Maria Stuart* (1800), Act III, Scene 4, 2447-49, my translation.
[12] Henrik Ibsen, *Ghosts* (1881). Translated by Peter Watts. In: Ibsen, *Ghosts and Other Plays*. Harmondsworth: Penguin, 1964, p. 101.

lence. It was about the events at Cawnpore during the Indian Mutiny, and reflected my ongoing interest in India. My template—though I wasn't aware of it at first—was probably Peter Shaffer's *The Royal Hunt of the Sun*, a ponderous and gloomy epic that had had great theatrical success in the Sixties, and which I had seen in its maiden production by the English National Theatre Company. My own play had not one, but two massacres, and for a new production in 2006 I added a scene of confrontation between the evil Sultana (lover of the villainous intriguer, Azimullah Khan) and the British general's wife, Lady Wheeler (who was once Azimullah's mistress), that owes more than a little, I admit, to *Maria Stuart*. But the most poignant moment in the play—in the original production, at least—was no more than a vignette.

The British garrison at Cawnpore is being besieged by the mutinous sepoys. Their situation is hopeless. A message arrives from the Nana Sahib, the leader of the rebels and self-declared Peshwa (a very important title in nineteenth-century India), offering the British an honorable withdrawal from Cawnpore. The message—which is actually intended to lure them into a trap—is carried by one of the sepoys' British captives, Mrs. Jacobi, whose children are being held as surety for her return to the rebel camp. Mrs. Jacobi, a minor character in the play, is in a desperate physical and emotional condition, but at first General Wheeler and his daughter Ulrica barely notice her, so interested are they in the message that she has brought. Then Wheeler instructs her:

> *General Wheeler.* Mrs. Jacobi, you must take my reply to the…to the Peshwa.
>
> *Ulrica.* Can't she stay here, Daddy? Can't we send someone else with the message?
>
> *Mrs. Jacobi.* I have to go back. They have my children.
>
> *General Wheeler [suddenly noticing her ears]* Poor woman, your ears are torn!
>
> *Mrs. Jacobi [tired and sad, touching her hands to her ears].* They wanted my earrings.
>
> *[Fade to black. Exeunt.]*[13]

---

[13] Francis Jarman, *A Star Fell: A Play* (1998). Third, revised edition. Rockville, MD: The Borgo Press, 2009, pp. 67-68.

My intention here was that Mrs. Jacobi's whispered understatement should *evoke* rather than show her abuse and humiliation at the hands of her captors, and the effect was brilliantly achieved. The actor playing General Wheeler lowered his voice and slowed his delivery, and there was a deep hush of emotional concentration as Mrs. Jacobi replied and the audience *felt* the pain and despair contained in her words, "They wanted my earrings."

Less is often more. In modern stage productions and films almost everything is shown, including acts of the grossest and cruelest kind. Even Shakespeare didn't spare his audience the blinding of Gloucester in *King Lear*: "Fellows, hold the chair. / Upon these eyes of thine I'll set my foot. [...] Out, vile jelly! / Where is thy lustre now?" (perhaps the most horrific lines that he ever wrote).[14] But Shakespeare's audiences were used to being entertained with "slasher movie" horrors in real life, at the places of public execution. As Dr. Johnson sagely observed, in the notes to his 1765 edition of Shakespeare's plays, "let it be remembered that our author well knew what would please the audience for which he wrote."[15] But whether the blood is real or only ketchup, the repeated viewing of cruelty will make us indifferent and blasé—I have caught myself laughing out loud at poorly executed, clichéd acts of violence in television films—whereas our imaginations hold a reservoir of nightmarish thoughts and images more terrifying to us than anything that we can be shown. The great Greek tragedians sensibly kept almost all acts of violence off-stage, probably because they were obliged to do so by "the small number of actors employed" and the "practical limitations of realistic staging and acting."[16] The second reason most definitely applies when the actors are incompetent, as I was when I played Cassius in the six performances of a school production of *Julius Caesar*. Every night, assisted by my servant Pindarus, I had to kill myself on stage; every night I fell awkwardly and unrealistically, bashing my head and genuinely hurting myself; and every night, adding insult to my injury, someone in the audience laughed.

To do justice to its subject matter, *A Star Fell* has to be brutal. There is a scene, later in the play, in which Mrs. Jacobi and Lady Wheeler are shown being verbally abused, kicked, and humiliated by their captors, and another scene in which the Sultana's servant

---

[14] William Shakespeare, *King Lear*, Act III, Scene 7, 66-67, 82-83.
[15] *Dr. Johnson on Shakespeare*, p. 126.
[16] Philip Whaley Harsh, *A Handbook of Classical Drama*. Stanford, CA: Stanford University Press, 1944, p. 33.

Husainee strikes Lady Wheeler. But the "earrings" vignette, with its quiet horror, is possibly more effective as theatre than either of these scenes. As for the really substantial violence: the play's two massacres invite and are given a "stylised" treatment; there is also a rape, but this takes place off-stage.

The applause at the end of each performance was deeply gratifying, but the comments made to me by members of the audience were more interesting. One gentleman confided in me how impressed he had been by the actress who played the wicked Sultana. I have already discussed her interpretation of the role once before, in a different context, describing it then as "a masterly study in seething vindictiveness."[17] The actress prowled the stage like a tigress, graceful (in her Indian sari) but threatening, spitting out hatred and (verbally) flashing her claws. The gentleman from the audience was absolutely fascinated. So, for the record, was I! I can understand how directors and playwrights can fall in love with "their" leading lady—though not so much with her as a person, as with what she is bringing to life—at least for the duration of the production. I had the pleasure of standing in for a missing actor at one of the rehearsals and experiencing, close up, how good she was. Her gentleman admirer noted how cunningly the Sultana manipulated those around her, but he was frustrated that she didn't receive her comeuppance at the end of the play. Instead, as so often happens—and as happened to the historical figure that my character is based upon—she got away with it (and with the money, too). He told me that he'd wanted to jump onto the stage and strangle the witch! A great compliment to the whole production, I told myself, but good that he didn't do it....

More disturbingly, I received an email from another member of the audience, who, after complimenting me on my play, expressed his admiration for my courage in revealing myself in public in such a manner: "A play like this is a kind of diary in which personal experiences and thoughts are indirectly, or perhaps sometimes directly, presented to the audience." No such thing! Writers have *plot* ideas, which they put into practice using the invented figures that we call *characters*. Even a historical personage has to be reinvented by the author, because playwrights are not biographers. Or we take one or more imagined characters as the starting point, and develop them by allowing them to show who they are and what they are like through

---

[17] Francis Jarman, "Writing about Evil." In: F. Jarman, *White Skin, Dark Skin, Power, Dream: Collected Essays on Literature and Culture*. Holicong, PA: The Borgo Press, 2005, p. 196.

the way that they behave in the plot. None of my plays is about me, though, and none of my characters represents me in any way.

I was indeed so open to other people's views and inputs when writing *A Star Fell* that it was originally intended to be a workshop production, in which I would develop and flesh out a plot in cooperation with the members of the cast. There followed hours of wasted rehearsal time as stances were adopted, positions clarified, and my text suggestions messed around with. For some, my take on the Indian Mutiny wasn't acceptable, *i.e.*, I wasn't portraying the Indian rebels as Third World freedom fighters and the colonial British as nineteenth-century Nazis. One of the actors objected to there being several non-white characters who were obviously villainous. (This was before 9/11, of course.) Under pressure, I agreed to modify the figure of Azimullah Khan, making him more complex and "torn." When, on the urging of the director, we finally closed the discussion about the play and agreed that my text, as it stood, would be our script, the revised version of Azimullah was allowed to stand. Since then I have researched the sources on Azimullah Khan very thoroughly, and published a long biographical article about him.[18] I can state with confidence that, although he was more multifaceted and interesting than I had originally intended to make him, he was undoubtedly wicked and spiteful—in short, a much nastier piece of work than the "Azimullah Khan" of *A Star Fell*. But I have no intention of further changing my play, which is neither history nor biography, but a drama.

What I learned from the experience is that actors should be discouraged from messing around with the text, and dealt with firmly in rehearsal if they try too energetically to "improve" their lines as they go along. As for those actors who think they can write too, and come up with rewrites of whole scenes or new ideas that they want to develop, I agree completely with Hollywood screenwriter Joe Eszterhas when he suggests: "Don't be open to too many ideas about changing your script." And why not? Because: "*You're* the writer; *they're* not. Plus this: Most of their ideas will be asinine. Believe me: I've heard thirty years of asinine ideas." The actors may be persistent. Actors are often actors precisely *because* of their obsessive need to be noticed. Eszterhas therefore advises (in the spirit of *A*

---

[18] Francis Jarman, "Azimullah Khan—A Reappraisal of One of the Major Figures of the Revolt of 1857." In: *South Asia: Journal of South Asian Studies*, Vol. XXXI, No. 3, December 2008, pp. 419-49.

Clockwork Orange): "If they mess with you, give them a little taste of the old ultraviolence."[19]

Seriously, though, if one of them is allowed to get away with it, soon they will all be playing games. They will lose sight of the play, and probably of the director's conception of it too, and then there will be as many "versions" out there being rehearsed as there are self-indulgent egos in the cast. Teamwork is necessary, but a play production is not an exercise in grassroots democracy, any more than an airline flight or a surgical operation is. The director needs to keep a tight grip on his production if he is going to bring it to market. Alfred Hitchcock understood this well:

> I was once quoted as saying that actors are cattle. My actor friends know I would never be capable of such a thoughtless, rude, and unfeeling remark; that I would never call them cattle.... What I probably said was that actors should be *treated* like cattle.[20]

Which means: herded in the right direction.

Actors can be completely shameless. I was once approached by an actress with the request that I add a romantic scene between her character and the character played by one of her male colleagues. There should be lots of kissing, she said. The audience would love it. "Why should there be a love scene between them?" I asked her, racking my brains to think whether I'd missed some deeply significant element of emotional involvement between the characters, and expecting her to tell me what I'd overlooked (after all, they'd been rehearsing the play for weeks, and she might indeed have spotted some intriguing possibility). "Oh, he's just *too cute*," she said—but it was the actor she meant, not my character.

The director is a different matter altogether. He probably knows what he is doing, and what he is talking about. There is a well-established, pragmatic tradition that plays can be edited, cut, adapted, adjusted, reorganized, and so on to meet the circumstances and needs of the production. Within reason, the director must be allowed to do this. (The writer probably won't be able to stop him anyway.) He carries the artistic responsibility for the production. If things go pear-shaped, the writer can slip away from the awfulness,

---

[19] Joe Eszterhas, *The Devil's Guide to Hollywood: The Screenwriter as God!* New York: St. Martin's Press, 2006, p .212.
[20] *Hitchcock on Hitchcock: Selected Writings and Interviews.* Edited by Sidney Gottlieb. Berkeley *etc.*: University of California Press, paperback edition 1997, p. 56.

but the director must stay with his troops. The director may ask for lines to be changed or scenes to be rewritten. He understands better than the writer does what his actors can do and what they can't. He may unilaterally change the text in small ways.

Yet I draw the line at "creative" directors who think that they know more about the play than the writer does. At its most extreme—for instance in German *Regietheater* ("direction-theatre," i.e., theatre in which the input of the director is more important than anything else)—the director upstages even his own actors, making himself the true star of the production, by doing "interesting" things with the play. Some spurious credibility for this has been sought with the argument that older plays must be made "relevant" (more accessible? Easier to digest? Or simply: easier?) for a modern audience. If this is the price that has to be paid for keeping such plays in the repertoire, then so be it, but let the "relevance" (please!) not be in the form of gags and stunts. The trapezes, boxes, and climbing frames, the actors bellowing and leaping like a caricature of asylum inmates, the addition of gratuitous, exhibitionistic nudity or provocative anachronisms (I once saw a production of Puccini's *Turandot* in which the action was transposed from a mythical China to the Beijing of Chairman Mao): unless the play was intended all along to be a flimsy vehicle for such experiments, the gimmicks should not be allowed to distract the audience's attention from the substance of the play.

Matching an older play to the taste of the times is nothing new. In the seventeenth century, Nahum Tate won approval for his "happy ending" version of *King Lear*, in which Lear regains his kingdom and Cordelia doesn't die, so much so that this "improvement" on Shakespeare held the stage from 1681 until 1823, when Edmund Kean restored the tragic ending (Macready brought back Shakespeare's version in full in 1838). In his notes on the play, Dr. Samuel Johnson remarked on the popularity of Tate's adaptation that "the public has decided". Adding his personal "sensations" to "the general suffrage," he revealed that he had been so shocked by Cordelia's death that he had long refrained from rereading the closing scenes of the play.[21] On the subject of "directorial improvements to Shakespeare," we might give George Bernard Shaw the last word. Shaw watched a spectacular but brutally edited version of *Hamlet* directed by and starring the actor-producer John Barrymore (1925). A year later, he published a crushing letter to him:

---

[21] *Dr. Johnson on Shakespeare*, p. 126.

> Shakespear [sic], with all his shortcomings, was a very great playwright; and the actor who undertakes to improve his plays undertakes thereby to excel to an extraordinary degree in two professions in both of which the highest success is extremely rare. Shakespear himself, though by no means a modest man, did not pretend to be able to play Hamlet as well as write it; he was content to do a recitation in the dark as the ghost. But you have ventured not only to act Hamlet, but to discard about a third of Shakespear's script and substitute stuff of your own [...].[22]

He advises Barrymore to "concentrate on acting"—a profession in which the American was undoubtedly brilliant—"rather than on authorship, at which, believe me, Shakespear can write your head off."[23]

However badly a director may need to make his mark, he shouldn't do it by cocking his leg against the play. Whatever their validity, the arguments for drastically reworking older, classic plays scarcely apply to modern ones by living authors. For the rape of a modern text, there is no excuse.

As well as actors and directors, there are other figures that playwrights will sooner or later encounter (and with whom they may have problems). Wherever serious money is involved—we're talking Broadway and London's West End, but also the mainstream theatres in other cities—people like producers, theatre company directors and theatre managers, and theatrical agents start to be important. The financial constraints in commercial theatre tend to make "unknown" writers the victims of the vicious circle of fame: they won't do your plays unless you're famous, but you won't become famous if they don't do your plays. It's hard for an outsider to break into the world of the theatre, and not really surprising that many successful playwrights were originally professional actors (who knew how to use their contacts).

There are only a limited number of types of play that are commercially relevant, some of the obvious ones being (a) musicals (overwhelmingly so), (b) farces and boulevard comedies (those reliable standbys of the middle-class, middle-aged theatre-goer), (c) "alternative," left-wing theatre (mostly in university towns, with a nu-

---

[22] George Bernard Shaw, "A Letter to John Barrymore". In: *Shakespeare's Tragedies: An Anthology of Modern Criticism*. Edited by Laurence Lerner (1963). Harmondsworth: Penguin, 1968, p. 87.
[23] *Op. cit.*, p. 88.

merically restricted but loyal clientele), (d) experimental, "art" theatre (ditto), and (e) the classics (strongly patronized by busloads of schoolchildren and tourists). It's rather awkward if, as a playwright, you're (a) unmusical, (b) serious-minded, (c) not stridently "progressive," (d) happy to let others push the envelope, and (e) still alive.

Anyone who writes plays for local theatre groups, university drama clubs, and other enthusiastic amateurs will find that they are expected to write for large casts, often with a high percentage of women. Plays like this are seldom commercially viable. As one agent wrote to me, he couldn't take my play to the appropriate people "because of the cost"; *i.e.*, they would not consider a play with such a large cast by an unknown author, because of the financial risk. This was an honest reaction, even though it revealed more about the commercial concerns of the agent than about his artistic commitment. Commoner is the agent's rejection slip that simply states that "due to an enormous workload we are unable to offer to take on any new clients at the moment." What this apparent lack of entrepreneurial curiosity really conceals is the vicious circle that I have already described.

I sent my musical *Girls Will Be Girls* to the office of a world-famous composer and producer of musicals. After a while a reply came, from the "assistant to the Head of Production," politely declining the play, thanking me, rather solipsistically, for my interest in their company (I had been hoping for *their* interest in *me*), and explaining that they felt that this was "not something for development" by their organization. It was a short-sighted view, because at the time their "organization" was going through a mediocre phase, serving up unconvincing productions with weak musical numbers. *Girls Will Be Girls* is full of great songs (I can allow myself to praise the music, since I didn't write any of it), and I do believe they could have done worse than take a closer look at it. But, in any case, writers don't want to be developed; they want to be discovered.

Surely the critics at least should be willing to place artistic considerations in the foreground? The relations between creative artists and critics (who themselves are often failed or timid would-be artists) have seldom been easy. The critics constantly express their views on the work of artists—not surprisingly, since it's their job. Asked what they think of the critics, artists will tend to say things like: "why not ask a lamp-post how it feels about dogs?," or: "critics think they know the way, but they just can't drive the car," or: "like eunuchs in a harem, they know what to do, but they haven't got the equipment to do it," or: "they're the gadflies that hinder the oxen from ploughing," or even: "people who piss into a river and say, oh look, what a big stream I made!"[24]

The newspaper reviews of my own plays have always been positive, but they've also never been perceptive (compared with the comments of my friends, which were sometimes the opposite in both cases!). I shall be tempted to ignore them in future. I shall certainly not react to them directly, as the composer Max Reger is claimed to have done, writing to the author of a negative review: "I am sitting in the smallest room of my house. I have your review before me. In a moment it will be behind me."[25]

Finally: I haven't really explained yet "how it's done"—how plays get written. It has helped me considerably to be able to work for a drama group, writing scripts for a team whose resources, possibilities, and weaknesses I'm broadly aware of. The downside of this (apart from producing plays that aren't seen as commercially viable) is that there are things that I can't expect the actors to be able to do, and so I don't write them. There are exceptions. Because I knew that we had an exceptional actress to play the wicked Sultana in *A Star Fell*, I took the risk of giving her a passionate dramatic monologue, in which she not only parodies a dialogue between two of the other characters, but concludes with a poetic and emotional peroration. The cosmic imagery was perhaps a little "literary" for modern tastes, but the actress carried it off.

The Sultana has just asked her slave-girl Husainee to go and fetch Azimullah Khan, with whom she has some anti-British plotting to do. She is angry and frustrated that her lover "Dondy," the local prince known as the Nana Sahib, is still a pensioner of the British, and treated like a child or a pet by the British General Sir Hugh Wheeler. Husainee is at first surprised that she has been told to bring Azimullah into the harem area of the palace:

> *Husainee [shocked].* Here? Into the ladies' quarters, mistress? He is a man. He is a man who has had many women, he is not a eunuch.
>
> *Sultana Oula.* Do as I say! *[Husainee salaams]* There is no danger. The Nana Sahib is busy with his British friends, may they rot! It will take a long time. "Hughie, shall we play billiards?" "Dondy, that would be so

---

[24] Attributed to: Christopher Hampton, Kenneth Tynan, Brendan Behan, Anton Chekhov, Robert Frost.
[25] Quoted in *Modernism and Music: An Anthology of Sources.* Edited by Daniel Albright. Chicago *etc.*: University of Chicago Press, 2004, p. 147.

wonderful! Will you come to the polo game this evening? There will only be British officers and their ladies present, no Indians, only the finest society!" "Oh Hughie, that would be absolutely topping! Please, please, let me be your poodle." "Dondy, you are such a well-behaved nigger, I shall ask John Company[26] to pay you two rupees more." "Oh Hughie, how generous you are!" Damn them to hell! God's curse on them all! *[Suddenly noticing Husainee again]* Fetch Azimullah. *[Husainee goes out]* The stars are turning on their backs. The world is out there waiting to be taken, and if I were a man I would take it.[27]

Beginnings and endings are of great importance. Productions by the drama group that I have often worked with tend to open quietly, with a masque, tableau, or single talking head, before exploding into action with a crowd scene or a song and dance number. Some plays are famous for their spectacular opening scenes. One of my favorites is *The Revenger's Tragedy* (1607), the Jacobean shocker by either Thomas Middleton or Cyril Tourneur. The revenger himself, Vindice, enters "carrying a skull." Then "the Duke, Duchess, Lussurioso her Son, Spurio the Bastard, with a train, pass over the Stage with Torch-light," and Vindice hurls his hatred and scorn at them:

> *Vindice.* Duke, royal lecher! Go, grey-haired adultery,
> And thou his son, as impious steeped as he:
> And thou his bastard, true-begot in evil:
> And thou his Duchess, that will do with Devil,
> Four ex'lent characters—[28]

For a dramatic opening, that is hard to beat! And as a bonus it conveniently introduces several of the main characters right from the start. (Curiously, the 2002 film version by Alex Cox failed to do much with this scene.)

The playwright can also make the opening of the play lyrically memorable, as Shakespeare does in *Twelfth Night* ("If music be the food of love, play on") and *Richard III* ("Now is the winter of our discontent"). More conventionally, he can use a dramatic Chorus to introduce the story, as in *Romeo and Juliet* ("Two households, both alike in dignity"), *Troilus and Cressida* ("In Troy, there lies the

---

[26] The British East India Company.
[27] *A Star Fell*, pp. 24-25.
[28] *The Revenger's Tragedy*, Act I, Scene 1, 1-5.

scene"), and *Henry V* ("O for a Muse of fire, that would ascend / The brightest heaven of invention"). Or he can go for a shock effect, like the Witches in *Macbeth* ("When shall we three meet again / In thunder, lightning, or in rain?") or the (for a Tudor audience) disturbing sight of a king *in extremis* in *1 Henry IV* ("So shaken as we are, so wan with care").

The plots of stage comedies tend to be driven by stubborn misunderstandings, and end with (and through) their resolution. In the final scenes of the play, rivals, enemies, and estranged friends are reconciled, those who belong together come together, and the world is a better, happier, and better-integrated place than it was before. There may be engagements or weddings. My own play *Girls Will Be Girls* (2000) ends, after many plot confusions and complications, with five happy couples (one of them a lesbian pair) on the stage—not quite a world record, I know (think *Seven Brides for Seven Brothers*), but difficult to organize plot-wise—and nobody is excluded from the celebratory circle of reconciliation.

> *Allan [looking at the reconciled couples].* Is this what they call a happy ending?
>
> *Sammie.* Perhaps…[29]

But some comedies are darker. Malvolio famously excludes himself in *Twelfth Night*: "I'll be reveng'd on the whole pack of you!" (though he is perhaps not irredeemably lost, since the Duke calls for someone to "Pursue him, and entreat him to a peace").[30] A play that makes any claim to being about serious matters in the real world cannot pretend that that world contains no evil. My second comedy, *Lip Service* (2001), which is about power struggles and sexual and ideological conflicts at a feminist cosmetics company, ends with the exclusion of the two "villains," the tyrannical chief executive Bella and the ultra-egotist and preening would-be Casanova Bill Bullock ("BAM! That's my company. Bullocks's Active Marketing. I'm Bullock!").[31] After Bella's reign of terror has been ended by a staff revolt, she storms out, taking Bill Bullock, whose services are also no longer required by the company, with her. It is

---

[29] Francis Jarman, *Girls Will Be Girls: A Play* (2000). Second edition. Rockville, MD: The Borgo Press, 2007, p. 112.
[30] William Shakespeare, *Twelfth Night*, Act V, Scene 1, 377, 379.
[31] Francis Jarman, *Lip Service: A Play* (2001). Second edition. Rockville, MD: The Borgo Press, 2007, p. 42.

hardly true love, but Bill and Bella deserve each other, and here too a kind of comedic "coming together" takes place:

> *Bella [half-heartedly]*. Come along, Bullock, I've got a business proposal for you.
>
> *Bill*. That's the spirit! Think positive, baby. Think constructive. Think *big*. There are big things we can do together. "Bill and Bella's Active Marketing"—BABAM!! That has a ring to it! *[On their way out]* You and I will make a great team. There are new worlds to conquer! Let's get our heads together over a drink. I know a fantastic little place, just round the corner from here....
>
> *[Exeunt Bella and Bill]*[32]

Bill has already been thwarted in three attempts to lure female members of the company staff to his favorite restaurant, or back to his apartment, "for drinkies by candle-light."[33] It seems that with Bella he has finally hit gold (she will eat him alive, of course, but he's too stupid to realize that).

My other male chauvinist is the rock music agent Ronnie de Silver in *Girls Will Be Girls*. In his very first scene he manages to offend each of the women on the stage, including his former girlfriend Elaine. The vulgar "joke" that he makes about her has not only always raised a laugh from theatre audiences, but has even gained a certain notoriety in other circles:

> *Rickie [with heavy sarcasm]*. You're so charming, Ronnie.
>
> *Ronnie [bowing]*. It's the company I keep.
>
> *Elaine*. While we're on the subject, don't you think, *at your age*, that it's rather tasteless...?
>
> *Ronnie*. Funny you should say that. Because you know what *you* remind me of, Elaine?
>
> *Elaine*. No?
>
> *Ronnie*. The British Museum.

---

[32] *Op. cit.*, p. 109.
[33] *Op. cit.*, p. 79.

> *Elaine [suspicious].* How come?
>
> *Ronnie.* It's got lots of interesting things to do and see, but everything's so *old*.
>
> *Sammie [unnecessarily].* Yeah, fossils and old bones.
>
> *Sally.* Ha, ha, look who's talking.
>
> *Ronnie.* No, that's a different museum. What I'm trying to say is: everyone's already *been there*. *[Leeringly]* If you know what I mean by that. They don't charge admission. People just go in and out as they please.
>
> *Elaine [very angry].* You bastard![34]

When the British Library (a sister organization to the British Museum, and once housed under its roof) acquired a copy of *Girls Will Be Girls* for their national copyright collection, the Head of the Modern English section wrote to me, "I notice the British Museum gets a mention!"

My "serious" plays, *A Star Fell* and *Invictus* (2006), both of which are based on historical events, end with the device of the future fates of the main characters being revealed. (This is an idea that was probably inspired by the information of this sort sometimes given at the end of films.) In *A Star Fell*, the different "villains" of the Indian Mutiny are dragged before a British military court to be sentenced. Azimullah Khan as Chorus describes what is going to happen to each of them, and the play then ends (as it also began) with his words. *Invictus*, a play about the Roman emperor Constantine, likewise begins and ends with monologues addressed directly to the audience, in this case by the Machiavellian court chamberlain and eunuch, Euphratas. In the final scene of the play, he invites the main characters to each "have their own last word", before revealing that he himself "was given many honours, and lived to be old. May you too die peacefully in your bed"—he tells the audience—"as I did."[35]

Openings and endings are indeed important, but a lot still has to be done in between. What is served up to the audience needs to have *some* quality, if only as a matter of politeness. It's easy for someone

---

[34] *Girls Will Be Girls*, pp. 53-54.
[35] Francis Jarman, *Invictus: A Play*. Rockville, MD: The Borgo Press, 2006, p. 103

to toss a novel aside, or switch channels on the television, but very few people have the courage to get up and walk out of a theatre performance. Once in their seats, the audience are committed to the play (at least until the interval), and they should be given something in return for that commitment, and for the price of the admission ticket. Neither the play nor the production should insult their intelligence.

On a more banal level, the plot of the play ought to make sense. It is a road map taking its characters from the opening scene to the final one. Although they are not real people with existences outside the scenes in the play in which they are shown interacting with each other, the characters should be so convincing (and the things that they do so plausible) that you could well imagine that they *might* be real. "He goes off at the end of scene 3," you tell yourself, "to make room for the intimate scene between B and C, but I need him again for scene 5 (with B), so how do I motivate his return (and engineer C's departure from the stage), and then get him off at the end of the scene, before bringing him back for scene 8? 'Oh, I think I'll go off and make myself a coffee'? 'Hello again, I was wondering where you were'?"

Clumsy entrance lines can quickly become clichés ("Anyone for tennis?"), far-fetched coincidences and *deus ex machina* effects should be used sparingly, and an imaginative stage direction like the notorious "Exit, pursued by a bear" (in Shakespeare's *The Winter's Tale*) can only ever be used once! To avoid embarrassing mistakes, I worked out the intricacies of the plot continuity of *Girls Will Be Girls* with a board representing the stage and my daughter's Lego figures standing in for the characters.

And yet—what matters most in a fast-moving play is that what the audience *perceives* (rather than what they deduce) should be plausible to them during the performance. Afterwards doesn't matter so much. One of my plays was only days away from dress rehearsal when one of the participant actors pointed out that "*this* character coming on at *this* moment, and for *these* reasons, doesn't make sense!" The director quickly replied that if no one in the cast had noticed it for weeks, it was unlikely that anyone in the audience would be perplexed by it during the two hours of the stage performance. He was right, too. (And does anyone actually watching *Othello*—as opposed to Shakespeare scholars analysing it—ever worry about how silly the plot is? It's still a marvellous play.)

The magic is what counts, and when the magic of the performance works, a play will reward its author with more joy and satisfaction than any other form of writing can.

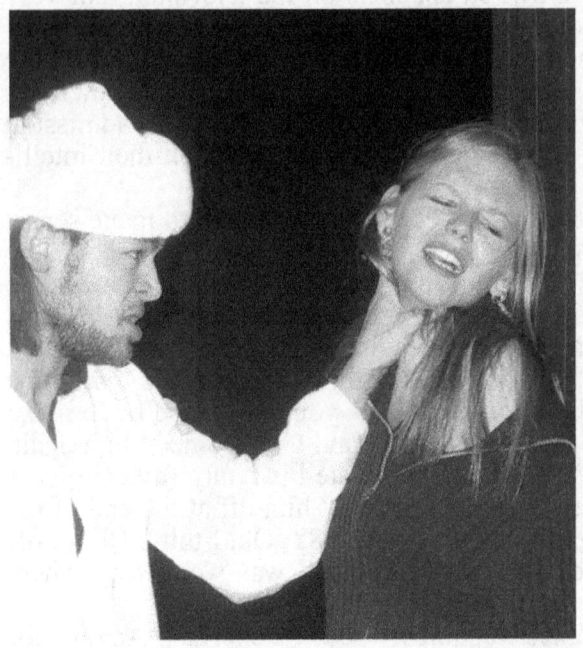

VIOLENCE—A rehearsal for the 2006 production of *A Star Fell* (with Björn Kassel and Katrin Fischer).

"THE ULTRA-EGOTIST and preening would-be Casanova Bill Bullock" (Christian Friedrich) in *Lip Service*.

ANOTHER MALE chauvinist—Ronnie de Silver (Paul Harrison) in the original production of *Girls Will Be Girls*.

XVII.

ON TRANSLATION

by Frank J. Morlock

How I Got into Translating

THERE'S AN OLD saying that patriotism is the last refuge of scoundrels. Perhaps translating is the last refuge of frustrated writers. At least it was for me.

I began translating quite accidentally. I had been writing plays since I was twenty-one, and in my forties still hadn't gotten any produced. The market for new plays is very difficult to break into. And it was expensive for the playwright. In the days before the internet a novice playwright sending his plays out had to copy them, mail them, and often pay a reading fee—and wait perhaps as long as a year for a decision. In an attempt to weed out a lot of wasted effort, query letters are recommended. The playwright describes his play, and the producer decides whether he actually is interested enough to want to read the play.

Producers usually employ a full-time dramaturge to read the submissions and select a few for the directors to read. But it still takes a while: the dramaturge is flooded with requests, and makes his selection of scripts he'd like to see.

For many years I followed the system outlined above. I sent out my query letters and, if the dramaturge was interested, I sent my play, waited, and waited some more, usually to get a rejection letter a year later, typically with no explanation.

For me, the last straw came after an unusually positive response from a very good theatre to a query letter of mine.

I was frankly surprised by his choices (I had described a half dozen plays), because they were not the sort of plays that the theatre he worked for usually performed. He probably wanted to do something different. So, I sent the plays requested and waited. Around a year went by. Just as I was about to call to inquire, I got the scripts back in the mail with a note from the *new* dramaturge expressing his astonishment that I had sent these scripts to his theatre in the first place. Obviously he hadn't read the correspondence. I refrained from sending him a poison pen letter, but I was furious, and I decided I was never going to send out plays in this way again.

But what to do? My joy in writing plays was seriously compromised. I felt after twenty years of frustration that the future didn't look very bright. I didn't know what to do exactly, but I knew I'd had enough of playing a game in which I constantly lost. Fortunately, I was not dependent on success as a writer to make a good living. I was a lawyer, and also taught undergraduate legal courses at the University of Maryland. One day I was in the Library of the University of Maryland, where I was teaching a course to paralegals, and went into the stacks to find something to read. At first I didn't see much of interest, until I came across a small, leather-bound book that appeared to be a couple of centuries old. Why the book was not in the Rare Book Department I do not know, but luckily for me it wasn't. It was a collection of French plays by a French writer I had never heard of by the name of Dufresny. My French, although not great, was still good enough (or perhaps the text was simple enough) for me to read a short little play called *The Spirit of Contradiction*. It was written in 1700. The piece was about a woman whose only goal in life is to thwart the ambitions of those around her (namely her husband, daughter, and family servants.) The others know her character, and she knows they know—and it's a cat-and-mouse game between them, each trying to conceal their real feelings from each other.

I thought the play hilarious and ingenious. As far as I could discover, it had never been translated into English. I did determine that as of 1900 it had been performed over 2,600 times by the Comédie Française, which was far more than any other writer except Molière. I had never had any ambitions as a translator, but I thought this would be a piece of cake. After all, it's less than thirty pages long, and the French is easy. So I'd give it a try. And so my nightmare began!

Like most people who've never actually translated anything, I had ideas and preconceived notions about what a good translation is and how to proceed. It didn't take long for me to realize that everything I thought I knew, I didn't.

My first delusion was that it would take, at most, a few days.

It actually took two months, and at several points I thought I would never finish. It's easy to become discouraged when words that make perfect sense in French sound awkward in English, and resist your best efforts to smooth them out.

And then there are the difficulties that you simply didn't foresee at all.

In translating an old play, the translator has several choices. First of all, he can do a straight translation. But how does one get a contemporary English-speaking audience interested in a play written in early eighteenth-century France by an unknown writer? It's hard enough to scare up an audience for a Molière play, and the numbers go down when the writer is Racine or Corneille. But Dufresny?

A second alternative would be to give the play a modern setting. Basically, it would be the same play, but set in modern Paris, or perhaps England. Sometimes this will work, but it didn't seem likely for the *Spirit of Contradiction*, where the mother is trying to thwart her daughter's choice of a husband.

A third alternative, and the one I opted for, was to set the play in England around 1700, where the social customs were similar, and parents had a lot of control over who their children would marry.

It seemed like a good choice. I'm very familiar with the English plays of the period. I like Restoration plays, especially those of Congreve, Cibber, Farquhar, Vanbrugh, and Mrs. Centilivre. I felt that setting the play in England would not involve any major problems. I felt an audience would feel more familiar and comfortable with eighteenth-century England than eighteenth-century France, and that it would be easy to transfer the action from one country to another. But I was wrong!

I soon discovered that if you change the country where the action takes place, you involve yourself in other problems which you did not foresee. For example, if in the original version the action takes place in Versailles, twenty miles from Paris, what is the English equivalent? And if a character has to travel from Versailles to Paris, how long does it take? A French audience knows the distance and understands pretty well how long it took in 1700. But what is the English equivalent in 1700? And if money is mentioned in the French original, what is the English equivalent? This may not seem terribly difficult, but it may take a little research—and when research fails, as sometimes happens—an educated guess.

Another question that is harder to categorize is this—is the character saying something polite or rude? Is the character saying "Be Quiet" or "Shut up"? The same verb might be used in French, but the context may suggest that the character is being rude. But if the context suggests the character is being rude, how do you convey this in English? "Shut up" is pretty strong language in English, and may seem *too* impolite for an English audience.

Another strange phenomenon is that people think they know how people talked in the eighteenth century or Roman times, or in Russia in the late 1600s. For example, if you use the word "Daddy" for Father in a play about Tsar Peter the Great and his son, Tsarevich Alexis, people will tell you that Russians didn't talk that way. Alexis would have referred to his Father as "Pater." Utterly absurd. The Russian language, then and now, abounds in diminutives. And Russians are very informal in family contexts anyway.

They certainly would not have used a Latin term which was an affectation introduced by English boarding schools in the eighteenth century. "Dad" was used in English in Shakespeare's time. Recently, someone questioned the use of the term "old geezer," because he thought it was a modern term. It's been around since Saxon times.

And then there is the question of foreign names. Should we keep the personal names used in the original? Generally speaking, I think we should, unless the name is so outlandish that it is off-putting. For example, in one play the heroine's name in French was "Cydalise." I thought it sounded rather strange, so I changed it to something that sounded more familiar, like Diane or Clarice. It really becomes a problem if the hero has a funny-sounding name.

Sometimes the name may sound alien—or worse, simply ridiculous—Germance, for example. Faced with this, I think it is reasonable to find a name that is more familiar to an English ear. I think one of the reasons that Molière has never really found an English audience is that he uses names for his characters that sound silly in English—for example, Tartuffe.

Another problem that is unique to dramatic works intended for performance is that there's no going back. There is no instant replay in the theatre. If the audience misses the point the dramatist is trying to make, the loss is irreparable.

There are no asterisks, no appendices. The translator has got to get the point across through the dialogue. Sometimes this may mean simplifying the text; at other times, it may mean adding a few words. For example, in the Lesage play, *La Tontine*, there is no explanation of what a "Tontine" is. So, in order to clarify the point, I had one character ask:

Character 1: Do you know what a Tontine is?

Character 2: A Tontine—of course I know, of course I know—it's a, it's a— (sheepishly) What is it?

Character 1: It's a kind of last man out club, where the survivor takes everything the other members have put in.

This is obviously not a translation, which is why most play translations are, in fact, adaptations. Of course, adaptations do not change the plot lines or characters in any way, but simply make what's going on plain to a modern audience.

It might even be necessary to do something along these lines in a modern French production, since I'm pretty sure the average modern-day Frenchman has no idea what a Tontine is. It derives its name from an Italian financier named Tonti who promoted this type of scheme, just as Ponzi contributed his name to the Ponzi scheme. But even if the example of Tontine is not well chosen, and the French to the last man standing know its meaning, there are other terms where similar action needs to be taken, not only in English translation, but in any modern production of the original text.

The benefits of translating are many. Most importantly, the translator develops his own language skills. It's not so important that you have an extraordinary command of the foreign language—you can almost always puzzle out the meaning. The real challenge is to rephrase the text in English in a dialogue that can be grasped by an audience immediately.

A second benefit, at least in America, is that you get more respect when presenting a translation to a publisher than you would if you were a novice or little-known writer. The general feeling amongst publishers is that if you are new, you are probably no good. Americans are not generally adept at foreign languages, and feel a bit intimidated by someone who can actually translate a work from a foreign language. Also, if you a translating an author who has a recognized name—*e.g.*, Voltaire—that also creates respect.

A third benefit, especially for novice writers, is that you will never suffer from writer's block. There's plenty of untranslated material in almost every language. The French, for example, produced some 30,000 plays in the nineteenth century, and very few have ever been translated. Some of these plays were by well-known writers and are quite excellent. In addition, unlike when you are writing an original work, you don't need to ponder: what happens next. All you need do is keep on translating. Having seen lots of writers jam up for long periods of time because their imagination failed them, I regard this as a benefit not to be despised.

A fourth benefit is that you learn to write by writing, even if the writing is translating. One Writer's School I heard of was managed by a woman who insisted that her students simply copy Hemingway or Fitzgerald. She was convinced that the act of copying, say, *The Sun Also Rises*, was an effective way, perhaps by some sort of literary osmosis or muscle memory, that would produce better works by the student. True or not, I don't know, but I do believe that translating involves a great deal of creativity on the part of the translator that goes beyond the mere choice of words.

The translator experiences the atmosphere of the translated work, feels the creative satisfaction, and in some sense makes the characters and plot his own, no matter how literal his translation might be.

Finally, the act of translating may not only polish the translator's style and improve his ability to write his own works, but actually open doors for him. That has certainly been the case with my own work. Go in with a translation of a work by a famous author, and you will be respectfully received. Then go in with an original work of your own. You will also be respectfully received. Don't underestimate the value of a translation as a door-opener.

Adaptations Versus Translations

LIKE OTHER ASPECTS of translating, the differences between adaptation compared to a straight translation are not as simple as they may appear, until you've actually done a translation or two. Generally, one thinks of a translation as being pretty literal, although not necessarily word for word.

On the other hand, an adaptation may be much freer. But as one examines these matters closely (usually by doing a translation or two), one finds the distinctions are not so clear cut. A simple example: until recently the French regarded every EXIT and ENTRANCE in a play as being a separate scene. English practice is to indicate a scene change only when there is a change of location or set change. The English system is easier to read, and is well established.

So when translating a French play, one employs the English system and gets rid of the "French Scenes," as they are called by theatre professionals. The French system, however, is extremely useful when actually producing a play. It's much easier to track what's going on and who's doing what to whom when you have specific set directions.

So it is not uncommon when a play is being prepared for staging to put in the "French Scenes," even in an English-language play. Also, the French have a way of mapping the stage very effectively, but the system is sufficiently different from the English system that to translate this literally would be confusing to English speakers, even to those trained in the theatre.

Things to Avoid

I BELIEVE THAT meaning trumps style in any translation.

Therefore, I avoid translating in a way that unduly celebrates style. I do not think that a translation needs to be literal, but it must emphasize content rather than verbal pyrotechnics. I think it's almost impossible (unless the languages are very closely related) to reproduce puns and foreign sounds. And I question whether inventing other puns than the one contained in the original is very useful.

The same applies to attempts to make English sound like French. While the sound of the French text may dazzle in French, it's unlikely to dazzle in English. If the French text is in rhyme or verse, it is *not* (at least if the text is a play) wise to translate the French verse into English verse. For the most part, the French use rhymed couplets (usually Alexandrines), and however effective this may be in French, it's hard to think of a play written in English in rhymed couplets since the time of the Elizabethans. English audiences gave up on rhyme long ago, the French only relatively recently.

Part of the reason for this difference is that English audiences expect plays to be acted, and that involves a kind of realism which rhyme interferes with. The French, on the other hand, were historically accustomed to their verse tragedies being *declaimed* rather than *acted.* Understanding that distinction explains a lot in the persistence of rhymed verse on the French stage—and its utter disappearance from the English stage. If you feel that verse is really necessary, I would suggest free verse even in preference to blank verse.

Another troubling question is the degree to which we are obligated to reproduce errors made by the original author.

Errors include factual errors and simple, clumsy mistakes and poor stagecraft. Occasionally, you will find that the author has made a mistake that is really a howler. This should be eliminated or corrected if possible.

For example, if the author, for some reason wrote that Columbus had sailed for America in 1482 rather than 1492, I think the mistake should simply be corrected—unless the "mistake" is intended by the writer (as a farcical comment, for example). Other, less glaring errors require a judgment call. I wouldn't hesitate to "fix" or simply eliminate an error by an unknown or forgotten writer, but tampering with a text by a major dramatist such as Victor Hugo or Gustave Flaubert is always questionable. Our first duty as translators is to the author of the original text. We must try to get his point across regardless of whether we agree with it, and even when we know that (in some instances) what he is saying is demonstrably false, and that he may not have known this at the time he wrote the work.

This leads to the question of censorship. Are we justified in censoring a writer simply because we feel his point of view is outrageous, unjust, or simply inflammatory?

Once I would have said absolutely not. But then I came across a situation that forced me—*in that instance*—to change my mind. I was translating a play about Jesus of Nazareth [published recently by Borgo Press—ed.].

On the whole, the drama adhered to the Biblical account (and that's the only account we have), and indeed provides insight that modern scholarship had only recently arrived at. Yet, there were several troubling comments that could be construed as *anti-Semitic*. Actually, only a couple instances really bothered me. In one, for example, a Jewish character and a follower of Jesus says, "The Jews have got him" [*i.e.*, Jesus].

That seems to me a rather strange way for one Jew to refer to his own people. In another case, the Commander of Herod's Guards (himself presumably Jewish) refers to the Jews as a "filthy race." Had a Roman or other foreigner made that statement, it would simply demonstrate a Roman or foreign *prejudice* against the Jews, rather than the attitude of the author. Again, this is a strange, even unacceptable, way for one Jewish character to refer to other Jews.

I agonized over what to do—make a change of some sort, or leave the text alone. I consulted several Jewish friends, who advised me to translate it the way I found it. I really wasn't convinced that the author was being *deliberately* anti-Semitic, but, on the other hand, I wasn't convinced either that the author wasn't *revealing* his own attitude through his characters. On the whole, I didn't think the play was anti-Semitic, but I still found these lines of dialogue troubling. Unable to decide what the author's true intent was, what decided me was that some readers or members of an audience (in the event the play was performed) would experience the work as a religious rather than an aesthetic or merely literary event.

I am sure that not everyone will agree with my decision, but I decided to change "The Jews have got him" to "The Sanhedrin has got him." After all, that statement was factually more specific and less subject to an anti-Semitic interpretation. The "Filthy race" comment I simply omitted. In the end, I felt I was merely removing a smudge from an otherwise excellent work.

What Should Be Our Goal in Translation?

REGARDLESS OF what others may think, my view is that a translator's role is to give the author being translated as good an English version as one is capable of, faithfully expressing the author's ideas, and attempting to make the work as sound in English as it is in the original. I try to give expression to the author's thoughts, as if the play had originally been written in English. Beyond that, everything else is simply a rule of thumb. Rules of thumb are useful—but should not dictate a procedure that must always be followed. And situations will arise, if you do a lot of translating, where every rule must bend to circumstance. Practicality rather than ideological purity is as desirable in a translator as in a statesman.

Some Tips on Translation

FIRST AND MOST important of all: be persistent. Try to set aside a bit of time every day for translating. Ten or twenty minutes multiplied by 365 days a year adds up to quite a bit of time over the course of a year. You will become more proficient as time goes by. Problems that stump you, or that you agonized over as a novice translator, will disappear with experience. A lot of work can be accomplished if you simply keep at it.

Second, never get hung up over your inability to translate a particular word or phrase. If a word or phrase stubbornly resists meaning or translation (and that will occur from time to time), just keep going. Meaning is largely determined by context. Go back over it later, and you will probably wonder why the meaning eluded you, because now you have a better context, and the author's intent suddenly seems plain.

If, however, a phrase is so obscure that even an educated French contemporary no longer understands it, the best thing to do may be simply to excise it. Rarely does plot or character hang on a simple word or phrase. There are on-line dictionaries that may be helpful, and it doesn't hurt to have cyber friends who are native speakers of the language you are translating from. They will often gladly try to help you resolve problems of meaning.

Occasionally, you will run into a writer who makes perfect sense in French, but that you find is very hard to translate their work into English. George Sand is my personal *bête noir*. I like her work, but hate translating her. There's something about her syntax that I find tongue-twisting in English. That may just be me, but it takes me much longer to arrive at a satisfactory and smooth translation of her work than almost any other French writer I can think of.

Don't Be Afraid of Slang

I THINK IT IS true that a translator is wise to recognize that in any language, and at all periods of time, there was, is, and always will be slang expression. Not every character uses the language perfectly, and some people deliberately misuse the language even though they are highly educated.

Puritanism is not as strong in some cultures as others, and things considered as rude or unmentionable in our culture may be matters of everyday conversation in others.

If you are translating plays, recognize that there is a difference between stage dialogue and the dialogue of ordinary speech and written language. Stage dialogue is meant to be spoken, heard, and easily understood by an audience. It is not necessarily perfect English. It is at once easier and more difficult to write than ordinary prose. Dialogue requires a special talent. And translated dialogue must sound like spoken English as well. But the foreign author may be writing clumsy dialogue. Since we are translating a work intended for performance, at this point our duty is both to the actors (to give them usable dialogue) and to the audience (to give them dialogue they can, as an audience, grasp), and if that means we have to tweak the text a bit, or edit it to provide clarity, I am all for it.

Great Writers Have Sometimes Been Translators

WE SOMETIMES think of translation as beneath the dignity of great writers. Baudelaire translated Poe, and his entire body of work was strongly influenced by him. Nobel Prize Laureates have done translations. That may not be the work for which they are most famous, but it may have been, and frequently was, a key factor in their development as writers.

Finally, work fast. Speed is usually friendly to style. You can always go back and correct minor errors of diction, meaning, or syntax.

Happy translating!

San Miguel de Allende
October 13, 2009

XVIII.

IN OTHER WORDS...

EDITING BORGO PRESS

by Robert Reginald

I WAS AN EDITOR from the very start of my professional career.

My first book, *Stella Nova*, which I wrote during my senior year in college (1968/69), was a work of compilation and anthologization, assembled from direct-mail questionnaires and research in a variety of printed sources and my own book collection. That I could successfully edit a 350-page page was a revelation to a twenty-year-old neophyte. I learned that the only true failure was never trying.

When I came to California in 1969 to earn my graduate degree at USC, I began haunting the bookstores in Hollywood, and soon encountered another collector, Douglas A. Menville. Doug was introduced to me by the owners of the Sunset-Vine Bookmart, located on Vine Street a third of a block up from Sunset.

Unbeknownst to me, the Saunders Brothers, owner of the Bookmart, had already decided to get out of the book *selling* business, and into the book *publishing* business—but they wanted to do everything on the cheap. They planned to issue a professional science-fiction magazine, since SF was very popular at the time; and also to start a line of trade paperbacks featuring self-help and occult nonfiction titles. Most of their material would be derived from public-domain sources (in other words, they wouldn't have to pay for rights).

But the Saunders Brothers possessed no editorial skills of their own. They were lifelong bookmongers, and knew how to peddle their wares just fine—but readers and writers, they were not. They needed willing workers who would work for very little—preferably nothing! And, lo and behold, there we were: Froggy and Toady, in the flesh!

This is not to imply that we were *unwilling* laborers in any way. Doug was Editor Prime, at least initially, which was only just and proper, since he was a decade older than *moi*, and at least had earned his *bona fides* in the film business. As for me, although I'd put together my first monograph the year before—and that was it! I had no other credentials whatsoever. So I talked my way through the back door, and Doug, bless his soul, accepted my help.

And what a wild ride that was!

The magazine was called *Forgotten Fantasy*, and it lasted just five bimonthly issues, but it was a blast and a half to put together. My contributions consisted of a few book reviews that I penned, and some public-domain materials that I found in *The Century Magazine* and similar publications in the library stacks. When the publication failed due to lack of distribution, we moved immediately into editing the book line, Newcastle Publishing Co., Inc.

Newcastle consistently published eight titles a year in its twenty-eight-year existence, usually four in the Fall season and four in the Spring. Most of the early titles were books whose copyrights had lapsed due to age or non-renewal. I had no interest whatever in the content of these volumes, but I learned how to put together a publishing line from the ground up.

I wrote cover copy and catalogue copy and introductions to the books by the gazillions. I prepared catalogues and helped select titles. I checked copyrights, managed the ISBN log, and wrote letters on behalf of the Saunders Brothers whenever we were challenged. I secured Cataloging-in-Publication data from the Library of Congress for some of the volumes. I did everything except market the line—which was the publishers' purview.

And so, of course, did Doug, and over the course of the decades, he actually picked most of the titles.

Along the way we managed to introduce a few SF and fantasy titles into the mix, and persuaded the Saunders Boys to allow us to create The Newcastle Forgotten Fantasy Library, which featured classic works of (mostly public domain) fantastic literature. We published twenty-four of these books before the series ended in 1980.

But I worked for other companies as well, beginning with Arno Press in 1973. That year I sold them the first of four packaged series of reprint and original books for the academic market, and brought Doug Menville in as my co-editor. I relied on my own and Doug's knowledge of classic SF, fantasy, and horror works, and used his extensive collection, and that of the J. Lloyd Eaton Collection at the University of California, Riverside, as sources for the physical copies. We eventually selected 200 volumes for reprinting, wrote the ad copy for the brochures, and put together nine original anthologies. It was great fun!

In mid-1975 I met my wife, Mary Wickizer Rogers, and she quickly became my personal and literary collaborator. Just a few months before then, I made a proposal to Al and Joe Saunders at Newcastle for a line of books that I would edit and publish and they would distribute. This venture became Borgo Press, the name a pun on the Borgo Pass (the pass nearest Castle Dracula!). Thus, Mary was involved with the planning for the new line almost from the beginning.

We envisioned producing short, original literary critiques on genre fiction, packaged together into a numbered series, and a similar line of booklets on popular music. Interspersed with these would be reprints and originals of classic SF and fantasy volumes. We issued our first list in the Spring of 1976, and eventually released exactly 300 titles before shutting our doors in early 1999. Newcastle distributed our books to the trade for the first four years, before we dropped the fiction titles and moved into the library market, with which I was intimately familiar.

We published a great many works that would never have seen the light of day, if it hadn't been for us—and not because they were unpublishable, either. That a particular work actually reaches market is often an accident of matching the right author with the right editor at just the right time.

We eventually shut down Borgo because we were beginning to plan for our retirement, and were both burned out at the frenetic pace, lack of financial return, and horrible stress.

In July 2003 I nearly died from a heart attack, and was forced to cut back severely on my schedule. A few months before then, on 23 January 2003, John Gregory Betancourt, Publisher of Wildside Press, had approached me, asking if he could buy the Borgo Press imprint, and suggested that he might be willing to reprint some of the old, out-of-print BP titles. I sold him the label for a dollar, but when I nearly died that summer, any plans for a revival of the list had to be put aside. I'd started working on a possible series of books a week before my collapse—now, however, just surviving in any form became my primary goal, and it took me a year to get any strength back. I began working anew on the project in 2004, but at a relatively low pace.

On 22 March 2006, John once again asked if I'd be willing to contact some of the old Borgo Press and Starmont House authors (Borgo had bought the remnants of SH after the death in 1991 of that line's Publisher, Ted Dikty, a close friend of mine), and secure the rights to reprint their books. As mentioned in my introduction to this volume, that very limited charge expanded within a year to encompass a full-fledged line of reprint and original volumes, both fiction and nonfiction, on any subject and encompassing any genre. As of November 2009, I've submitted and seen published more than 750 titles for the revived BP program at Wildside Press, about half of my lifetime editorial output.

* * * * * * *

PAST IS PRELUDE to future, and I mention these parts of my vita only to establish that I've paid my dues in full over the past forty-one years. Mostly unmentioned here is my career as an academic librarian and administrator, which has paralleled the other half of my life for the last thirty-nine years, with cross-pollination and reinvigoration occurring in both directions.

But perhaps it needs to be noted in some fashion, because there are some lessons that I learned throughout my University existence that directly pertain now.

I served, among many other roles, as Head of Collection Development for eleven years at the local state university, and was ultimately responsible for purchasing perhaps a third or a fourth of the entire collection of 800,000+ volumes, frequently through my own efforts, with orders or purchases that I generated myself.

Over the decades I gradually developed a philosophy of acquisition that was very broadly based. It was not enough, I felt, for the campus to acquire only materials that directly supported the curriculum, as worthy and necessary as that goal might be. I also thought that I had a responsibility as chief acquisitions officer to purchase books that added depth to our collection, that completed our holdings of major and minor authors reflective of the history of civilization, that rounded out areas of knowledge in which we might otherwise be deficient, that included materials that seemed interesting or vital or unusual to me, and just…*because*. That was my prerogative, and it was never challenged by my superiors, since I made certain that I fulfilled all the other requirements of the position *first*.

So I cast my net very widely indeed.

I've followed a similar, broadly based philosophy in assembling the titles for the Borgo Press Imprint of Wildside Press. A print-on-demand (POD) line has a far different set of parameters than any comparable trade program. With trade books, or monographs targeted for specific markets (libraries, for example—this was the orientation of the original BP imprint for much of its history), the editor attempts to acquire materials that fit a particular set of guidelines, formal or informal, for that series.

With POD, however, the only three questions that an editor asks are:

1. Is the ms. under consideration worthy of being published?
2. Is there a niche market identifiable for this title?
3. Is the author or literary estate easy to work with?

For me, "easy to work with" often becomes the paramount issue, since I have no staff, no money to pay advances, very limited time, and even more limited patience and energy.

But what does this mean in reality?

I mostly deal primarily with old (usually older than I), established professionals who know the score, still possess a fan following (large or small), have previously published books in legitimate venues (the more titles, the better), are courteous and undemanding, are capable of providing me with e-copy compatible with my word-processing program—or, in some cases, clean copies of previously-published volumes that can be cannibalized for reprinting—and aren't constant pains-in-the-butt.

I'm enough of a curmudgeon myself that I don't want to see myself constantly reflected in a literary mirror.

So, while I *have* published neophytes in the program, I don't do so very often—and that's certainly *not* because their materials are somehow less worthy of publication, or because I wish to discourage such folks. It's more a matter of time and energy and effort. I have relatively little left of such things these days, and must conserve what I have to get the most out of what I do—as editor, as writer, and individual—and new writers tend to require a greater amount of education.

I've now published science fiction, fantasy, horror, westerns, mysteries, suspense novels, romances, historicals, gay classics, cookbooks, humor, plays, poetry (including one epic!), translations, books on cats and dogs, biography and autobiography, writing manuals, literary and film critiques, serious history, political science, Holocaust memoirs, short story and nonfiction collections and anthologies, gemology, genealogy, popular music guides, and a fair number of books that simply defy any attempts at classification.

* * * * * * *

THE SUDDEN, PARTIAL implosion of trade publishing at the beginning of 2009 has left many authors literary orphans, unable to find trade outlets for publications that would, in normal times, have sold without difficulty.

But this situation actually began developing more than a decade ago, with the collapse of the mass-market independent distributors in the mid-to-late 1990s. As a direct result of this, average print runs for smaller-sized paperback books declined markedly, and many midlist writers gradually lost access to the publishing lines that had harbored them in the past, with some of the survivors being forced to pen media tie-ins or other such litglop just to survive. Their own original fictions became harder and harder to peddle, with publishers no longer being willing to give writers much sales leeway beyond two or three books. If they didn't "measure up," they were cut off, and either had to change writing names (many authors went this route), or find some other, lesser-paying markets.

The result for me has sometimes been a sad reaping of literary riches. I cannot help thinking on such occasions that I'm picking the bones of writers and books that I could never have acquired in previous years. This hasn't stopped me from issuing those contracts, of course, but the situation is far from ideal for the authors.

But I also feel that what I'm doing is helping to preserve the lifetime output of some genuinely talented individuals. When a quality writer such as Ardath Mayhar first came knocking at my door, I truly experienced an epiphany of revelation, saying to myself: "Wow! This woman is *really* good!" I'd never read Ardath's work before, and one of the joys of this job has been savoring her novels *now*, as well as providing permanent homes for them. I was able to acquire more than fifty of her seventy monographs (the ones for which rights were available); of these, perhaps twenty had never been issued in print form before, so *my* versions are actually their First Editions. Some of these titles have done fairly well in POD, selling a hundred or more copies annually. These aren't high numbers by trade standards, of course, but they're a good sale for an unpromoted work that's produced on demand.

I try to work closely with my authors, to give them whatever they need in terms of minor concessions to style or format—subject, however, to the requirements of our printers and the dictates of my publisher. Everything at Borgo/Wildside is oriented towards producing the maximum number of titles as quickly and efficiently as possible.

I issue all the agreements for the titles that we acquire, and have been given a fairly free rein to acquire those works that I think worthy of adding to the line.

I employ a standard format to prepare the internal copy of the books—and I don't vary from this very often. Through trial and error, John Betancourt and I have determined what parameters work best with the two POD printers that handle most of our publications.

I also prepare cover copy, and record the metadata for the titles on our printers' websites; this information is used by them to distribute title data to the sales sites of Amazon.com and similar on-line bookmongers. Wildside does the actual packaging of the books.

And, somehow, the process actually works! The final product is both attractive and professional, inside and out, a package certainly worthy of the content. And the quality of the content has been consistently high throughout the course of the program.

Authors seem to find me and Borgo without difficulty, although I make very little effort to solicit materials, other than glad-handing at conventions. And they often return to publish a second or third—or even fortieth—book with us. That's very gratifying to me.

Increasingly this past year, I've been passing out ideas to the authors on my list to generate original works—this anthology is one of them—that might be constituted from new or reprint material in their backlist. I intend to be more proactive in the future in the collaborative creation of such materials.

I'll continue editing books for Wildside as long as they'll have me, and for as long as I feel capable of making a positive contribution, both to them and to my writers. I don't ever want to retire—not really! Writing and editing are, and always have been, a necessary part of my life.

In other words…whenever I put down my pen for the last time, I'll finally be ready to go.

XIX.

HOW NOT TO STARVE AS A WRITER

by Ardath Mayhar

ALMOST EVERY writer who has attained professional status has at some time had an enthusiastic beginner approach him, starry-eyed, to say something like this:

> "I have just sold a story to __! They are paying me three hundred dollars! I'm going to quit my job and write for a living!"

My first instinct, always, is to grab the youngster by his collar and shout, "Don't!" with all my might.

To those who have not yet experienced the illogical ups and downs, not to mention the irregular and undependable nature of payment for material that has been bought and delivered, it seems that once you have sold professionally, it will become easy to sell more. That, sadly, is not necessarily true.

There are several reasons. First, of course, is the fact that there are limited commercial markets for short fiction these days. Though many magazines do publish fiction, most pay modestly for the privilege. For every market like *Omni*, which paid fabulous rates (and no longer exists), there are a hundred less remunerative publications.

In the science fiction-fantasy field, which I know best, standard rates vary from four to perhaps seven cents a word. At this rate, even a novella will bring only a relatively small sum.

Below markets paying that scale are the semiprofessional and "little" magazines. Their standards, usually, are high, but their capitalization is limited, which forces their rates to remain low. A half cent to a penny a word is usually their offer. While this can buy postage, it isn't going far toward making a living, believe me. The best thing these markets can do for a beginner is to showcase his work and put his name before those who may later recognize it.

If you write mystery, horror, and science fiction/fantasy stories, there are fewer than two dozen profitable markets for you to approach. There are many lesser ones, of course, that may bring in the grocery money (if you eat lightly), so that may bring the sum total of possible markets for stories in the above categories to about thirty or forty. Those markets are flooded with submissions, and the competition for space is fierce. But if you could sell a story to each of them five or six times a year, you might make a very modest living.

It doesn't usually work that way. To make a living from short fiction is almost impossible, and those who work mainly in that field often teach writing classes or something similar in order to live and work. The competition for those spaces may allow you to sell only a couple of stories a year to one of the really viable markets, if you are extremely good and fairly well known in the field.

So you dissuade that young writer from trying to make it selling short stories. "I will write books, instead. That will give me a better income, once I have sold a couple and have established my name," he will say.

Unfortunately, even after you have sold well over twenty, as I have [this was written a long time ago!], you still will not have the sort of dependable income that our economy demands of those who intend to survive without going to the woods and becoming hermits.

You cannot, for instance, count on drawing any royalties on a novel, no matter what genre is involved. Many books never make more than enough to pay back your advance (and some don't even do that well). Some companies, who shall remain nameless, write more creatively in their bookkeeping than their authors do in their novels. And if you should earn royalties, they will only be paid twice a year, in almost all cases.

This means that you are going to have to write enough books in any given year (at mid-list rates for advances) to sustain your personal economy. If your usual advance is from three to five thousand dollars, which was for a long time fairly average, you are going to have to write at least five novels a year in order to live at all. And when you are forced to work that quickly and steadily, writing becomes a chore instead of a joy.

Even if you are able to crank out that many books in twelve months, however, that doesn't mean that you will have a steady and dependable income. You're going to get great lumps of money at unpredictable intervals, with long droughts between them. It is almost impossible to explain to a bank, a utility company, or a finance company that you are not paid weekly. Not monthly. Not even quarterly.

"I may have ten thousand dollars by June," you might say to your banker in February. "But it may take until August to get my money."

Bankers do not understand that. If you need a loan to sustain you while you wait for the advance to come through, you are not going to get it. You may have to take a temporary job pumping gas or cleaning houses in order to eat in the interval.

And that is the best reason I know to hold onto any job that pays the bills, no matter if it does cut into your writing time. Nothing, believe me, discourages the Muse like starvation.

When I wrote my first two novels, I lived in Oregon, worked as a proofreader for an afternoon newspaper, commuted seventeen miles (one way) to work. I made a two-acre garden and canned the produce, besides helping my husband in his service station in the evenings.

When, you may ask, did I find the time to write? I had every Monday off. After zooming through my house with the vacuum cleaner like a demented bee, in the mornings, I sat down every Monday afternoon and completed ONE CHAPTER of the book in hand.

I thought about that book while driving, waiting at stoplights, between rushes on the job, waiting in doctors' offices. By the time I had the physical time to sit down at my (manual portable) typewriter, I had organized the material so well that what hit the paper was actually a second draft. I had gone over everything, not only waking but in my dreams, and the story had built up such a head of steam that it erupted onto paper.

Anyone can organize his life so as to leave some time for writing. Nobody can do it for you, of course, for only you understand your schedule and any possible holes it might contain. But you can manage it, if you devote effort to doing it, and you can find time to write, if it is only an hour a week.

When you have done that and are writing (as well as eating) regularly, you also have to begin marketing on a steady basis. If your output is of professional quality, you will begin, sooner or later, to sell. One indication of the approach of that era will be the arrival of personal letters of rejection...even "sorry" scribbled onto a form rejection is a sign that SOMEBODY LIKED what you sent to them. Editors are busy. If one takes the time to do that, he/she liked the work and may well recall your name when you present him with another story. Which, if you are wise, you will do pretty promptly.

Sales will become fairly frequent, as you go along, and you may earn larger amounts. With novels this is particularly true, for most first novels draw very small advances, which can grow modestly with each additional book. There are few of us who have blockbuster best-sellers, and we must content ourselves with persistent, unspectacular growth in income.

The income from your job is going to be more than welcome, particularly if you have a family. This is going to remove the stress of worry about meeting bills, emergencies, and other demands, and that will relieve your mind, letting it relax into its creative mode.

One who quits a steady job to write full time, unless he has outside income, may find himself worrying full time and writing less than he would have done by working it into his job schedule.

Unless you are independently wealthy or married to a professional with a solid yearly income—or like to chew your fingernails and tear your hair—KEEP THAT JOB!

When you begin grossing six figures a year—that is the time to quit.

INDEX

by Mary Wickizer Burgess

I Henry IV (Shakespeare), 162
Ace Doubles, 46
Ackerman, Forrest J, 56, 58, 61-62
Adelbert Ames, Jr.: A Life of Vision and Becomingness (Bamberger), 54-55
AggieCon (SF convention), 17
Albright, Daniel, 160
Alexandrines (couplets), 175
Alexis, Tsarevich, 172
Alpha Yes, Terra No! (Petaja), 46
Amazon.com, 40, 186
American Psychiatric Association, 76
Ames, Adelbert, Jr., 42-55
Ames, Gen. Adelbert, Sr., 49
Ames, Dr. Adelbert, III, 51-54
"Ames Rooms," 48, 51
"And He Not Busy Being Born..." (Stableford), 103
The Annotated Lolita (Nabokov and Appel), 88
Angels and Demons (Brown), 81, 83, 88
Appel, Alfred, Jr., 88
Ariadne Press, 10
Arno Press, 181-182
The Art and Craft of Poetry: Twenty Exercises Toward Mastery (Collings), 9
"Art and Life: A Mennipean Paean to the Flea, or Did Dostoevsky Kill Trotsky?" (Klonsky), 47
"Art and the Subjective Visual Sensation" (Ames), 53
The Art of Fiction (Gardner), 22
Asimov, Isaac, 36
Atria Books, 88
Avon Books, 88
Azimullah Khan, 152, 154, 160-161, 164

"Azimullah Khan—A Reappraisal of One of the Major Figures of the Revolt of 1857" (Jarman), 154
The Ballad of Beta-Two (Delany), 46
Bamberger, Aja, 44
Bamberger, W. C., 10, 42-55
Banis, Victor J., 9, 11, 13, 18-32
Barker, Clive, 33
Barnes & Noble, 40, 50
Barrymore, John, 157-158
Barthelme, Donald, 47
Baudelaire, Charles, 178
Beattie, Ann, 48
Behan, Brendan, 160
Bellow, Saul, 46
Berry, Halle, 149
Betancourt, John Gregory, 11-12, 182-183, 186
Biggers, W. Watts, 47
Boleyn, Ann, 151
Bonham Carter, Helen, 149
Borderline (Vercors), 102
Borges, Jorge Luis, 47
Borgo Pass, Transylvania, 182
Borgo Press, 9-14, 152, 154, 162, 176, 180-186
Borzoi Books/Alfred A. Knopf, 22
Bradbury, Ray, 36, 56-58, 61, 65
Bradley, Marion Zimmer, 19
Brando, Marlon, 149
British Library (and Museum), 164
Broderick, Damien, 9, 11, 81-88
Brooks, Terry, 66
Brown, Dan, 81-84, 88
Burgess, Mary Wickizer, 11-13, 67, 69, 182, 192
Burke, James Lee, 31
Byline Magazine, 41
California State University, San Bernardino, 183
Capote, Truman, 71
Card, Orson, Scott, 44
Carter—See: Bonham Carter
Castle Dracula, 182
Catherine, Princess of Aragon, Queen of England, 151
Catton, Bruce, 95
Cawnpore, Sultana of, 152, 154, 160-161
Centilivre, Mrs. (Susannah), 171
The Century Magazine, 181
Cheever, John, 29, 48
Chekhov, Anton, 160

"Choice Cuts" (Reginald), 10-14, 66-70
Choice Words (ed.: Reginald), 13
Cibber, Colley, 171
City Lights, 148
Clarke, Arthur C., 86
A Clockwork Orange (film), 156
Collier's Encyclopedia, 43
Collings, Michael R., 9, 11, 9-92, 104-108
Comédie Française, 170
Congreve, William, 171
Constantine I, Emperor of Rome, 164
Copernicus, 83
Corneille, Pierre, 171
Cox, Alex, 161
The Crying of Lot 49 (Pynchon), 43
da Vinci, Leonardo, 49
Dann, Jack, 66
Darwin, Charles, 44
Delany, Samuel R., 42, 44, 46-47
The Demon Box (Kesey), 42
The Devil's Guide to Hollywood: The Screenwriter as God! (Eszterhas), 156
Dewey, John, 50
Diagnostic and Statistical Manual of Mental Disorders (American Psychiatric Association), 76
Dikty, Ted, 11, 183
"Dispatch from the Front: Never Waste Anything" (Mayhar), 9, 15-17
"Distorted Rooms"—See: "Ames Rooms"
Doubleday, 88
Dr. Johnson on Shakespeare (ed. Wimsatt), 150, 153, 157
Du Bois Irvin—See: Irvin
Duchamp, Marcel, 48
Dufresny, Charles, 170-171
Eastlake, William, 44, 47
Eaton Collection—See: J. Lloyd Eaton Collection
The Elements of Style (Strunk & White), 19
Eliot, T. S., 148
Elizabeth I, Queen of England (Elizabethan Era), 150-151, 175
Elkin, Stanley, 47
Ellison, Harlan, 19, 36
Elm Tree Books, 10
Elmslie, Kenward, 46-47
"Emotion and Intellect in Poetry" (Collings), 9, 89-92
The Empire of Fear (Stableford), 103
Empire Star (Delany), 46-47
English National Theatre Company, 152

Escher, M. C., 51
Eszterhas, Joe, 155-156
Evans, E. Everett, 56
Farquhar, George, 171
Faulkner, William, 44
Ferocious Minds: Polymathy and the New Enlightenment (Broderick), 9
"A Few Words, a Very Few Words, on Writing" (Reginald), 10, 66-70
Filippo Lippi, Fra, 87
Finnegans Wake (Joyce), 83
Fischer, Katrin, 166
Fitzgerald, F. Scott, 174
Flaubert, Gustave, 176
For a New Novel (Robbe-Grillet), 47
Forgotten Fantasy (magazine), 181
"French scenes," 174-175
Friedrich, Christian, 167
Frost, Robert, 160
Galilei, Galileo, 82
García Lorca, Federico, 148-149
Gardner, John, 22, 24-25
Garon, Jay, 20
Ghosts, and Other Plays (Ibsen), 151
The Gila Queen's Guide to Markets (Ptacek), 41
Gillespie, Bruce, 86
Ginsberg, Allen, 148
Girls Will Be Girls: A Play (Jarman), 159, 162-165, 168
Gottlieb, Sidney, 156
Gramlich, Charles Allen, 9, 11, 33-41, 71-80
Great Wave (Hokusai), 47
Greek drama, 101, 153
Greenleaf (Classics), 19-20
"The Growth of the House of Usher" (Stableford), 103
Hamlet (Shakespeare), 88, 157-158
Hammer, Elliott D., 9, 74-80
Hampton, Christopher, 160
A Handbook of Classical Drama (Harsh), 153
Haraway, Donna, 42
Harlequin Romance novels, 144, 146
Harper (Colophon), 20, 22
Harrison, Paul, 168
Harsh, Philip Whaley, 153
Haruf, Kent, 29
Hawking, Stephen, 82
Heinlein, Robert A. ("basic plot"), 99-102
Hemingway, Ernest, 19, 29, 48, 71, 79-80, 87, 174
Henry V (Shakespeare), 162

Henry VIII, King of England, 151
Herod, King, 176
Hitchcock, Alfred, 156
Hitchcock on Hitchcock: Selected Writings and Interviews (ed. Gottlieb), 156
Hokusai, 47
"How Not to Starve as a Writer" (Mayhar), 9, 187-190
Howl and Other Poems (Ginsberg), 148
Hugo, Victor, 176
Hunter, Evan, 19
"I Have No Mouth, and I Must Scream" (Ellison), 36
Ibsen, Henrik, 151
Illuminati, 82
"Images" (Broderick), 981-88
Images of Tomorrow (Nuetzel), 58
"In Other Words...: Editing Borgo Press" (Reginald), 10, 180-186
In Search of Duende (García Lorca), 149
Indian Mutiny, 152, 154, 164
Interzone (magazine), 10
"Introduction"—See: "Choice Cuts"
Invictus: A Play (Jarman), 164-165
Irvin, Y. Du Bois, 9, 74-80
J. Lloyd Eaton Collection, 182
Jakes, John, 19
James, Jesse, 49
Jarman, Francis, 10-11, 147-168
"Jerry Was a Man" (Heinlein), 101-102
Jesus of Nazareth, 176
Johnson, Dr. Samuel, 150, 153, 157
Jones, James, 19, 22
Jones, Little Hat, 45
Joyce, James, 83
Julius Caesar (Shakespeare), 153
Kafka, Franz, 45
Kassel, Björn, 166
Katz, Steve, 47
Kean, Edmund, 157
Kellerman, Jonathan, 22
Kennedy, John F., 49
Kerouac, Jack, 50
Kesey, Ken, 42
King, Stephen, 24, 36, 66, 71, 79
King Lear (Shakespeare), 153, 157
Klonsky, Milton, 47
Koontz, Dean, 33-34
Kuttner, Henry, 58

L'Enfant, Pierre, 84
Lesage, Alain-René, 172-173
Lerner, Laurence, 158
"A Letter to John Barrymore" (Shaw), 158
Lip Service: A Play (Jarman), 162-163, 167
Lippi—See: Filippo Lippi
Literary Market Place (*LMP*), 40
Lolita (Nabokov), 84, 87-88—See also: *The Annotated Lolita*
Lorca—See: Garcia Lorca
The Lost Symbol (Brown), 82-84, 88
"Love, Anyone? or, How to Write Sex Scenes" (Maltese), 10, 116-146
"Low-Lands" (Pynchon), 47
Lynn (publisher), 80
Macbeth (Shakespeare), 162
Macready (playwright), 157
Mahu, or the Material (Pinget), 47
"Making Things Happen" (Mayhar), 9, 93-96
Maltese, William, 10-11,116-146
The Man Inside (Biggers), 47
"Manga" books, 44
Mao, Tse-tung, Chairman, 157
Maria Stuart (Schiller), 150-152
Marvel Comics, 45
Marx, Carl, 45
Masons, 82
The Master Tanner Heads West (Bamberger), 50
Matthew, Saint, 100
Maugham, W. Somerset, 22
Maurer, Christopher, 149
Maxwell, James Clerk, 42-43
Maxwell's Demon, 42-55
Mayhar, Ardath, 9-11, 13, 15-17, 93-96, 185, 187-190
McGraw-Hill, 88
McGuane, Thomas, 47
Menville, Douglas A., 180-182
Meredith, Scott, 20, 22, 99
Middleton, Thomas, 161
Mills & Boon, 98
Modernism and Music: An Anthology of Sources (ed. Albright), 160
Molière, 170-172
Monster's Ball (film), 149
Morlock, Frank J., 10-11, 169-179
The Morning Notes of Adelbert Ames, Jr. (Ames), 48-55
Mosley, Walter, 28
Mystery Ridge (roadside attraction), 43-44, 48, 51, 55
Nabokov, Vladimir, 83-84, 87-88

Naked Came the Stranger (collaborative novel), 110
New Directions, 149
Newcastle Forgotten Fantasy Library, 181
Newcastle Publishing Co., Inc., 181-182
Nicholson, Jack, 26
Nobel Prize for Literature, 178
Norton, Andre, 45, 47
Novel and Short Story Writer's Market, 40
Nude Descending a Staircase (painting; Duchamp), 48
Nuetzel, Charles, 10-11, 56-65
O'Connor, Flannery, 29
Omni (magazine), 187
On Becoming a Novelist (Gardner), 22
On the Waterfront (film), 159
"On Translation" (Morlock), 10, 169-179
On Writing (King), 66
Oprah (TV), 71
The Orchid Stories (Elmslie), 47
Othello (Shakespeare), 165
Ozick, Cynthia, 47
"Paperback Writer" (Banis), 9, 18-32
Penguin Books, 150-151, 158
Petaja, Emil, 46
Peter I the Great, Tsar of Russia, 172
Pinget, Robert, 47-48
"Play and Theory of the Duende" (García Lorca), 148-149
"Plotting a Science Fiction Story" (Stableford), 10, 97-103
Pocketbook Writer: Confessions of a Commercial Hack (Nuetzel), 10
Poe, Edgar Allan, 71, 178
Ponzi (scheme), 173
Prelude to Eternity (Stableford), 103
"Preparing and Writing" (Gramlich, *et al.*), 9, 74-80
Print on Demand Publishing (POD), 184-186
Profiles in Courage (Kennedy), 49
Ptacek, Kathryn, 11, 41
Puccini, Giacomo, 157
Pynchon, Thomas, 43, 47
Quipu (Broderick), 86-88
Racine, Jean, 171
Reed, Ishmael, 47, 50
Reger, Max, 160
Regietheater ("direction-theatre"), 157
Reginald, Robert, 10-14, 66-70, 180-186
Restoration era, 171
The Revenger's Tragedy (Middleton/Tourneur), 161
Richard III (Shakespeare), 161

Rimbaud, Arthur, 45
Robbe-Grillet, Alain, 47
Robinson, Edward G., 21
"Rocket Summer" (Bradbury), 36
Rogers, Mary—See: Burgess, Mary
Romeo and Juliet (Shakespeare), 161
A Room with a View (film), 149
The Royal Hunt of the Sun (Shaffer), 152
San Bernardino Mountains, 111
Sand, George, 178
Saunders Brothers (Al and Joe), 180-182
"Saying Much with Little: Some Practical Suggestions for Tightening Bulky Lines in Poetry" (Collings), 9, 104-108
Schiller, Friedrich, 150-151
Schrödinger, Erwin, 51
Scott Meredith Agency ("basic plot" formula), 20, 98-100, 102-103
Seven Brides for Seven Brothers (film), 162
"Sexual Chemistry" (Stableford), 103
Shaffer, Peter, 152
Shakespeare, William (Shakespearean), 88, 101, 148, 150, 153, 157-158, 161-162, 165, 172
Shakespeare in Love (film), 148
Shakespeare's Tragedies: An Anthology of Modern Criticism (ed. Lerner), 158
Shaw, George Bernard, 157-158
Shepard, Sam, 47
The Shining (film), 26
Simenon, Georges, 25
Simpsons (TV), 75
"Slanting Can Be Fun and Dangerous; or, Art vs. All That Other Stuff" (Nuetzel), 10, 56-65
Sometimes the Magic Works (Brooks), 66
South Asia: Journal of South Asian Studies, 154
Spine Intact, Some Creases: Remembrances of a Paperback Writer (Banis), 9
The Spirit of Contradiction (Dufresny), 170-171
St. Martin's Press, 156
Stableford, Brian, 10-11, 97-103
Stanford University Press, 153
Stanwyck, Barbara, 22
A Star Fell: A Play (Jarman), 151-155, 160-161, 164, 166
Starmont House, 11, 183
Stegner, Wallace, 18
Stella Dallas (film), 22
Stella Nova (Reginald), 180
Strong Opinions (Nabokov), 83, 88

Stuart, Mary, Queen of Scots, 150-151
The Summing Up (Maugham), 22
The Sun Also Rises (Hemingway), 174
Sunset-Vine Bookmart, 180
"A Supermarket in California" (Ginsberg), 148
Tate, Nahum, 157
Texas A&M University, 17
Theroux, Alexander, 47
Thomas, William S., 109-115
Through a Stone Wall: Lessons from Thirty Years of Writing (Mayhar), 10
"Tipping the Odds in Your Favor" (Gramlich), 9, 33-41
La Tontine (Lesage), 172-173
Tourneur, Cyril, 161
Trilobite Dreams; or, The Autodidact's Tale: A Romance of Autobiography (Reginald), 10
Troilus and Cressida (Shakespeare), 150, 161-162
Turandot (Puccini), 157
Twain, Mark, 71
Twelfth Night (Shakespeare), 161-162
"The Two-Headed Author: The Challenges, Risks, and Rewards of Collaboration" (Weeks), 10, 109-115
Tynan, Kenneth, 160
University of California Press, 156
University of California, Riverside, 182
University of Chicago Press, 160
University of Maryland, 170
University of Southern California (USC), 180
Updike, John, 48
Vanbrugh, John, 171
Vercors, 102
Vidor, King, 22
Voltaire, 173
Waterwheels (Bamberger), 47
Watts, Peter, 151
The Way to Write Science Fiction (Stableford), 10
Weeks, John Howard, 10, 109-115
Westlake, Donald, 19
What Is Life? (Schrödinger), 51
Whipple, Kimball, 51
The White Abacus (Broderick), 88
White Skin, Dark Skin, Power, Dream: Collected Essays on Literature and Culture (Jarman), 154
Whitehead, A. N., 50
Whitman, Walt, 148
Wildside Press, 11-12, 182-186
Wimsatt, W. K., 150

Window Beyond the World (Weeks and Thomas), 109-115
The Winter's Tale (Shakespeare), 165
Winterson, Jeanette, 44
The Woman in the Window (film), 21
Write with Fire: Thoughts on the Craft of Writing (Gramlich), 9
The Writer (magazine), 41
Writer's Digest, 41
Writer's Digest Books, 20, 40
The Writer's Handbook, 40
Writer's Market, 40
"Writing about Evil" (Jarman), 154
"Writing for the Stage" (Jarman), 10, 147-168
Writing in Psychology: A Guidebook (Gramlich, et al.), 9, 75
"Writing Is Fighting the Familiar; or, 47 Years in the Wake of Adelbert Ames, Jr." (Bamberger), 10, 42-55
Writing to Sell (Meredith), 20
"Writing with Purpose" (Gramlich), 9, 71-73
"Yellow Backs" (adventure Westerns), 50
Yellow Back Radio Broke-Down (Reed), 50
Zebrowski, George, 66

ABOUT THE AUTHORS

W. C. BAMBERGER is the author or editor of twelve books, including the collection, *And, in Conclusion, I Would Like to Mention Hydrogen: 11½ Essays and 1½ Stories* (2009); two critical studies, *43 Views of Steve Katz* (2007) and *William Eastlake: High Desert Interlocutor* (1993); and a bibliography, *The Work of William Eastlake* (1994)—all published by the Borgo Press Imprint of Wildside Press—plus a revisionist cowboy novel, *The Master Tanner Heads West*. He lives in semi-rural Michigan with his daughter.

VICTOR J. BANIS is the critically acclaimed author ("the master's touch in storytelling..."—*Publishers Weekly*) of more than 150 published books and numerous short stories in a career spanning nearly a half century, twenty-nine of them published by the Borgo Press Imprint of Wildside Press. A native of Ohio and a longtime Californian, he lives and writes now in West Virginia's beautiful Blue Ridge. You can visit him at:

http://www.vjbanis.com

DAMIEN BRODERICK, Ph.D., is an Australian science fiction and science writer and critical theorist, and a Senior Fellow in the School of Culture and Communication at the University of Melbourne, Australia, although these days he lives in San Antonio, Texas. His scholarly books include *The Architecture of Babel* (1994), *Reading by Starlight* (1995), *Transrealist Fiction* (2000), *x, y, z, t: Dimensions of Science Fiction* (2004), *Unleashing the Strange: Twenty-First Century Science Fiction Literature* (2009), and *Chained to the Alien* (2009), the latter three published by Borgo Press. In 2005, he received the Distinguished Scholarship Award of the International Association for the Fantastic in the Arts. He has also published a number of award-winning novels.

MICHAEL R. COLLINGS is an Emeritus Professor of English at Seaver College, Pepperdine University, where he directed the Creative Writing Program for over two decades. He has published multiple volumes of poetry, novels, short fiction, and scholarly studies of such contemporary writers as Stephen King, Dean R. Koontz, Orson Scott Card, and Piers Anthony, fifteen of them published by the Borgo Press Imprint of Wildside Press. He is now retired and lives in his native state of Idaho.

CHARLES ALLEN GRAMLICH grew up on a farm in Arkansas, near the foothills of the Ozark Mountains, but moved to the New Orleans area to teach psychology at a local university. He's since sold four novels and numerous short stories. His stories, while mostly in the genres of horror, science fiction, and fantasy, have included westerns, children's tales, mainstream, slipstream, and experimental fiction. Charles has also published poetry and nonfiction, the latter ranging from reference works to articles on writing, and including five books from the Borgo Press Imprint of Wildside Press. He is an editor for *The Dark Man: The Journal of Robert E. Howard Studies*, and produces a regular column on writing for an online newsletter called *The Illuminata*. He lives with his wife in Abita Springs, Louisiana, and has a son named Joshua. His blog can be found at:

http://charlesgramlich.blogspot.com/

ELLIOT D. HAMMER is an Associate Professor of Psychology and the John LaFarge Professor in Social Justice at Xavier University of Louisiana. He regularly teaches courses in research, statistics, and writing, as well as social psychology. He conducts research on stereotyping and prejudice, as well as person perception and the scholarship of teaching and learning. He and his wife Elizabeth spend their free time traveling, relaxing with their pets, and celebrating the culture of New Orleans.

Y. DU BOIS IRVIN is the granddaughter of the late well-known civil rights activist and writer, W. E. B. Du Bois (1868-1963), and a prominent speaker, commentator, teacher, editor, and writer in her own right.

FRANCIS JARMAN is (according to family tradition) a descendant of the Thracian slave Androcles (of "Androcles and the Lion" fame). He grew up in North London and Essex, England, but lives in Germany, teaching comparative cultural studies and intercultural communication at the University of Hildesheim. He has published more than forty books, as well as a large number of essays, articles, and reviews. His four plays (*A Star Fell*, *Girls Will Be Girls*, *Lip Service*, and *Invictus*) and *White Skin, Dark Skin, Power, Dream*, a collection of essays on literary and cultural topics, are available from the Borgo Press Imprint of Wildside Press.

WILLIAM MALTESE was born in the Pacific Northwest. He has a B.A. in Marketing/Advertising and spent an honorable tour of duty in the U.S. Army, achieving the rank of E-5. He started his authorial career writing for the men's pulp magazines, and has since penned more than 200 books, both fiction and nonfiction. According to queerhorror.com, this included the first gay werewolf novel ever published. He also has written a number of bestselling women's romances under the name "Willa Lambert" for houses such as Harlequin and Carousel, including *Love's Emerald Flame*, the internationally acclaimed Harlequin SuperRomance #2, which has been published by the Borgo Press Imprint of Wildside Press along with twenty-one of his other titles. He encourages his fans to visit his websites:

www.williammaltese.com
and
www.myspace.com/williammaltese

ARDATH MAYHAR is the author of more than seventy books. She began her career in the early eighties with science fiction novels from Doubleday and TSR. Atheneum published several of her young adult and children's novels. Changing focus, she wrote westerns (as Frank Cannon) and mountain man novels (as John Killdeer), four prehistoric Indian books under her own name, and the historical western *High Mountain Winter* under the byline Frances Hurst. Fifty of her titles are now available from the Borgo Press Imprint of Wildside Press and Amazon.com. Mayhar was widowed in 1999, after forty-one years of marriage, and has four grown sons. She works at her home in East Texas, writing short fiction and nonfiction, and doing professional book and story doctoring. Her main web pages can be found at:

w2.netdot.com/ardathm/
and
http://ofearna.us/books/mayhar.html

FRANK J. MORLOCK has written and translated over 200 French plays since retiring from the legal profession in 1992. His translations have appeared on Project Gutenberg, the Alexandre Dumas Père web page, Literature in the Age of Napoléon, Infinite Artistries.com, Munsey's (formerly Blackmask). More than thirty-five have now been published by the Borgo Press Imprint of Wildside Press. In 2006 he received an award from the North American Jules Verne Society for his translations of Verne's plays. He lives and works in México. He invites you to visit his website at:

http://frankjmorlock.com

CHARLES NUETZEL writes: "As long as I can remember, I wanted to be a writer. It was a dream I never thought would materialize. But with the help of Forrest J Ackerman, who became my agent, I managed to finally make it into print.

"I was lucky enough not only in selling my work to publishers but also ending up packaging books for some of them, and finally becoming a 'publisher' much like those who had bought my first novels. From there it as a simple leap to editing not only a science-fiction anthology, but also a line of SF books for Powell Sci-Fi back in the 1960s. Throughout these active professional years, I had the chance to design some covers and do graphic cover layouts for pocket books & magazines."

Over forty of his books have been published by The Borgo Press Imprint of Wildside Press, including the classic Noomas fantasy trilogy.

In retirement he has become involved in swing dancing, being a long-time lover of Big Band jazz. But more interestingly, world travels have taken him (and his wife Brigitte) across the world, to Hawaii, Caribbean, Mexico, Kenya, Egypt, Peru, having a lifelong interest in ancient civilizations. His website is full of thousands of pictures taken during these trips:

http://haldolen.com

ROBERT REGINALD (Michael Burgess) was born in Japan in the Year of the Rat, and lived in Turkey as a youth. He starting writing as a mere child, and penned his first book during his senior year in college. He's been infected with terminal logorrhea ever since, churning out more than 12 million words of professional fiction and nonfiction. He settled in Southern California in 1969, working as an academic librarian at California State University, San Bernardino for 40 years. In his spare time he edits a line of books for the Borgo Press Imprint of Wildside Press, and has penned 114 volumes of his own, as well as 13,000 short pieces. His recent books include the three Nova Europa historical fantasy novels, *The Dark-Haired Man* (2004), *The Exiled Prince* (2004), and *Quæstiones* (2005); the science-fiction trilogy, *Invasion! Earth vs. the Aliens* (2007); two period mystery novels featuring the Phantom Detective, *The Phantom's Phantom* (2007) and *The Nasty Gnomes* (2008); the story collection, *Katydid and Other Critters* (2001); two literary essay collections, *Xenograffiti* (1996 & 2005) and *Classics of Fantastic Literature* (with Douglas Menville, 2005); two guides to the Deryni universe, *Codex Derynianus I and II* (with Katherine Kurtz, 1998 & 2005); and two historical anthologies, *San Quentin* (edited with Bonnie L. Petry, 2005) and *¡Viva California!* (edited with Mary Wickizer Burgess, 2006). He's currently finishing a new Nova Europa fantasy, *The Fourth Elephant's Egg*, and *The Coyote Chronicles*, a lengthy history of his campus. In 1993 he received the Pilgrim Award from the Science Fiction Research Association for his literary criticism. You can find him at:

http://www.millefleurs.tv/Robert_Reginald.html
and
http://www.millefleurs.tv/Michael_Burgess.html

BRIAN STABLEFORD was born in Yorkshire in 1948. He taught at the University of Reading for several years, but is now a full-time writer. He has written many science fiction and fantasy novels, including *The Empire of Fear*, *The Werewolves of London*, *Year Zero*, *The Curse of the Coral Bride*, *The Stones of Camelot*, and *Prelude to Eternity*. Collections of his short stories include a long series of *Tales of the Biotech Revolution*, and such idiosyncratic items as *Sheena and Other Gothic Tales* and *The Innsmouth Heritage and Other Sequels*. He has written numerous nonfiction books, including *Scientific Romance in Britain, 1890-1950*, *Glorious Perversity: The Decline and Fall of Literary Decadence*, *Science Fact and Science Fiction: An Encyclopedia* and *The Devil's Party: A Brief History of Satanic Abuse*. Forty-two of his books have been published by the Borgo Press Imprint of Wildside Press. He has contributed hundreds of biographical and critical entries to reference books, including both editions of *The Encyclopedia of Science Fiction* and several editions of the library guide, *Anatomy of Wonder*. He has also translated numerous novels from the French language, including several by the feuilletonist Paul Féval and numerous classics of French scientific romance by such writers as Albert Robida, Maurice Renard, and J. H. Rosny the Elder.

JOHN HOWARD WEEKS is an author and satirist whose work appears in newspapers throughout Southern California. He is Features Editor of San Bernardino County's two largest dailies, *The Sun* in San Bernardino, and *The Inland Valley Daily Bulletin* in Ontario, and also a staff contributor to the Los Angeles Newspaper Group, which includes five other dailies. His popular humor column, which takes a satirical look at regional topics and issues, has earned him the nickname, "Emperor of the Inland Empire."

A forty-year career journalist, he also is the author of two books, *Inland Empire*, a pictorial history of inland Southern California, and the novel, *Window Beyond the World*, a supernatural thriller set in the San Bernardino Mountains. A fantasy novel is forthcoming from the Borgo Press Imprint of Wildside Press.

Born in Oklahoma, he is a graduate of Loma Linda Academy in Loma Linda, Calif., the University of California, Riverside, and Birmingham University in England, where he earned his master's degree in English literature. Except for one year abroad, he has been a resident of the Inland Empire since 1963. He has lived in Loma

Linda, Redlands, Riverside, Lake Arrowhead, and San Bernardino, where he now makes his home.

Books published by the Borgo Press Imprint of Wildside Press can be purchased through the websites of all the major on-line book vendors, or via the on-line catalog of Wildside Press:

www.wildsidebooks.com

www.ingramcontent.com/pod-product-compliance
Lightning Source LLC
LaVergne TN
LVHW041617070426
835507LV00008B/288